Hiking Waterfalls in North Carolina

A Guide to the State's Best Waterfall Hikes

LORRIE —
HAPPY TRAILS !!

Melissa Watson

ü m.

FALCONGUIDES

GUILFORD, CONNECTICUT
HELENA, MONTANA
AN IMPRINT OF GLOBE PEQUOT PRESS

For Johnny, my beloved brother.
With special thanks to Mom and all my family for giving me the love and freedom
to chase my dreams—and to my friends for giving me the support and
encouragement needed to follow through with those dreams.

To buy books in quantity for corporate use
or incentives, call **(800) 962-0973**
or e-mail **premiums@GlobePequot.com.**

FALCONGUIDES®

FalconGuides is an imprint of Globe Pequot Press.

Falcon, FalconGuides, and Outfit Your Mind are registered trademarks of Morris Book Publishing, LLC.

Maps: Mapping Specialists © Morris Book Publishing, LLC
TOPO! Explorer software and SuperQuad source maps courtesy of National Geographic Maps. For information about TOPO! Explorer, TOPO!, and Nat Geo Maps products, go to www.topo.com or www.natgeomaps.com.
Photos: Melissa Watson
Project editor: Julie Marsh
Layout: Sue Murray

Library of Congress Cataloging-in-Publication Data

Watson, Melissa.
  Hiking waterfalls in North Carolina : a guide to the state's best waterfall hikes / Melissa Watson.
      p. cm.
  Includes index.
  ISBN 978-0-7627-7150-9
  1. Hiking–North Carolina–Guidebooks. 2. Waterfalls–North Carolina–Guidebooks. 3. North Carolina–Guidebooks. I. Title.
  GV199.42.N66W38 2011
  917.56–dc23
                                                              2011026401

Printed in the United States of America
10 9 8 7 6 5 4 3 2 1

Contents

The Hikes

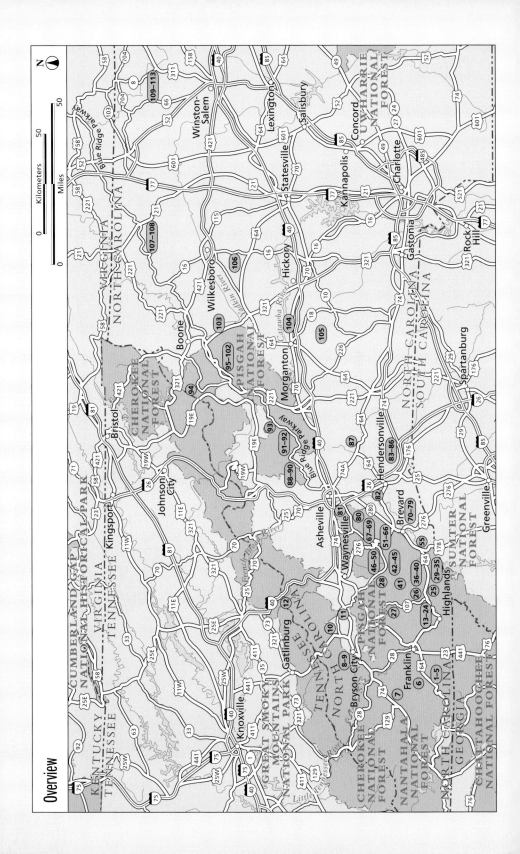

Overview

Acknowledgments

I'd like to thank my family for their love, patience, and support: Terri Sansonetti; Maria, Frazier, Christina, and Cory Payton; Doug Watson; Sue, Tom, Frank, Amy, Thomas, Joe, Kristen, Rebecca, Nathaniel, Katilee, Mark, Jonathon, and Joshua Strazza; Michelle, Roland, and Lucas Arisolo; Maris Herold; and Rachel Saunders. I love you all!

Many people were helpful in confirming the accuracy of the hikes in this guide. I'd like them all to know how thankful I am for their investment of time and their wealth of knowledge: Randall Burgess, Joe Narsavage, and Jean Tate at the Pisgah Ranger District of the Pisgah National Forest; Bruce MacDonald and Roberta Belcher at DuPont State Forest; Dave Cook at Hanging Rock State Park; Steve Pagano at Gorges State Park; Edward Farr at Stone Mountain State Park; Jonathon Griffith at South Mountains State Park; Curtis Phillabaum and Melissa Dolinsky at the Palm Beach Zoo; and Kathleen Stuart and Patrick Miller at Great Smoky Mountains National Park.

Finally, I'd like to thank the following people for covering my shifts at the firehouse so that I could spend six weeks in the woods, rehiking every trail in this book: Jeff McCord, George Donechie, Donny Brown, Joe Bostic, Travis Thomas, and of course my crew at Station 51—Craig Hatton, Chris Uzzo, Jody Miedema, Jason Alexander, and Mike Osuna—for their patience and tolerance while I diligently worked on this project.

Introduction

Waterfalls are magical, mysterious wonders of nature. From small cascades to tall, free-falling water, each has a character and beauty of its own.

I have been entranced by the magic of waterfalls my entire life, and now, after spending the past twenty years seeking out new falls and revisiting old favorites, I'm sharing that passion. For months at a time I have hiked and camped and reveled in the waterfalls of North Carolina. Some of this time was spent in frustration, though, due to inaccurate trail or driving directions. And so I began writing this book with one goal in mind—accuracy. Setting out with my dog Mikey in tow, I hiked and rehiked each trail in this book while documenting the details along the way. I ended up hiking hundreds of miles and driving thousands of miles so that you wouldn't have to.

Once I gathered my field notes together, I began the laborious task of putting them into writing. I've provided specific trail directions and thorough driving directions. I've also included GPS coordinates and *DeLorme: North Carolina Atlas & Gazetteer* map page and coordinates to assist you on your quest to find the falls.

While I was finishing up some of the more entertaining text of this guidebook, I discovered the strangest thing—my muse, which happened to come in the form of champagne and show tunes. I found my fingers tip tapping away on the keyboard to the likes of *The Phantom of the Opera* and *The Sound of Music.* I can't tell you how many times I heard Julie Andrews sing "Do-Re-Mi" as the words flowed onto my computer screen. Pandora radio really is fabulous but repetitive, and I can now say with a smile that I know every word to *The Jungle Book* song, "The Bare Necessities."

I hope you find this book entertaining as well as accurate. Within these pages you will find a collection of more than 150 waterfalls for your viewing pleasure—from roadside beauties to those set deep in the forest. Enjoy this user-friendly guide as it leads you to the most magnificent waterfalls in North Carolina. Don your hiking boots and grab your camera—a world of discovery lies ahead.

How to Use This Guide

The waterfalls in this guide have been divided into geographic areas. This way, when you plan to visit a certain town, you can easily see which waterfalls are nearby. A detailed map of the trails and their surroundings are provided for each area.

Along with each map you'll find the hikes shown on that map. Each hike in this guide is presented in the same format, which begins with a brief description of the waterfall, from the author's perspective.

Next come the hike "specs": important information such as waterfall height; my personal beauty rating for each waterfall; trail distance (always for the total out-and-back hike, unless otherwise noted), difficulty, surface, and blaze color; approximate hiking time for the entire recommended hike; and other trail users you might encounter. I have also noted the county in which the waterfall is located, land status (national forest/park, private owner, etc.), trail contacts, and FYI (for your information) for additional information on the area and any other important information, such as park hours and fees.

Lastly you will find the relevant page and coordinates in *DeLorme: North Carolina Atlas & Gazetteer* (2010, 9th edition) to supplement the maps provided in this guide. I highly recommend getting the *DeLorme Atlas & Gazetteer* for any state in which you plan to hike. They've been of great help to me on my explorations. The *National Geographic Trails Illustrated* topographic maps are another useful tool and an invaluable resource when navigating through the mountains of the Pisgah and Nantahala National Forests.

Following the hike specs you will see "Finding the trailhead." Because you can't enjoy the hike if you can't find the trailhead, I have provided explicit driving directions, usually from two points of reference, using either a main intersection or a state line as your starting point.

Many of the trailheads are located on USDA Forest Service roads, most of which are unmarked dirt roads, and there may be several of these in a given area. For this reason I have given specific driving distances in mileage rounded to the nearest 0.1 mile. I've also tried to give you the best route to the trailhead. So if you see what appears to be a shortcut on the map, chances are there's a good reason I didn't send you that way. **Note:** When parking near a Forest Service gate, be sure not to block the gate, and try to leave room for others when parking in pull-offs.

While I prefer a good old-fashioned map and compass, more and more people are becoming adept at using the Global Positioning System. I therefore have provided GPS coordinates for both the trailheads and waterfalls.

The Hike is where you'll find a general description of what to expect along the trail. I've also included a brief history for each waterfall, perhaps how the falls got its name, or some interesting information about the area. I personally learned quite a bit while researching this portion of the book and found some of the folklore to be thoroughly entertaining. I hope you do as well.

The **Miles and Directions** provide thorough hiking directions. Any questionable turn, every fork, and every T junction has been documented. I've given you the distance at which you will reach them and also provided left/right directions with corresponding compass direction. If the waterfall can be viewed from the roadside, no Miles and Directions are needed or given.

I've worked very hard to keep you from getting lost, but please remember that trails do change over time, as do the waterfalls. The appearance of a waterfall may change with each rainfall, or lack thereof, and with every season. This is the reason I return to the same waterfalls time and time again, and yet I'm always greeted with a new experience.

For Your Safety

Before you hit the trails, there's some important information you should know to help keep you safe and sound.

Know your limits. If I say that a trail or portion of trail is for experienced hikers only, I mean it. This means no children either. Some of the trails presented in this book are extremely steep and potentially dangerous. Please heed my warnings and hike within your limits.

Carry the essentials. Next are the "10 Essential Items" every hiker should carry: map, compass, flashlight, first-aid kit, knife, waterproof matches, candle or fire starter, extra clothing, food, and lots of water. Better to have these things and not need them than to need them and not have them. You will find every one of these items (plus some others) in my day pack at all times.

Give someone your itinerary. Whether you hike in a group or especially if you hike by yourself, always tell people where you'll be hiking and when you expect to return. If there's a place to sign in at the trailhead, please do so prior to hiking. And don't forget to sign out when you return.

Watch for the blazes. For those of you new to hiking, blazes are colored markers on a tree or other natural surface that indicate where the trail goes. Not all trails have blazes, but for those that do I have listed the blaze color in the hike specs. Be aware that the blazes on some trails may be few and far between. And two blazes together on the same surface indicate that there is a sharp turn in the trail ahead.

Dress in layers, and always bring rain gear; it can protect you from rain, wind, and cold. Weather conditions can change rapidly and drastically in the mountains, so try to get a weather report prior to hiking. It pays to be prepared.

Wear the right footwear. It's so easy to twist an ankle or stub a toe while hiking. Hiking boots are a simple way to prevent this. Wear good hiking boots or trail runners, and break them in prior to hiking—you don't want to ruin your hike with blisters.

Carry a towel in your pack. Some trails call for fording creeks, and you don't want to hike with cold, wet feet. Not to mention that you may want to take a dip. I swear by chamois-style pack towels, available at local outfitters or REI. They're lightweight, compact, and dry very quickly.

Know where you've been. Here's a helpful hint when hiking on unfamiliar trails: Make it a habit to turn around and look at the trail from the other direction after taking a fork or T. This way, when you're hiking back out, it will look familiar and you won't miss any crucial turns.

Be careful at the brink. Do not play at, around, or near the brink of any waterfall! I cannot stress this enough. Every year people die at waterfalls, and I guarantee they never thought it would happen to them.

Do not climb the face of any waterfall. Countless injuries, even deaths, have been attributed to this as well. Always remember that the rocks and terrain around any waterfall are dangerously slippery, regardless of how surefooted you may be.

Respect the water. Lastly, be aware of how strong the currents can be at both the brink and the base of waterfalls. Never cross at the brink of a waterfall; and if you choose to take a dip at the base, look before you leap. Rocks and trees might lie beneath the surface, and currents may be strong. Choose your swimming holes wisely.

Taking Care of Mother Nature

Many creatures make their home in the forest. As you hike, remember that you are a guest on their terrain; respect them and the forest that harbors them. Try to live by the philosophy of "Take nothing but pictures; leave nothing but footprints." Every stone in the creek, every wildflower along the trail, has its purpose within the ecosystem. Please do not remove these or any items, except litter, from the forest.

A camera is an added bonus to your pack. When you see wildflowers in bloom, you can take their beauty home with you on film or memory card while leaving them for others to appreciate as well.

Note: Federal law prohibits picking wildflowers; removing stones, feathers, or any other natural artifacts; and harassing wildlife in national parks.

Practice "pack it in, pack it out" hiking. If you bring food into the woods, also bring a trash bag to carry out the wrappers and remnants, including orange peels. There's nothing worse than arriving at the base of a stunning waterfall and finding it littered with human debris. I especially ask that you not litter the trails I have shared with you.

Last but not least, please do not shortcut the trails. If you see a shortcut between switchbacks, I implore you to resist the temptation to take it. Stay on the main trail. Shortcutting not only destroys valuable vegetation and creates erosion but also makes the trails much harder to follow.

Happy trails!

Trail Finder

Roadside Waterfalls

Take a moment to ponder the reflections on a mountain lake.

Map Legend

Transportation

≡40≡   Interstate Highway

≡19≡   U.S. Highway

≡175≡   State Highway

≡97≡   Forest Road

Trails

- - - - - -   Featured Trail

- - - - - -   Trail

→   Direction of Travel

Water Features

Body of Water

River/Creek

Waterfall

Land Management

- - - - -   State Line

National Park/National Forest

Local/State Park/Wildlife Refuge

Symbols

⌣   Bridge

||||| Boardwalk/Steps

▲   Campground

•—•   Gate

▲   Mountain Peak/Summit

🛈   Picnic Area

■   Point of Interest/Structure

🚻   Restroom

○   Town

①   Trailhead

   Viewpoint/Overlook

❓   Visitor/Information Center

1 Bull Cove Falls

Solitary! Almost aloof, Bull Cove Falls stands out in a stately manner, above and different from the rest of the many playful cascades on the creek. Although Bull Cove Falls is located in North Carolina, you must drive through Tate City, Georgia, to access the trailhead.

Height: 40 feet
Beauty rating: Good
Distance: 2.2 miles out and back
Difficulty: Strenuous
Trail surface: Hard-packed dirt
Approximate hiking time: 1 hour, 30 minutes
Blaze color: Blue
County: Clay

Land status: National forest
Trail contact: Nantahala National Forest, Tusquitee Ranger District; (828) 837-5152; www .fs.usda.gov/nfsnc
Maps: DeLorme: North Carolina Atlas & Gazetteer: Page 51 F6; DeLorme: Georgia Atlas & Gazetteer: Page 16 A1

Finding the trailhead: From the junction of US 76 west and US 441 in Clayton, GA, drive west on US 76 for 7.9 miles. Turn right onto Persimmon Road at the TALLULAH RIVER CAMPGROUND sign and travel 4.0 miles. Turn left onto Tallulah River Road (FS 70) and travel for 1.4 miles to the Tallulah River Campground. Bypass the campground and continue straight ahead on the unpaved Tallulah River Road for another 5.95 miles (entering North Carolina) to a parking area on your left, signed for BEECH CREEK TRAILHEAD.

From the junction of US 76 and GA 197 near Lake Burton, GA, drive east on US 76 for 3.0 miles and turn left onto Persimmon Road at the sign for TALLULAH RIVER CAMPGROUND. After turning onto Persimmon Road, follow the directions above.

The trailhead for Bull Cove Falls is located on the opposite (east) side of the road from where you parked and approximately 50 feet to the south. GPS: N34 59.895 / W83 33.385

The Hike

The trail to Bull Cove Falls is marked with blue blazes on the trees and a sign for TRAIL #378, which is the Beech Creek Trail. The dirt path heads steeply uphill and into the woods. Once in the forest, the trail leads you around several switchbacks as you slowly climb. When you finally reach the top of the hill, the trail flattens out to give you a breather before making a steep descent to Beech Creek.

Ford the creek and follow it upstream to a T junction. Go left here and soon rock-hop across a tributary. As you head upstream, bypass the many small cascades and continue until you reach the creek again. Cross the creek and head right (upstream) on the narrow, overgrown path. You will pass several smaller falls, but don't be fooled. Continue to bushwhack your way upstream to the much larger and more powerful Bull Cove Falls.

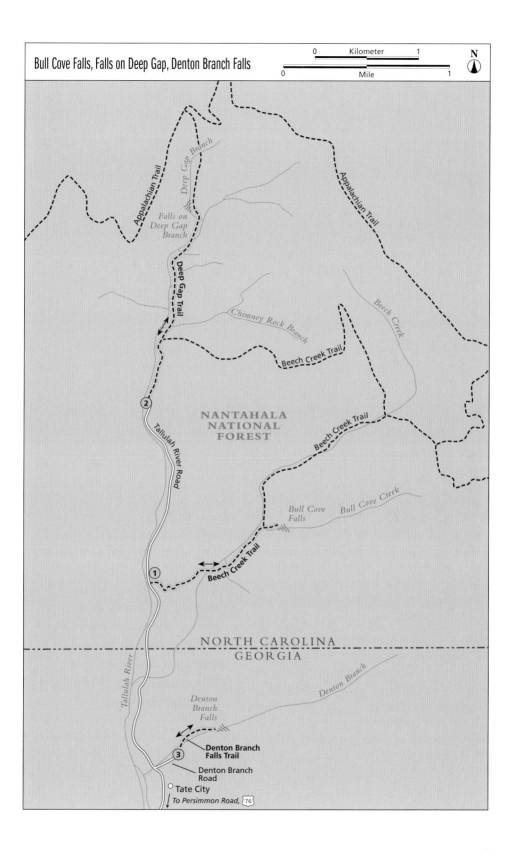

Bull Cove Falls, Falls on Deep Gap, Denton Branch Falls

0   Kilometer   1
0   Mile   1

N

Appalachian Trail

Deep Gap Branch

Falls on
Deep Gap
Branch

Deep Gap Trail

Appalachian Trail

Chimney Rock Branch

Beech Creek

Beech Creek Trail

②

Tallulah River Road

NANTAHALA
NATIONAL
FOREST

Beech Creek Trail

Beech Creek Trail

Bull Cove
Falls

Bull Cove Creek

①

Beech Creek Trail

NORTH CAROLINA
GEORGIA

Tallulah River

Denton Branch

Denton
Branch
Falls

Denton Branch
Falls Trail

③   Denton Branch
Road

○ Tate City

To Persimmon Road, 76

Wonderful views can be enjoyed from a country road.

Beware! While hiking the final bushwhack portion of this trail, my dog and I were viciously attacked by yellow jackets from an underground nest. I highly recommend carrying some Benadryl with you. If you have known allergies, carry an EpiPen, just in case.

As you make your way to the trailhead, you can't help but notice Tate City as you pass through it. What really stands out is the barn with SEE TATE CITY painted on it in bold letters and the official road sign that reads TATE CITY—POPULATION 32+/-. This sleepy little town is said to be one of the old-est settled areas in the Southern Appalachians. It was once a thriving community, known for its corundum mines. When the mines dried up, the town became a lumber camp. When the lumber boom ended, Tate City eventually evolved into what you see today.

▶ The southern yellow jacket is commonly mistaken for a bee when, in fact, it's not a bee at all but a wasp. These sinister stingers often live in underground nests, which can hold nearly 100,000 wasps in a single colony.

Miles and Directions

0.0 From the trailhead, follow the dirt path east, heading steeply uphill and into the woods. Almost immediately come to a fork; go left (north).

0.1 Arrive at a T junction in the trail. Go left (east) at the T junction; the trail continues to climb before leading you to a fork. Go right (south-southeast) here; the trail takes you around a few switchbacks as you head uphill.

0.3 Reach the top of the hill; the trail bends left (northeast).

0.6 The trail leads down to Beech Creek. Ford the creek and then head left (east), following the creek upstream.

0.7 Come to a T junction in the trail. Go left (east-northeast) at the T junction and soon come to a tributary. Rock hop across, and continue hiking north-northeast.

1.0 The rocky path leads across the creek one last time. After crossing, head right (east) and follow the very narrow path upstream.

1.1 Arrive at the base of Bull Cove Falls (GPS: N35 00.184 / W83 32.561). Return the way you came.

2.2 Arrive back at the trailhead.

2 Falls on Deep Gap Branch

Challenging! With a unicorn-like tree standing out from the top of the falls, hiking this trail is nearly as challenging as capturing a real unicorn. While it begins easy enough, the trail ends up as a hard-core bushwhack. Although the Falls on Deep Gap Branch are located in North Carolina, you must drive through Tate City, Georgia, to access the trailhead.

See map on page 9.
Height: 40 feet
Beauty rating: Fair
Distance: 2.6 miles out and back
Difficulty: Strenuous
Trail surface: Hard-packed dirt
Approximate hiking time: 2 hours
Blaze color: Blue

County: Clay
Land status: National forest
Trail contact: Nantahala National Forest, Tusquitee Ranger District; (828) 837-5152; www.fs.usda.gov/nfsnc
Maps: DeLorme: North Carolina Atlas & Gazetteer: Page 51 F6; DeLorme: Georgia Atlas & Gazetteer: Page 16 A1

Finding the trailhead: From the junction of US 76 west and US 441 in Clayton, GA, drive west on US 76 for 7.9 miles. Turn right onto Persimmon Road at the Tallulah River Campground sign and travel for 4.0 miles. Turn left onto Tallulah River Road (FS 70) and travel on Tallulah River Road for 1.4 miles to the Tallulah River Campground. Bypass the campground and continue straight ahead on the unpaved Tallulah River Road for another 7.0 miles (entering NC) to where the road ends.

From the junction of US 76 and GA 197 near Lake Burton, GA, drive east on US 76 for 3.0 miles. Turn left onto Persimmon Road at the Tallulah River Campground sign and follow the directions above.

The trailhead is located at the north end of the parking area. GPS: N35 00.834 / W83 33.378

The Hike

The trail begins by going around the boulders at the trailhead and heading uphill. As you enter the Southern Nantahala Wilderness, the trail soon narrows and then leads across an open area and then up to a fork. Head left at the fork and follow the Deep Gap Trail (#377).

The trail crosses over a creek as you continue to follow the Tallulah River upstream for another 0.3 mile. Along the way you will rock-hop a few tiny tributaries before returning to the river. Do not cross it. Instead head right and continue to follow the blue-blazed Deep Gap Trail upstream. You will cross another stream and a wet weather tributary as the trail narrows and you lose the blazes.

As you continue your uphill trek, rock-hop the creek once more. Continue climbing for less than 0.25 mile more and come to the creek one last time. Do not cross the creek; instead head left and bushwhack your way upstream to the falls.

Miles and Directions

0.0 From the trailhead, go around the boulders and uphill to a trail information sign for the Southern Nantahala Wilderness. Continue hiking north, past the sign.

0.3 The trail crosses an open area. Continue hiking on the rocky path as you head northwest and upward.

0.4 Come to a fork and go left (north), following the Deep Gap Trail (#377). Cross a creek and continue hiking northeast as you follow the river upstream.

0.7 Arrive at the river, but do not cross it. Instead head right (east), still following the trail upstream.

0.8 Come to another small stream crossing. Rock-hop across, and continue northwest.

1.0 Rock-hop across another small, wet-weather tributary. Pick up the trail on the other side as it heads to the right (northeast). The trail, now unblazed, narrows as you trek uphill.

1.1 Come to another creek crossing. Cross the creek and head right (north) as you begin to climb steeply.

1.2 Reach the creek one last time but do not cross. Instead head left (north) and bushwhack your way upstream toward the falls.

1.3 Arrive at the base of Falls on Deep Gap Branch (N35 01.812 / W83 33.096). Return the way you came.

2.6 Arrive back at the trailhead.

Options: If you've got some extra energy after visiting Falls on Deep Gap Branch, you could continue hiking on the Deep Gap Trail for less than a mile to where it dead-ends near Deep Gap on the Appalachian Trail (AT). If you really want to spruce up the adventure, the Standing Indian Shelter sits less than a mile north on the AT. You could make this an overnight trip and stay at the shelter, but be prepared—this area tends to get quite cold at night.

While Big Laurel Falls sits geographically near Falls on Deep Gap Branch, you must drive several miles to access it. Denton Branch Falls, however, lies right around the bend. If you've come all the way out through Tate City, Georgia, to see this one, I recommend making a day of it and visiting Denton Branch and Bull Cove Falls as well. Big Laurel and Mooney Falls could be coupled as a separate outing.

3 Denton Branch Falls (Georgia)

Splendid! You'll probably have Denton Branch Falls to yourself, and a splendid experience it should be. While Denton Branch is actually located in Georgia, it's included in this guide due to its proximity to Bull Cove Falls and Falls on Deep Gap Branch.

See map on page 9.
Height: 40 feet
Beauty rating: Very good
Distance: 0.6 mile out and back
Difficulty: Easy
Blaze color: No blazes
County: Rabun

Land status: National forest
Trail contact: Chattahoochee National Forest, Blue Ridge Ranger District; (706) 745-6928; www.fs.fed.us
Maps: *DeLorme: North Carolina Atlas & Gazetteer: Page 51 F6; DeLorme: Georgia Atlas & Gazetteer: Page 16 A1*

Finding the trailhead: From the junction of US 76 west and US 441 in Clayton, GA, drive west on US 76 for 7.9 miles. Turn right onto Persimmon Road at the Tallulah River Campground sign and travel for 4.0 miles. Turn left onto Tallulah River Road (FS 70) and travel for 1.4 miles to the Tallulah River Campground. Bypass the campground and continue straight ahead on the unpaved Tallulah River Road for another 5.0 miles to a right turn onto Denton Branch Road. An unmarked dirt road, Denton Branch Road is the first right turn after Chapple Lane, a short distance past the Valley Community Church. Follow Denton Branch Road for approximately 0.2 mile to where it dead-ends at the creek.

From the junction of US 76 and GA 197 near Lake Burton, GA, go east on US 76 for 3.0 miles. Turn left onto Persimmon Road at the Tallulah River Campground sign and follow the directions above.

GPS: N34 59.030 / W83 33.174

The Hike

The Denton Branch Trail follows the old roadbed north and crosses the creek. Once on the other side, continue upward on the old road, which soon becomes a narrow path and leads to a fork. Head right at the fork and follow the footpath toward the creek. Follow the creek upstream until the large and powerful Denton Branch Falls comes into view.

Located within the Southern Nantahala Wilderness, Denton Branch is part of the Tallulah River Basin, meaning that, along with many other creeks in the area, it flows into and feeds the mighty Tallulah River. As you make your way to the trailhead, be sure to take a moment and appreciate the grand final product of this basin as you pass it by. With its plentiful cascades, this riverside drive is always a pleasure.

Bulbs like this iris are quite common in the mountains of North Carolina.

Miles and Directions

0.0 From the trailhead, head north across the creek. Continue upward on the old roadbed as it bends right (east) and becomes a narrow path.

0.1 Come to a fork with an overgrown old roadbed leading up and to the left (north) and a narrow footpath leading to the right (southeast) and toward the creek. Go right (southeast), following the narrow footpath uphill and upstream.

0.3 Cross the creek east-southeast to reach an island at the base of Denton Branch Falls (N34 59.136/W83 32.941). Return the way you came.

0.6 Arrive back at the trailhead.

4 Big Laurel Falls

Tantalizing! This beauty invites you to bask in the cool waters at the base. An ideal swimming hole awaits those willing to brave the chill.

Height: 30 feet
Beauty rating: Excellent
Distance: 1.2 miles out and back
Difficulty: Easy to moderate
Trail surface: Rooty, rocky path
Approximate hiking time: 30 minutes
Blaze color: Blue

County: Macon
Land status: National forest
Trail contact: Nantahala National Forest, Nantahala Ranger District; (828) 524-6441; www.fs.fed.us
Maps: *DeLorme: North Carolina Atlas & Gazetteer:* Page 51 F6

Finding the trailhead: From the junction of US 64 and Business US 441 in Franklin, drive west on US 64 for 11.7 miles. Turn left onto West Old Murphy Road at the WALLACE GAP sign, and travel for 1.8 miles to FR 67. Turn right onto FR 67 at the sign for STANDING INDIAN CAMPGROUND, and travel 6.8 miles to a pull-off on the right at the sign for TIMBER RIDGE TRAIL AND LAUREL FALLS TRAIL.

From the junction of US 64 and NC 175 near Murphy, drive east on US 64 for 16.2 miles. Turn right onto West Old Murphy Road at the sign for WALLACE GAP and follow the directions above.

The trailhead is located at the west end of parking area. GPS: N35 01.321 / W83 30.217

The Hike

The Laurel Falls Trail leads you down into the woods under the cool, damp cover of the forest before it dead-ends at the base of Big Laurel Falls.

The site of a lumber camp in the late 1800s, nearby Standing Indian Campground is named for Standing Indian Mountain. At 5,499 feet, this peak is the highest point in the Southern Nantahala Wilderness.

Legend has it that an Indian scout was keeping watch atop the mountain after a small village child was snatched up and taken away in the talons of a great flying beast. In answer to the villagers' prayers, the Great Spirit sent down thunderbolts to destroy the monster. The lone sentinel was turned to stone where he stood, and to this day he keeps watch over the valleys below.

Miles and Directions

0.0 From the trailhead, hike southeast down the hill. Almost immediately come to a T junction. Go right (southwest) at the T junction, following the blue blazes.

0.1 Cross a footbridge and head right (northwest). Follow the creek downstream as the trail climbs, bypassing any side trails shooting off toward the creek.

0.6 Arrive at the base of Big Laurel Falls (N35 01.098 / W83 30.391). Return the way you came.

1.2 Arrive back at the trailhead.

Big Laurel Falls, Mooney Falls

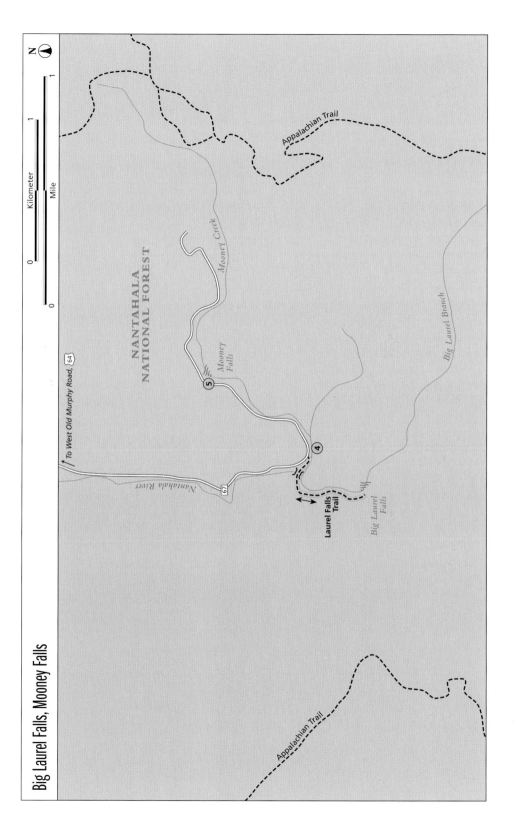

5 Mooney Falls

Intriguing! The mass of downed trees in the area truly makes you wonder about the storms, and ages, this waterfall has witnessed through the years.

See map on page 17.
Height: 30 feet
Beauty rating: Good
Distance: 0.4 mile out and back
Difficulty: Easy
Trail surface: Hard-packed dirt
Approximate hiking time: 15 minutes
Blaze color: No blazes

County: Macon
Land status: National forest
Trail contact: Nantahala National Forest, Nantahala Ranger District; (828) 524-6441; www.fs.fed.us
Maps: *DeLorme: North Carolina Atlas & Gazetteer:* Page 51 F6

Finding the trailhead: From the junction of US 64 and Business US 441 in Franklin, drive west on US 64 for 11.7 miles. Turn left onto West Old Murphy Road at the WALLACE GAP sign and travel for 1.8 miles to FR 67. Turn right onto FR 67 at the sign for STANDING INDIAN CAMPGROUND; travel for 7.4 miles to a small pull-off on the right at the MOONEY FALLS TRAIL sign.

From the junction of US 64 and NC 175 near Murphy, drive east on US 64 for 16.2 miles. Turn right onto West Old Murphy Road at the WALLACE GAP sign and follow the directions above.

GPS: N35 01.758 / W83 29.868

The Hike

Mooney Falls is audible from the parking area. The Mooney Falls Trail (#31) makes a rapid descent into the woods and leads to the middle section of Mooney Falls.

The falls were named for James Mooney, an anthropologist who lived among the Cherokee for years. Mooney had applied for employment with the Bureau of American Ethnology in Washington, D.C., for three years in a row, being denied each time. So determined was he, however, that in 1885 he made the journey in person, met with the director, and was hired on the spot as an ethnologist for the Smithsonian Institution. Mooney is fondly remembered for how well he chronicled the Cherokee culture and opened, to many, a better understanding of them as a people.

Sunset in the mountains of North Carolina sets the sky ablaze.

Miles and Directions

0.0 Start at the trailhead and hike southwest, down and into the woods.

0.1 Come to a T intersection. Go right (southwest) and follow the trail around a switchback. (The left leads east-northeast to the brink of the falls.)

0.2 Arrive in the middle of Mooney Falls (N35 01.706 / W83 29.870). Return the way you came.

0.4 Arrive back at the trailhead.

6 Rufus Morgan Falls

Poised! Tall, stony-faced Rufus Morgan Falls stands poised above, flowing fully and freely into the creek below.

Height: 70 feet	**County:** Macon
Beauty rating: Very good	**Land status:** National forest
Distance: 1.0 mile out and back	**Trail contact:** Nantahala National Forest,
Difficulty: Moderate	Nantahala Ranger District; (828) 524-6441;
Trail surface: Hard-packed dirt with rocky	www.fs.fed.us
sections	**Maps:** *DeLorme: North Carolina Atlas & Gazet-*
Approximate hiking time: 40 minutes	*teer:* Page 51 E6
Blaze color: Blue	

Finding the trailhead: From the junction of US 64 and Business US 441 in Franklin, drive west on US 64 for 3.7 miles. Turn right onto Old Murphy Road at the Wayah Bald sign and travel for 0.2 mile. Just before Old Murphy Road bends to the right, turn left onto Wayah Road (SR 1310). Follow Wayah Road for 6.3 miles; turn left onto FR 388 and travel for 2.0 miles to a small parking area on the right.

From the junction of US 64 and NC 175 near Murphy, drive east on US 64 for 24.2 miles. Turn left onto Old Murphy Road at the Wayah Bald sign and follow the directions above.

GPS: N35 08.798 / W83 32.854

The Hike

The easily followed Rufus Morgan Trail rises and falls as it winds through the forest. Along the way you will pass a wonderful small sliding rock before following a side path to the base of Rufus Morgan Falls.

The falls were named for Reverend Albert Rufus Morgan, a poet, naturalist, minister, and avid hiker. Morgan spent most of his life working to improve miles of trails in this area, including the Appalachian Trail (AT). One of the founding fathers of the Nantahala Hiking Club, he served as a board member for the AT Conservancy for more than twenty years. Also named in his honor is a section of the Mountains-to-Sea Trail and a shelter on the AT.

Morgan lived to be ninety-seven years old. Perhaps it was all that fresh air.

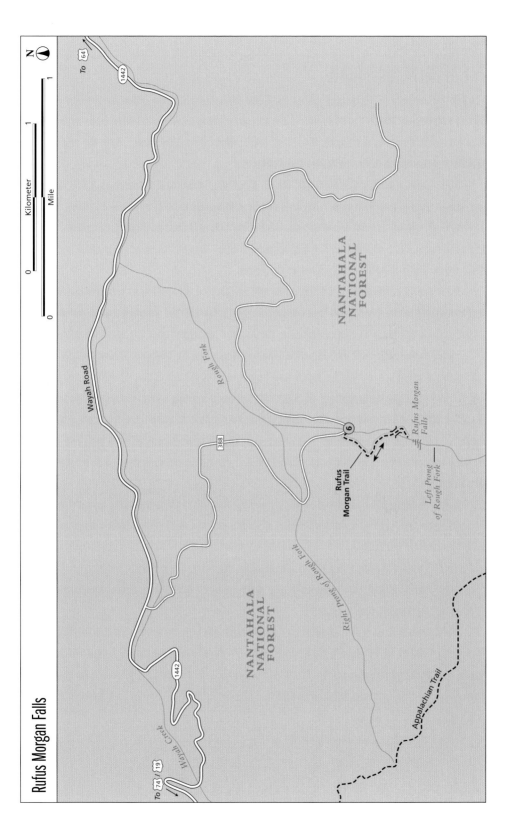

Rufus Morgan Falls

THE APPALACHIAN TRAIL

The Appalachian Trail (AT) stretches more than 2,000 miles, from Springer Mountain in Georgia to Mount Katahdin in Maine. The AT is one of the longest marked continuous hiking trails in North America—second only to the Pacific Crest Trail (PCT), which runs 2,650 miles along the western seaboard of the United States from Mexico to Canada.

While the PCT spans the West Coast, the AT is the king of the East. It traverses 2,175 miles and passes through fourteen states. The trail was first conceived in 1921 by Benton McKaye, who saw the trail as a way to promote wilderness by offering a place for people to seek refuge from the trials and tribulations of daily life. The first Appalachian Trail Conference was held in 1925, and in 1937 the trail was completed and opened to the public.

Today the AT is officially part of the National Park Service, although it is privately managed and maintained by the Appalachian Trail Conservancy (ATC). The ATC is a volunteer-based, nonprofit organization dedicated to the preservation, protection, and management of the Appalachian Trail.

Every year, three to four million people hike portions of the AT, while the annual average for "thru-hikers" (people who hike the entire trail from end to end) teeters around 400 a year. Just over 11,000 people have completed this task since the trail's inception. This demanding feat takes several months to complete and also requires very careful planning. From weather concerns to lodging, food, water, and gear, every detail must be addressed before attempting a thru hike. The majority of people who have successfully hiked the AT from end to end have done so in a south to north direction.

There are about 260 designated shelters along the AT, each about a day's hike from the next. Of course this trail sees so much traffic, that often the shelters are full, and hikers must set up their own camp for the night.

Whether you thru-hike or just visit a section at a time, you're in for a treat. Over the distance of the trail, there are over 2,000 species of rare plants and over 500 different animal species, not to mention the amazing scenic vistas.

Several informative guides about the AT are available, but I also recommend Bill Bryson's *A Walk in the Woods* for its sheer entertainment value. If you've ever spent a day on the trail, you should find the book entertaining. It chronicles the author's very amusing experiences on the AT. For trail maps, trail updates, and everything else AT, visit the ATC's website at www.appalachian trail.org.

With the average pack of a thru-hiker weighing forty pounds, my hat's off and my utmost respect to every one of you!

Miles and Directions

0.0 The trail heads west and uphill from the center of the parking lot. Come to a T junction and go right (north), following the trail as it climbs and winds through the forest.

0.4 Cross the footbridge and head upstream to a wonderful little sliding rock. Go left at the sliding rock, and head uphill.

0.5 A little more than halfway up the hill, come to a side trail that turns sharply to the right as the main blue blazed trail continues on. Turn right (west) onto this side trail and arrive at the base of Rufus Morgan Falls (N35 08.582 / W83 32.869). Return the way you came.

1.0 Arrive back at the trailhead.

7 Camp Branch Falls

Simplicity! Like a ewer in the hands of a handmaid, the flowing waters of Camp Branch Falls feed and cleanse the river.

See overview map on page iv.
Height: 200 feet
Beauty rating: Good
Distance: Roadside
Difficulty: Easy
Blaze color: No blazes
County: Macon

Land status: National forest
Trail contact: Nantahala National Forest, Nantahala Ranger District; (828) 524-6441; www.fs.fed.us
Maps: *DeLorme: North Carolina Atlas & Gazetteer:* Page 51 C5

Finding the trailhead: From the junction of US 19 and US 129 north near Andrews, drive north on US 19 for 2.1 miles. Turn right onto Wayah Road (SR 1310) and travel for 2.7 miles to a pull-off on your left.

From the junction of US 19 and NC 28 north near Bryson City, drive south on US 19 for 11.9 miles. Turn left onto Wayah Road (SR 1310) and follow the directions above.

From the junction of US 64 and Old Murphy Road near Franklin, follow Old Murphy Road for 0.2 mile. Turn left onto Wayah Road (SR 1310) and travel for 25.2 miles to a pull-off on the right.

GPS: N35 15.220 / W83 39.200

The Hike

Camp Branch Falls is viewed from the roadside and can be seen on the opposite side of the river, where Camp Branch flows into the Nantahala River.

Aptly named by the Cherokee, Nantahala means "land of the noonday sun." Being that the Nantahala gorge is very narrow, with many trees overhead, it seems true that the sun only shines upon the river at midday.

Camp Branch Falls freely flows into the Nantahala River.

8 Juneywhank Falls

Refreshing! The way the water trickles, bounces, and shoots off the mossy rocks of Juneywhank Falls is a lively treat.

Height: 30 feet
Beauty rating: Good
Distance: 0.5 mile out and back
Difficulty: Moderate
Trail surface: Gravel and hard-packed dirt
Approximate hiking time: 20 minutes
Blaze color: No blazes

County: Swain
Land status: National park
Trail contact: Great Smoky Mountains National Park; (865) 436-1200; www.nps.gov/grsm
Maps: *DeLorme: North Carolina Atlas & Gazetteer:* Page 51 A7

Finding the trailhead: From the junction of US 19 and US 441 south in Cherokee, drive south on US 19 for 9.55 miles. Turn right onto Everett Street and travel through downtown Bryson City for 0.2 mile. Turn right onto Depot Street (immediately after the railroad tracks) and travel 0.2 mile to a stop sign. Turn left onto unsigned Ramseur Street, which soon becomes Deep Creek Road. Follow Deep Creek Road for 0.3 mile to a fork in the road at West Deep Creek Road. Bear left at the fork, and follow West Deep Creek Road for 2.55 miles to the trailhead and parking area on your left (before the road takes you back to the right and over a bridge).

From US 74/US 19 (Great Smoky Mountains Parkway), drive east to exit 64 (this is where US 74 and US 19 split). Take the exit and follow US 19 north toward Bryson City for 3.0 miles. Turn left onto Everett Street and follow the directions above.

The signed trailhead is on the north side of the parking lot. GPS: N35 27.871 / W83 26.049

The Hike

Hike up the gravel hill from the trailhead. The trail bends left as it takes you to a T junction. Go right at the T junction; the trail continues to climb before leading to a stairway that takes you down to a footbridge that passes over Juneywhank Falls. From the falls you can either return the way you came or make a loop by continuing past the falls and ending up on the Deep Creek Trail.

If you plan on also hiking to nearby Tom's Branch or Indian Creek Falls, I recommend making the loop to avoid needless backtracking. After passing Juneywhank Falls, you soon come to a T junction. Go right (southeast) at the T junction and almost immediately come to a fork. Go right (southeast) at the fork as well, following the gravel trail steeply down to where it ends at a T junction along the Deep Creek Trail. Turning right at the T junction takes you to the Deep Creek Trailhead. A left (northeast) at the T junction takes you to Tom's Branch Falls in less than 0.1 mile.

Juneywhank is presumably named for Junaluska Whank, a local man who was named for the famous Cherokee chief Junaluska. In the early 1800s Chief Junaluska assisted Andrew Jackson in a fierce battle against the Creek. He led the Cherokee

Juneywhank Falls, Tom's Branch Falls, Indian Creek Falls

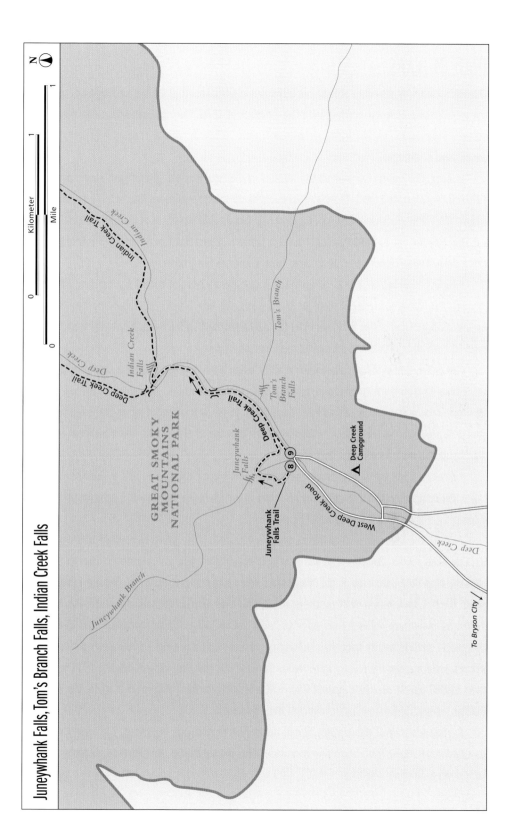

TRAIL OF TEARS

The official date for the "Trail of Tears" is 1838, but in truth this Native American saga began at the turn of the nineteenth century with the Compact of 1802. This compact was a contract in essence between the United States government, under the leadership of Thomas Jefferson, and the citizens of Georgia.

In brief, the compact promised the citizens of Georgia that the government would extinguish all Cherokee land titles. These early threats lay dormant for decades. But in 1829 someone struck gold! What soon followed was the first significant gold rush in U.S. history. Needless to say, greed set in, and in 1830 President Andrew Jackson signed the Indian Removal Act into law. This spawned the beginnings of what came to be known as the Trail of Tears.

Although thousands of U.S. citizens and Native Americans petitioned against the Indian Removal Act, Congress ignored their pleas and passed it into law. In 1831 the Choctaw, who occupied Mississippi at the time, were the first to be rounded up for expulsion. A year later, the removal continued with the Chickasaw, Creek, and Seminoles.

The Indian Removal Act culminated in 1835, when a small group from the Cherokee tribe signed the Treaty of New Echota. In a nutshell, this treaty between the U.S. government and the Cherokee people was a trade agreement. Essentially, those who signed it agreed to trade their land in Georgia for "suitable" land in Oklahoma. The problem of course was that even those who didn't sign this treaty were affected by it.

For years prior, the U.S. government had ignored treaty after treaty. Bit by bit they had taken more and more land that rightfully belonged to the Cherokee. But now the government had a treaty they were more than willing to honor.

In 1838 President Martin Van Buren began implementing the forced removal of the remaining Cherokee people. The Cherokee were not only required to give up their land in Georgia but also any land they held east of the Mississippi River. Under the direction of General Winfield Scott, the U.S. Army began swift roundups of the Cherokee, corralling them into stockades that served as temporary holding cells prior to "deportation." From these stockades, the Cherokee people were forced to take their belongings and march more than 2,000 miles west. Even women, children, and the elderly were forced to make this grueling journey. During 1838 more than 15,000 people marched against their will, and nearly a third of them died along the way. Hunger, disease, and exhaustion decimated their numbers.

In remembrance of this tragedy, the National Park Service has designated the route taken as a National Historic Trail, which now commemorates the survival of the Cherokee people in the face of overwhelming adversity.

troops alongside the white men and is even credited with saving Jackson's life. Oddly enough, Andrew Jackson still signed the Indian Removal Act of 1830, which led to the infamous "Trail of Tears." Chief Junaluska is buried in downtown Robbinsville, North Carolina, where a monument in his honor still stands today.

Miles and Directions

0.0 From the trailhead, hike north up the gravel hill. The trail soon bends left (southwest). Continue hiking and reach a T junction in the trail. Go right here, continuing to follow the Juneywhank Falls Trail uphill. (The trail to the left is the Deep Creek Horse Trail.)

0.2 Come to a fork in the trail. Go right (northeast) at the fork and head down the steps toward the falls.

0.25 Arrive at Juneywhank Falls (N35 27.991 / W83 26.100). Return the way you came. (*Option:* Continue past the falls and hike another 0.3 mile to connect with the Deep Creek Trail.)

0.5 Arrive back at the trailhead.

9 Tom's Branch and Indian Creek Falls

Phenomenal! The Deep Creek Trail gives you two waterfalls along the same trail. The first is Tom's Branch Falls. The waters of Tom's Branch flow so softly into Deep Creek that they soothe the senses and calm the soul. Indian Creek Falls is next to come. Much like Mother Nature's spa, it has a perfect plunge pool at the base and what seems to be a Jacuzzi on the right. The only thing missing here is a masseuse.

See map on page 27.

Height: Tom's Branch, 80 feet; Indian Creek, 35 feet

Beauty rating: Good for Tom's Branch Falls; very good for Indian Creek Falls

Distance: 1.8 miles out and back (Tom's Branch Falls, 0.4 mile)

Difficulty: Easy

Trail surface: Wide gravel road

Approximate hiking time: 1 hour

Other trail users: Trail runners, equestrians

Blaze color: No blazes

County: Swain

Land status: National park

Trail contact: Great Smoky Mountains National Park; (865) 436-1200; www.nps.gov/grsm

Maps: *DeLorme: North Carolina Atlas & Gazetteer:* Page 51 A7

Finding the trailhead: From the junction of US 19 and US 441 south in Cherokee, drive south on US 19 for 9.55 miles. Turn right onto Everett Street and travel through downtown Bryson City for 0.2 mile. Turn right onto Depot Street (immediately after the railroad tracks) and travel 0.2 mile to a stop sign. Turn left onto unsigned Ramseur Street, which soon becomes Deep Creek Road. Follow Deep Creek Road, for 0.3 mile to a fork in the road at West Deep Creek Road. Bear left at the fork, and follow West Deep Creek Road for 2.55 miles to the trailhead and parking area on your left (before the road takes you back to the right and over a bridge).

From US 74/US 19 (Great Smoky Mountains Parkway), drive east to exit 64 (this is where US 74 and US 19 split). Take the exit and follow US 19 north toward Bryson City for 3.0 miles. Turn left onto Everett Street and follow the directions above.

The trailhead for the Deep Creek Trail is at the far north end of the parking area, by the signs for the "unloading zone." GPS: N35 27.888 / W83 26.013

The Hike

The roadlike trail follows the creek's edge and leads to an open area where you see Tom's Branch Falls on the opposite side of the creek. From Tom's Branch, the path continues upstream, bringing you over one bridge and then to a second. Do not cross the second bridge. Instead go right and soon arrive at the base of Indian Creek Falls. On weekends you're likely to see many people on inner tubes in the creek. If you'd like to tube the creek yourself, there are tube rental stands just outside the park.

Indian Creek Falls is one of several waterfalls found within the North Carolina portion of the Great Smoky Mountains National Park.

This area is remembered for the Battle of Deep Creek, a Civil War battle in which William Thomas was able to convince the Cherokee to fight with the Confederates. Fighting alongside Thomas and his troops, the Cherokee helped win the bloody battle.

Miles and Directions

0.0 From the trailhead, hike around the gate and follow the Deep Creek Trail upstream (northeast).

0.1 Bypass the trail to Juneywhank Falls on your left, and continue straight ahead (northeast).

0.2 Arrive at Tom's Branch Falls (N35 28.003 / W83 25.811). (*Option:* Return to the trailhead.)

0.5 Cross the bridge and continue north-northeast.

0.8 Come to a second bridge. Do not cross this one. Instead go right (east-northeast) and soon see some steps on your left (east) that lead down toward the falls.

0.9 Arrive at the base of Indian Creek Falls (N35 28.355 / W83 25.669). Return the way you came.

1.8 Arrive back at the trailhead.

10 Mingo Falls

Brilliant and bright! Like a goddess atop the Parthenon, Mingo Falls stands out above all others in the area. The water truly shines as it flows freely over her mossy face.

Height: 150 feet	**County:** Swain
Beauty rating: Excellent	**Land status:** Owned by Eastern Band of
Distance: 0.4 mile out and back	Cherokee
Difficulty: Easy to moderate	**Trail contact:** Eastern Band of Cherokee
Trail surface: Wooden stairs and hard-packed	Indians Parks and Recreation; www.chero
dirt	kee-nc.com
Approximate hiking time: 15 minutes	**Maps:** *DeLorme: North Carolina Atlas & Gazet-*
Blaze color: No blazes	*teer:* Page 29 F8

Finding the trailhead: From the junction of US 441 north and US 19 in Cherokee, drive north on US 441 for 2.2 miles. Turn right onto Acquoni Road at the sign pointing to Big Cove Road. Travel on Acquoni Road for 0.1 mile and turn left onto Big Cove Road. Continue for 4.7 miles and turn right at the Mingo Falls sign onto Mingo Falls Bridge. Cross the bridge and go straight ahead to the parking area.

From the junction of US 441 and the Blue Ridge Parkway in Cherokee, drive south on US 441 for approximately 0.4 mile. Turn left onto Acquoni Road at the sign pointing to Big Cove Road, and follow the directions above.

The trailhead is at the south end of the parking lot. GPS: N35 32.034 / W83 16.562

The Hike

The trail begins by climbing a steep staircase. When you reach the top of the steps, the trail follows the creek upstream to the base of Mingo Falls.

Mingo Falls is located within the Qualla Tract of the present-day Cherokee Indian Reservation. The "Qualla Boundary" that forms its border was actually named in 1876 for what was then known as Quallatown. It was occupied by about 1,000 Cherokee who lived outside the boundaries of the Cherokee Nation. Because of this technicality, these people were allowed to remain in North Carolina, unlike their Cherokee brothers and sisters who were forced to emigrate to Oklahoma on the infamous "Trail of Tears." Many of the people residing here today are direct descendants of those lucky few.

Mingo Falls

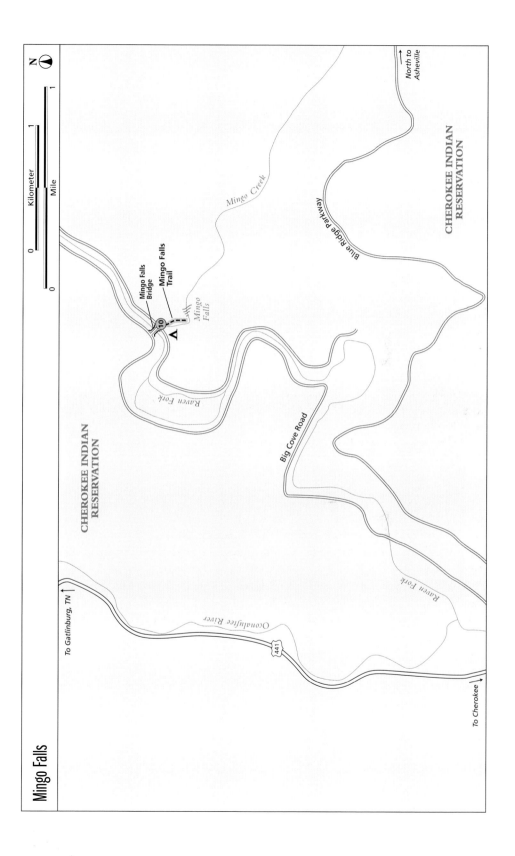

N

0   Kilometer   1
0   Mile   1

To Gatlinburg, TN

CHEROKEE INDIAN RESERVATION

Oconaluftee River

441

To Cherokee

Big Cove Road

Raven Fork

Raven Fork

Mingo Falls Bridge

Mingo Falls Trail

Mingo Falls

Mingo Creek

Blue Ridge Parkway

CHEROKEE INDIAN RESERVATION

North to Asheville

Mingo Falls flows with confidence.

Miles and Directions

0.0 From the trailhead, hike south up the 150+ stairs. Once at the top of the steps, follow the creek upstream.

0.2 Arrive at Mingo Falls (N35 31.915 / W83 16.541). Return the way you came.

0.4 Arrive back at the trailhead.

11 Soco Falls

Convergence! Like songbirds at the wake of dawn complete each other's songs, two waterfalls converge here, forming one creek, and completing each other in a similar way.

Height: 50 feet
Beauty rating: Very good
Distance: 0.2 mile out and back
Difficulty: Easy to moderate
Trail surface: Hard-packed dirt
Approximate hiking time: 10 minutes
Blaze color: No blazes
County: Jackson

Land status: National forest
Trail contact: Nantahala National Forest, Nantahala Ranger District; (828) 524-6441; www.fs.fed.us
FYI: No pets are allowed on the trail
Maps: *DeLorme: North Carolina Atlas & Gazetteer:* Page 52 A1

Finding the trailhead: From the junction of US 19 and the Blue Ridge Parkway near Maggie Valley, drive south on US 19 for 1.4 miles to a large pull-off on the left at the small sign for Soco Falls.

From the junction of US 19 and US 441 north in Cherokee, drive north on US 19 for 10.4 miles to a large pull-off on the right at the small sign for Soco Falls.

The trailhead is located at the northeast end of the parking area, at the split in the guardrail. GPS: N35 29.574/W83 10.180

The Hike

The narrow dirt path makes a few quick switchbacks before leading to an observation deck overlooking Soco Falls.

It is said that the Cherokee threw one of Hernando de Soto's men from the top of the falls, all the while shouting "Soco, Soco." Presumably this incident occurred at Soco Falls, since the Cherokee word *askwan,* or "where the Spaniard is thrown in the water," refers to a place near Soco Gap.

White tail deer are commonly seen at dusk.

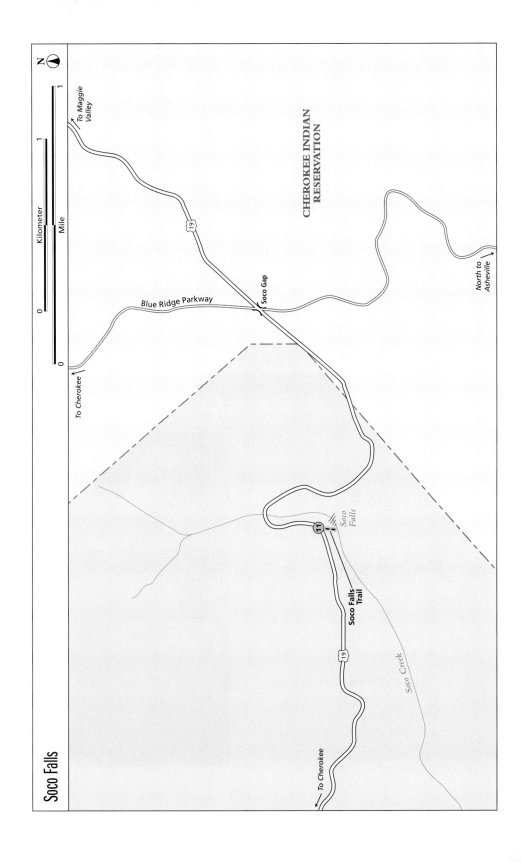

Soco Falls

Red-tailed hawks, one of the most common hawks in North America, feed primarily on small mammals.

Miles and Directions

0.0 Start at the trailhead, following the dirt path northeast and around some switchbacks.

0.1 Arrive at an observation deck overlooking Soco Falls (N35 29.555 / W83 10.187). Return the way you came.

0.2 Arrive back at the trailhead.

12 Midnight Hole and Mouse Creek Falls

Vivid and vibrant! This trail gives you two of the most colorful waterfalls in this book. First you come to Midnight Hole. Like the full moon, the pool of Midnight Hole captures your gaze and will not release it. The vivid colors of the water here are captivating. Next along the trail is Mouse Creek Falls. This lively waterfall will put a spring in your step.

Height: Midnight Hole, 6 feet; Mouse Creek Falls, 35 feet
Beauty rating: Excellent for both
Distance: 4.0 miles out and back (Midnight Hole, 3.0 miles)
Difficulty: Moderate
Trail surface: Wide gravel road
Approximate hiking time: 2 hours, 15 minutes
Other trail users: Mountain bikers, equestrians

Blaze color: No blazes
County: Haywood
Land status: National park
Trail contact: Great Smoky Mountains National Park; (865) 436-1200; www.nps.gov/grsm
Maps: DeLorme: North Carolina Atlas & Gazetteer: Page 30 D2

Finding the trailhead: From the junction of US 276 and US 19 in Waynesville, drive north on US 276 for 5.9 miles to where US 276 becomes I-40 west. Continue on I-40 west for 20.5 miles into Tennessee and take exit 451 (Waterville Road). Turn left off the exit ramp onto Waterville Road (SR 1332) and travel 2.3 miles to a stop sign. Continue straight ahead at the stop sign and enter Great Smoky Mountains National Park. (**Note:** Once inside the national park, you will pass the trailhead at 0.8 mile at the BIG CREEK TRAIL sign.) Follow this road for 0.9 mile to where it dead-ends at a parking area. The trailhead is located off the main park road, northwest of the parking area. GPS: N35 45.100 / W83 06.625

The Hike

The trail follows an old roadbed and the creek upstream from high above the entire way. After hiking for 1.1 miles, you finally come back near the creek's edge before arriving at the blue-green pool known as Midnight Hole. A perfect swimming hole awaits those daring enough to brave the chilly water.

From Midnight Hole, the trail continues to follow the road for another 0.5 mile to the base of vibrant Mouse Creek Falls, where Mouse Creek flows into Big Creek.

Located in the Big Creek area of Smoky Mountains National Park, this trail is actually an old logging road, originally built by the Crestmont Logging Company during the early 1900s logging boom. The road was later improved by the Civilian Conservation Corps in the 1930s and became the gravel roadway it is today. The trail now welcomes foot, bicycle, and horse traffic, but no dogs or other pets are allowed. There are restrooms, trash cans, and a picnic area near the parking lot.

Midnight Hole and Mouse Creek Falls

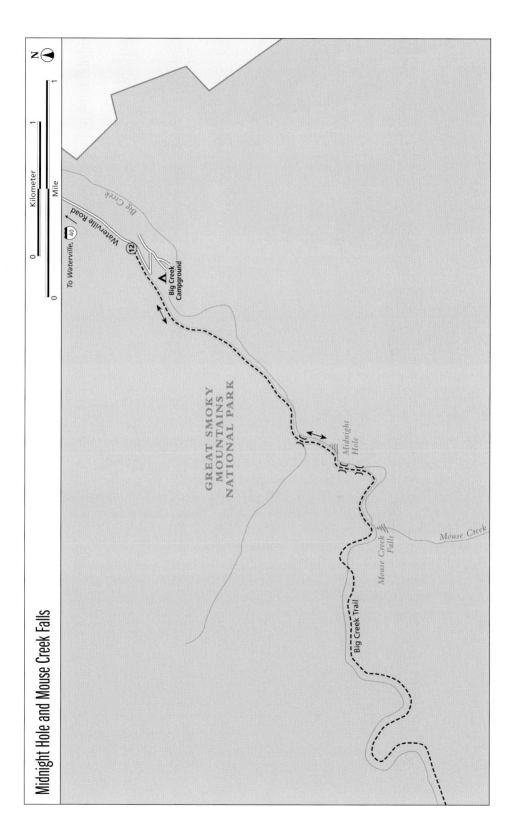

Midnight Hole is always awe inspiring.

Miles and Directions

0.0 From the trailhead, go around the rocks, and head west on the old roadbed.

0.25 Bypass the side trail on your left, and continue hiking straight ahead (southwest).

1.3 Hike across the tiny footbridge and then rock hop a tributary.

1.5 Follow the rocky side trail that leads south-southeast to Midnight Hole (N35 44.302 / W83 07.643). Continue hiking upstream on the old roadbed. (**Option:** Return to the trailhead for a 3-mile hike.)

1.6 Cross back-to-back small footbridges. Continue hiking south-southwest.

2.0 Come to horse hitching posts off to your left and head left (south) toward the creek. You will see Mouse Creek Falls flowing in from across the creek (N35 44.124 / W83 08.019). Return the way you came.

4.0 Arrive back at the trailhead.

13 Cullasaja Falls

Postcard perfect! You can't appreciate the beauty of this waterfall by driving by, even at only 10 miles per hour. As difficult as it is to pull off here, the view is well worth it, but please use caution!

See map on page 44.
Height: 250 feet
Beauty rating: Phenomenal
Distance: Roadside
Difficulty: Easy
Blaze color: No blazes
County: Macon

Land status: National forest
Trail contact: Nantahala National Forest, Nantahala Ranger District; (828) 524-6441; www.fs.fed.us
Maps: DeLorme: North Carolina Atlas & Gazetteer: Page 51 E8

Finding the trailhead: From the junction of US 64 and US 441 Bypass in Franklin, drive east on US 64 for 7.8 miles to a very small pull-off on the right.

From the junction of US 64 and NC 106 in Highlands, drive west on US 64 for 8.5 miles to a very small pull-off on the left. (**Note:** If traveling west on US 64, I recommend continuing past the falls until you can find a place to turn around. The pull-off is much safer to approach from the west, driving eastward.)

GPS: N35 07.056 / W83 16.238

The Hike

Cullasaja Falls is viewed from the roadside, but please use caution; it is located along a very narrow and busy section of US 64.

The name Cullasaja is derived from the Cherokee word *kulsetsiyi*, which translates to "honey locust place" or "sugar town." In the 1700s there were three North Carolina towns known as Sugartown, one of which was located within the Cullasaja Gorge near the mouth of Ellijay Creek. It is for this Sugartown that the gorge and river are said to be named.

> Of the four National Forests within North Carolina, the Nantahala is the largest. It encompasses well over a half million acres.

The rather impressive Cullasaja Falls is visible from the roadside.

14 Cascades on the Cullasaja River

Swift! Sitting just upstream from the mighty Cullasaja Falls, the cascades move swiftly through the gorge as the river gains power and builds strength for the climax that awaits just downstream.

Height: 25 feet
Beauty rating: Very good
Distance: Roadside
Difficulty: Easy
Blaze color: No blazes
County: Macon

Land status: National forest
Trail contact: Nantahala National Forest, Nantahala Ranger District; (828) 524-6441; www.fs.fed.us
Maps: *DeLorme: North Carolina Atlas & Gazetteer:* Page 51 E8

Finding the trailhead: From the junction of US 64 and US 441 Bypass in Franklin, drive east on US 64 for 9.0 miles to a small pull-off on the right.

From the junction of US 64 and NC 106 in Highlands, drive west on US 64 for 6.4 miles to a small pull-off on the left.

GPS: N35 05.572 / W83 15.942

The Hike

Cascades on the Cullasaja are viewed from the roadside as the Cullasaja River flows through Macon County. The river begins at Lake Sequoyah and cuts its way through the gorge to its terminus, where it flows into the Little Tennessee River. As US 64 follows alongside the river, six fabulous waterfalls—all of which can be seen from the roadside—can be found over a 6-mile stretch of highway between Lake Sequoyah Dam and Cullasaja Falls. Wow, that's one per mile.

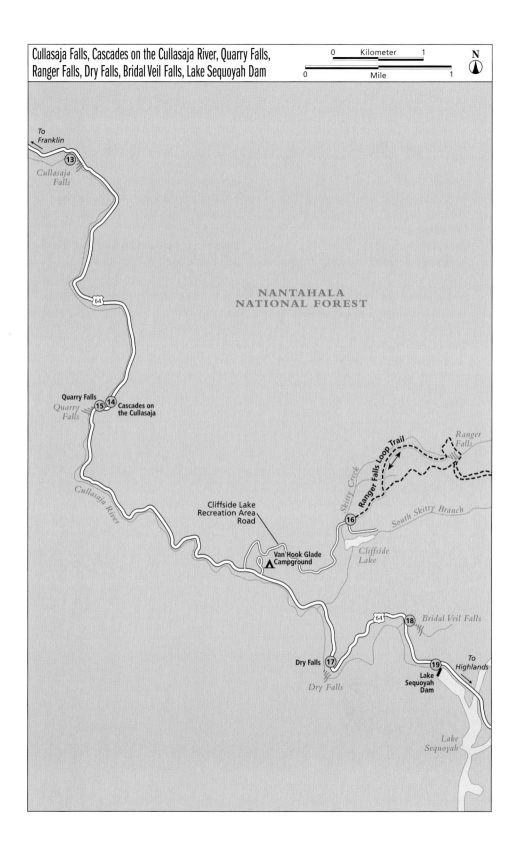

Cullasaja Falls, Cascades on the Cullasaja River, Quarry Falls, Ranger Falls, Dry Falls, Bridal Veil Falls, Lake Sequoyah Dam

To Franklin

13 Cullasaja Falls

64

NANTAHALA NATIONAL FOREST

Quarry Falls
Quarry Falls
15 14 Cascades on the Cullasaja

Ranger Falls

Cullasaja River

Skitty Creek

Ranger Falls Loop Trail

South Skitty Branch

Cliffside Lake Recreation Area Road

16

Cliffside Lake

Van Hook Glade Campground

64 18 Bridal Veil Falls

Dry Falls 17

19

To Highlands

Lake Sequoyah Dam

Dry Falls

Lake Sequoyah

0   Kilometer   1

0   Mile   1

N

15 Quarry Falls

Fanciful! The unique characteristics of pools and the lines carved through the rocky face of the falls make this inviting swimming hole a great place to spend the day. Don't expect to have it to yourself though; this one sees a lot of traffic.

See map on page 44.
Height: 20 feet
Beauty rating: Excellent
Distance: Roadside
Difficulty: Easy
Blaze color: No blazes
County: Macon

Land status: National forest
Trail contact: Nantahala National Forest, Nantahala Ranger District; (828) 524-6441; www.fs.fed.us
Maps: *DeLorme: North Carolina Atlas & Gazetteer:* Page 51 E8

Finding the trailhead: From the junction of US 64 and US 441 Bypass in Franklin, drive east on US 64 for 10.1 miles to a large pull-off on your left.

From the junction of US 64 and NC 106 in Highlands, drive west on US 64 for 6.4 miles to a large pull-off on your right.

There is a trailhead information sign at the far west end of the pull-off. GPS: N35 05.566 / W83 15.969

Quarry Falls is a very popular swimming hole with the locals.

More than fifty species of sunflowers (Helianthus annuus) *are native to North America. Some can grow as tall as 9 feet.*

The Hike

From the parking area, *carefully* cross US 64 and follow the creek downstream to view Quarry Falls. The locals call this waterfall Bust Your Butt Falls, perhaps a more fitting name given the very slick nature of the rocks surrounding the cascade.

16 Ranger Falls

Spry! Ranger Falls recently graduated to the ranks of named waterfalls located within the Nantahala National Forest. While the newly cut trail can be challenging, the rewards of this lively, youthful waterfall are well worth the effort.

See map on page 44.
Height: 40 feet
Beauty rating: Good
Distance: 2.2 miles out and back
Difficulty: Moderate to strenuous
Trail surface: Hard-packed dirt
Approximate hiking time: 1 hour, 15 minutes
Blaze color: No blazes

County: Macon
Land status: National forest
Trail contact: Nantahala National Forest, Nantahala Ranger District; (828) 524-6441; www.fs.fed.us
Maps: *DeLorme: North Carolina Atlas & Gazetteer:* Page 52 A1

Finding the trailhead: From the junction of US 64 and US 441 Bypass in Franklin, drive east on US 64 for 12.1 miles. Turn left into the Cliffside Lake day-use area, and drive on the paved road to the gate at the self-pay station. After paying the fee, continue for another 0.3 mile and turn left into the parking area by the restrooms.

From the junction of US 64 and NC 106 in Highlands, drive west on US 64 for 4.2 miles. Turn right into the Cliffside Lake day-use area and follow the directions above.

The trailhead is located at the northeast corner of the parking area at the Ranger Falls sign. GPS: N35 04.904 / W83 14.148

The Hike

Follow the trail steeply uphill to a fork. Head left at the fork; the trail now begins to make a steep descent. After crossing a small tributary, continue hiking along the interpretive trail for another 0.5 mile until you arrive at the base of Ranger Falls where the trail crosses the creek near Signpost 9. From the falls you can either return the way you came or continue on. The trail makes a loop that leads back to the fork mentioned above. This route adds another 1.0 mile to your hike but takes you past a lovely orchard along the way.

After hiking the many trails within the Cliffside Lake Recreation Area, you may want to take advantage of some of the other activities. The lake is a popular summertime swimming spot, or you can try your hand at fishing from the shoreline. Picnic sites are located throughout the area, and if you'd like to extend your stay, primitive camping is available right next door at Van Hook Glade Campground. A special thanks to Henry Buerkert and Brandon Byrd for sharing this waterfall with us.

Suspension bridges are always fun.

Miles and Directions

0.0 From the trailhead, hike southeast and uphill into the forest.

0.3 Come to a fork at the top of the hill. Go left (northwest) at the fork and begin your descent.

0.4 Cross a small tributary and continue hiking north-northwest.

1.1 Reach the base of Ranger Falls (N35 05.272 / W83 13.469). Return the way you came. (*Option:* Continue past the falls to loop back to the fork in an additional 1.0 mile.)

2.2 Arrive back at the trailhead.

17 Dry Falls

Not dry at all! The sheer mass of water crashing down in front of you is quite an amazing experience—a damp one that is. The Cullasaja River drops in a pure freefall, misting those who dare to walk behind the falls. That's right, you can walk behind this one, and she's definitely more powerful than any other waterfall you've gone behind around here.

See map on page 44.

Height: 80 feet

Beauty rating: Excellent

Distance: 0.2 mile out and back

Difficulty: Easy

Trail surface: Paved path

Approximate hiking time: 15 minutes

Blaze color: No blazes

County: Macon

Land status: National forest

Trail contact: Nantahala National Forest, Nantahala Ranger District; (828) 524-6441; www.fs.fed.us

FYI: There is a small fee to park and visit the falls.

Maps: *DeLorme: North Carolina Atlas & Gazetteer:* Page 52 F1

Finding the trailhead: From the junction of US 64 and US 441 Bypass in Franklin, drive east on US 64 for 13.3 miles. Turn right into the parking area for Dry Falls.

From the junction of US 64 and NC 106 in Highlands, drive west on US 64 for 3.0 miles. The parking area is on the left, just past the National Forest Service sign for DRY FALLS RECREATION AREA.

The trailhead is located at the north end of the parking area. GPS: N35 04.104 / W83 14.313

The Hike

Follow the path down the stone steps, and it soon leads you to an observation deck overlooking Dry Falls. From here the path continues on to where you can go behind Dry Falls and come out to view it from the opposite bank.

To fully experience this one, you must go behind the falls. The rush of the water and wonderful views of the river simply cannot be appreciated from the observation deck alone.

Located along the 61.3-mile Mountain Waters Scenic Byway, this stretch of US 64 from Franklin to Highlands is most impressive, displaying several noteworthy waterfalls.

Notice the trail behind Dry Falls.

Miles and Directions

0.0 From the trailhead, go down the stone steps and hike northeast to an observation deck. The paved path continues southwest to where you can go behind the falls.

0.1 Arrive behind Dry Falls (N35 04.127 / W83 14.323). Return the way you came.

0.2 Arrive back at the trailhead.

18 Bridal Veil Falls (Highlands)

Delicate! The soft and easy freefall of Bridal Veil Falls is a unique experience for the area. You can actually drive behind this one.

See map on page 44.
Height: 60 feet
Beauty rating: Good
Distance: Roadside
Difficulty: Easy
Blaze color: No blazes
County: Macon

Land status: National forest
Trail contact: Nantahala National Forest, Nantahala Ranger District; (828) 524-6441; www.fs.fed.us
Maps: *DeLorme: North Carolina Atlas & Gazetteer:* Page 52 E1-F1

Finding the trailhead: From the junction of US 64 and US 441 Bypass in Franklin, drive east on US 64 for 14.0 miles to a pull-off on the left at Bridal Veil Falls.

From the junction of US 64 and NC 106 in Highlands, drive west on US 64 for 2.2 miles to a pull-off on the right at Bridal Veil Falls.

GPS: N35 04.312 / W83 13.725

The Hike

Bridal Veil Falls is viewed from the roadside, and you can actually drive behind the falls.

For several years the area behind the falls was closed to vehicular traffic due to a boulder that came crashing down from above and landed in the fortunately unoccupied pull-off. The Forest Service has now deemed the area safe, and you can once again have the wonderful experience of driving behind Bridal Veil Falls.

According to Cherokee legend, a maiden who walks behind these falls in spring will be wed before the year's passing. Hence the name, Bridal Veil Falls.

A car drives behind the sweet veil of Bridal Veil Falls near Highlands, NC.

19 Lake Sequoyah Dam

The calm before the storm! The tranquil waters of Lake Sequoyah transform in an instant, falling fiercely as it forms a raging river.

See map on page 44.
Height: 30 feet
Beauty rating: Very good
Distance: Roadside
Difficulty: Easy
Trail surface: Hard-packed dirt
Approximate hiking time: 5 minutes
Blaze color: No blazes

County: Macon
Land status: National forest
Trail contact: Nantahala National Forest, Nantahala Ranger District; (828) 524-6441; www.fs.fed.us
Maps: *DeLorme: North Carolina Atlas & Gazetteer:* Page 52 E1–F1

Finding the trailhead: From the junction of US 64 and US 441 Bypass in Franklin, drive east on US 64 for 14.4 miles to a pull-off on the right, just before the dam.

From the junction of US 64 and NC 106 in Highlands, drive west on US 64 for 1.8 miles to a pull-off on your left, just past the dam.

GPS: N35 04.065 / W83 13.498

The Hike

The falls are visible from the roadside, or you can follow the very short path down to the base of Lake Sequoyah Dam.

Known as the "Father of the Cherokee Language," Sequoyah was the first Native American for whom a statue stands in the National Statuary Hall in Washington, D.C. He was born in 1776 in Tennessee and given the name Sikwo-ya, which may imply that he had some sort of handicap (*sikwo-yi* is Cherokee for "pig foot").

Lake Sequoyah flows over the dam creating this wonderful man-made waterfall.

Sequoyah later moved to Georgia and became a silversmith. This is where his genius may have been inspired. It was customary for silversmiths to sign their work, but at the time there was no written language for the Cherokee. So, he began the laborious task of creating the *Syllabary,* a dictionary containing eighty-six symbols representing consonants and vowels. No easy task, it took him over fifteen years, during which time he was ridiculed for his work and slipped into reclusion. Over time, however, the *Syllabary* gained vast acceptance and is still in use to this day.

20 Glen Falls

Mystical! The cool, misty breeze created by Glen Falls is almost like the hand of God is fanning you Himself. It mimics the emotions felt when standing atop a mountain range on a crisp autumn day.

See map on page 59.
Height: Upper Falls, 70 feet; Middle Falls, 60 feet; Lower Falls, 20 feet
Beauty rating: Excellent for all
Distance: Upper Falls, 1.0 mile out and back; Middle Falls, 1.6 miles out and back; Lower Falls, 2.0 miles out and back
Difficulty: Strenuous
Trail surface: Very rooty trail

Approximate hiking time: 1 hour
Blaze color: No blazes
County: Macon
Land status: National forest
Trail contact: Nantahala National Forest, Nantahala Ranger District; (828) 524-6441; www.fs.fed.us
Maps: *DeLorme: North Carolina Atlas & Gazetteer:* Page 52 F1

Finding the trailhead: From the junction of NC 106 and US 64 in Highlands, drive south on NC 106 for 1.7 miles. Turn left onto Glen Falls Road (SR 1618) at the Glen Falls sign. Immediately turn right and follow Glen Falls Road for 1.0 mile to where it dead-ends.

From the junction of GA 246 and US 441 in Dillard, Georgia, drive north on GA 246 for 12.3 miles. Turn right onto Glen Falls Road at the Glen Falls Recreational Area sign and follow the directions above. (**Note:** GA 246 becomes NC 106 once inside North Carolina.)

The trailhead is located at the southwest corner of the parking area. GPS: N35 02.000 / W83 14.152

The Hike

I must highlight the scenic overlooks this trail affords you. Below sits the Blue Valley Experimental Forest, and some of the best views of this 1,400-acre hardwood forest can be seen from the Glen Falls Trail. Along with amazing views of the surrounding mountains, this trail passes three distinct sections of the waterfall as it makes a continual descent around several switchbacks and leads you to Upper, Middle, and Lower Glen Falls. The rewards here are hard earned though. Not only is the terrain covered with tree roots but also the grade is steeper than it seems, which you quickly realize on your way back to the trailhead.

Upper Glen Falls sparkles even on a foggy day.

Miles and Directions

0.0 From the trailhead, hike south on the wide gravel trail, ignoring the Chinquapin Mountain Trail to the right (north).

0.1 Come to a makeshift bench offering incredible scenic views. Go right (northwest) at the bench and head downhill around several switchbacks.

0.2 Arrive at an observation deck atop Glen Falls. Continue southwest and downhill, heading deeper into the forest.

0.3 Come to a T junction; go right (north-northwest) and reach another observation deck at the brink of Glen Falls.

0.4 Return to the T junction; go left (south-southeast) and continue until you come to a three-way fork. Go straight ahead (south) at the fork, ignoring the small trails to the right and left, and make your way deeper into the valley.

While the trail to Middle Glen Falls is strenuous, it's well worth the effort.

0.5 Arrive at the base of Upper Glen Falls (N35 01.881/W83 14.304). Continue hiking south. (*Option:* Return to the trailhead for a 1-mile hike.)

0.8 After making your way around a few switchbacks, arrive at the base of Middle Glen Falls (N35 01.847/W83 14.326). Continue hiking south and downstream. (*Option:* Return to the trailhead for a 1.6-mile hike.)

0.9 Come to a fork in the trail; go right (west-southwest) and immediately come to a T junction. Turn right (northwest) at the T junction.

1.0 A short distance from the T junction, arrive at Lower Glen Falls (N35 01.773/W83 14.362). Return the way you came.

2.0 Arrive back at the trailhead.

21 Picklesimer Rock House Falls

Pacifying! As the water makes a freefall and then dances on the rocks below, it brings an inner peace to the soul. Cliffs jut out overhead, creating a mammoth cave below. Such rocky outcroppings and the caverns they create came to be known as "rock houses."

Height: 40 feet
Beauty rating: Very good
Distance: 1.2 miles out and back
Difficulty: Easy
Trail surface: Wide, dirt and grassy roadway
Approximate hiking time: 30 minutes
Blaze color: No blazes

County: Macon
Land status: National forest
Trail contact: Nantahala National Forest, Nantahala Ranger District; (828) 524-6441; www.fs.fed.us
Maps: *DeLorme: North Carolina Atlas & Gazetteer:* Page 52 F1

Finding the trailhead: From the junction of NC 28 and US 64 in Highlands, drive south on NC 28 for 5.8 miles. Turn right onto Blue Valley Road (SR 1618) at the sign for the Blue Valley Campground. Travel for 3.6 miles until you get to a fork in the road at a Backcountry Information sign. Go left at the fork and travel 0.6 mile to an old logging road on your right. Go right here and park.

From the junction of GA 28 and Warwoman Road in Pine Mountain, GA, drive north on GA 28, for 5.8 miles. Turn left onto Blue Valley Road (SR 1618) at the sign for Blue Valley Campground and follow the directions above. (**Note:** Along the way, you enter into North Carolina, and GA 28 becomes NC 28.)

GPS: N35 00.756/W83 14.955

The Hike

The trail takes you up the old logging road, around a gate, and into the forest. Continue to follow the grassy road until you reach the creek. Once at the creek, the trail transforms into a narrow dirt path. Follow this path upstream to the base of Picklesimer Rock House Falls.

Note: There is also an area known as the Picklesimer Fields, located within the Pisgah Ranger District of Pisgah National Forest.

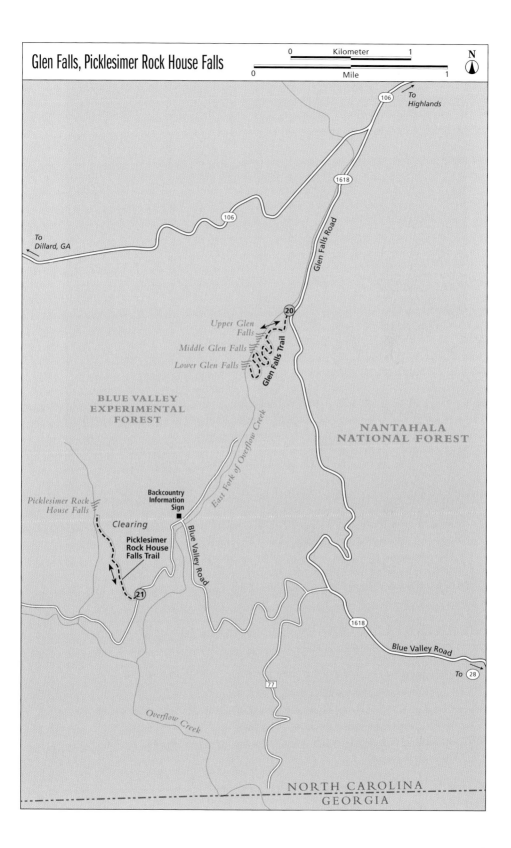

Glen Falls, Picklesimer Rock House Falls

0   Kilometer   1
0   Mile   1

N

To Highlands
106

1618

106

Glen Falls Road

To Dillard, GA

20

Upper Glen Falls
Middle Glen Falls
Lower Glen Falls

Glen Falls Trail

BLUE VALLEY
EXPERIMENTAL
FOREST

East Fork of Overflow Creek

NANTAHALA
NATIONAL FOREST

Picklesimer Rock House Falls

Backcountry
Information
Sign

Clearing

Picklesimer
Rock House
Falls Trail

Blue Valley Road

21

1618

Blue Valley Road

To 28

77

Overflow Creek

NORTH CAROLINA
GEORGIA

A "Rock House" is formed below Picklesimer Falls.

Miles and Directions

0.0 From the trailhead, hike west up the old logging road.

0.1 Go around the gate and continue hiking northwest up the grassy road.

0.4 Cross a clearing; continue hiking north-northwest.

0.45 Arrive at the creek, but do not cross it. Instead go right (northeast) and follow the obscure dirt path upstream toward the sound of the falls.

0.6 Arrive at the base of Picklesimer Rock House Falls (N35 01.108 / W83 15.206). Return the way you came.

1.2 Arrive back at the trailhead.

22 Lower Satulah Falls

Stoic! Hiding away across the valley, Lower Satulah Falls waits silently in solitude for those who pass a glance her way. Although it is visible with the naked eye, you can get a much better view of the falls with binoculars or through a good zoom lens. Personally, I think the spectacular views of the surrounding mountains tend to overshadow the beauty of the falls.

Height: 100 feet
Beauty rating: Good
Distance: Roadside
Difficulty: Easy
Blaze color: No blazes
County: Macon

Land status: National forest
Trail contact: Nantahala National Forest, Nantahala Ranger District; (828) 524-6441; www.fs.fed.us
Maps: *DeLorme: North Carolina Atlas & Gazetteer:* Page 52 F1

Finding the trailhead: From the junction of NC 28 and US 64 in Highlands, drive south on NC 28 for 3.5 miles to a pull-off on the right.

From the junction of GA 28 and Warwoman Road in Pine Mountain, Georgia, drive north on GA 28 for 8.1 miles to a pull-off on the left. (**Note:** Along the way, you enter into North Carolina, and GA 28 becomes NC 28.)

GPS: N35 01.444 / W83 11.191

The Hike

Lower Satulah Falls is viewed from the roadside and can be seen across the valley. Lower Satulah Falls is also known as Clear Creek Falls, for the creek it's located on, and Hidden Falls, for obvious reasons. The Satulah name came from Satulah Mountain, from which the creek flows.

At 4,543 feet, this impressive heath bald is known for its plant diversity. Also to its credit are massive cliffs and rocky outcrops, which make it a fabulous place for viewing peregrine falcons and other birds of prey.

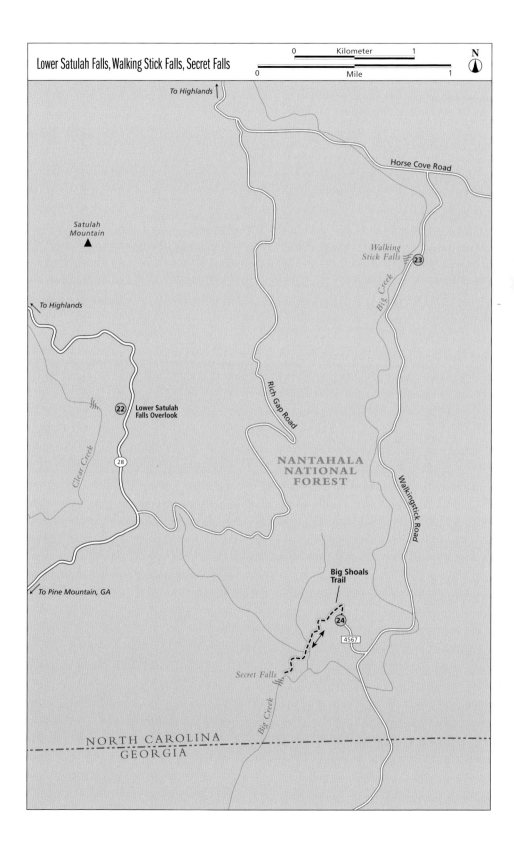

Lower Satulah Falls, Walking Stick Falls, Secret Falls

0   Kilometer   1

0   Mile   1

N

To Highlands

Horse Cove Road

Satulah
Mountain

Walking
Stick Falls   23

Big Creek

To Highlands

22   Lower Satulah
Falls Overlook

Rich Gap Road

Clear Creek

28

NANTAHALA
NATIONAL
FOREST

Walkingstick Road

Big Shoals
Trail

To Pine Mountain, GA

24

4567

Secret Falls

Big Creek

NORTH CAROLINA
GEORGIA

See these amazing views from Lower Satulah overlook.

REGAL RAPTORS

The peregrine falcon was almost eradicated in the mid 1900s by the widespread use of the pesticide DDT. Their numbers began to rise with DDT's ban in the 1970s, and these regal raptors were removed from the Endangered Species List in 1999. This magnificent bird of prey now has one of the widest ranges of all bird species and can be found on every continent except Antarctica. The name peregrine means wanderer, which seems fitting since they are migratory. The peregrine falcon is the fastest bird in the world, diving after its prey at speeds of up to 200 miles per hour. It's no wonder these skilled hunters were the birds used by nobles in the days of medieval falconry.

23 Walking Stick Falls

Ambiguous! Located on private property, this waterfall is obscured from the public eye. Unless you visit in winter, you're probably not going to get a decent view of the falls—without trespassing, that is. And I certainly don't recommend that.

See map on page 62.
Height: 40 feet
Beauty rating: Fair
Distance: Roadside
Difficulty: Easy

Blaze color: No blazes
County: Macon
Land status: Private property
Maps: *DeLorme: North Carolina Atlas & Gazetteer:* Page 52 F1

Finding the trailhead: From the junction of US 64 (Main Street) and NC 28 in Highlands, drive east on Main Street and pass through the light at Fifth Street. After approximately 0.2 mile, Main Street becomes Horse Cove Road. Follow Horse Cove Road for 3.7 miles and turn right onto Walkingstick Road. Continue for 0.6 mile to get a glimpse of Walking Stick Falls on the right. GPS: N35 02.062 / W83 09.644

The Hike

Walking Stick Falls is viewed from the roadside. I suggest taking a quick peek at Walking Stick Falls and then heading down the road to view Secret Falls.

Also worth seeing while you're in the area is the Bob Padgett tulip poplar tree on nearby Rich Gap Road. It's the second biggest tree in North Carolina and the third biggest tree in the eastern United States. Padgett is a naturalist who fought long and hard to preserve the natural heritage of this magnificent tree and the area surrounding it.

▶ The brilliant yellow, green, and orange colors of the tulip poplar blossom resemble candy corn at Halloween. While the sweet confection may seem medicinal to those with a sweet tooth, the tulip poplar itself has been known to serve several medicinal purposes.

24 Secret Falls

Conquest! The water here falls valiantly, cutting its way over and through the rocks, as it creates a surging wave pool at the base. Named for its obscurity, for years, many had heard of it, but few knew its prized location.

See map on page 62.
Height: 75 feet
Beauty rating: Excellent
Distance: 1.4 miles out and back
Difficulty: Easy
Trail surface: Narrow, hard-packed dirt
Approximate hiking time: 1 hour, 30 minutes
Blaze color: Blue

County: Macon
Land status: National forest
Trail contact: Nantahala National Forest, Nantahala Ranger District; (828) 524-6441; www.fs.fed.us
Maps: DeLorme: North Carolina Atlas & Gazetteer: Page 52 F1

Finding the trailhead: From the junction of US 64 (Main Street) and NC 28 in Highlands, drive east on Main Street and pass through the light at Fifth Street. After approximately 0.2 mile, Main Street becomes Horse Cove Road. Follow Horse Cove Road for 3.7 miles and turn right onto Walkingstick Road. Continue for 2.9 miles and turn right onto FR 4567. Travel for 0.2 mile to a small parking area on the left. The Big Shoals Trailhead is located at the northwest corner of the parking area. GPS: N35 00.523 / W83 09.996

The Hike

The narrow trail takes you around a gate and then winds its way through the forest. You will cross two tributaries before the sound of the falls grow nearer.

A long-kept "secret" among locals and a few privileged outsiders, Secret Falls has recently been outed both on websites and in other hiking books. So, I too shall join the unfaithful in revealing its location. Special thanks to Jinny Hawkins and Lillian for sharing this one with me years ago.

Secret Falls was once Mother Nature's best kept secret, but the cat's out of the bag now.

Miles and Directions

0.0 Go around the gate at the Big Shoals Trailhead and hike northwest. The narrow trail winds through the forest while making a descent.

0.4 Cross a small tributary and continue straight ahead (southwest) to a second tributary. After crossing this tributary, the trail begins to climb.

0.5 A fork awaits. Go left (south), continuing to follow the blue blazes.

0.7 Take the steps down to the base of Secret Falls (N35 00.281 / W83 10.310). Return the way you came.

1.4 Arrive back at the trailhead.

25 Silver Run Falls

Smooth as silk! Although small in height, Silver Run Falls represents grace and beauty in the purest of forms.

Height: 25 feet
Beauty rating: Excellent
Distance: 0.4 mile out and back
Difficulty: Easy
Trail surface: Gravel
Approximate hiking time: 20 minutes
Blaze color: No blazes

County: Jackson
Land status: National forest
Trail contact: Nantahala National Forest, Nantahala Ranger District; (828) 524-6441; www.fs.fed.us
Maps: *DeLorme: North Carolina Atlas & Gazetteer:* Page 52 E2–F2

Finding the trailhead: From the junction of NC 107 and US 64 in Cashiers, drive south on NC 107 for 4.0 miles to a small pull-off on your left at the sign for SILVER RUN FALLS.

From the junction of NC 107 and the North Carolina–South Carolina state line, drive north on NC 107 for 4.1 miles to a small pull-off on your right at the SILVER RUN FALLS sign.

The trailhead is at the southeast end of the pull-off. GPS: N35 04.018 / W83 04.023

The Hike

Follow the trail back into the woods toward the creek. Cross the creek and soon come to a side trail on your right that leads to the base of Silver Run Falls. You may have to share this waterfall—it's not only easy to get to but also makes a great swimming hole.

Silver Run Creek flows into the mighty Whitewater River just a few miles from the town of Cashiers (pronounced *CASH-ers*). The town was settled around 1830, although Native Americans resided there for more than one hundred years prior. Among the first settlers of this now-booming resort town was a man named McKinney.

Of the many theories on how the town came to be named, I prefer this one for its sheer entertainment purposes. According to this version, McKinney had a white stallion named Cash. One year as autumn approached, it was time to herd the horses and cattle south for winter. Cash was nowhere to be found, and McKinney was forced to leave without him. When spring arrived and they returned to town, there was Cash feeding in the valley, as happy and healthy as ever before. From that day on they called the area Cash's Valley, which over time transformed into Cashiers Valley.

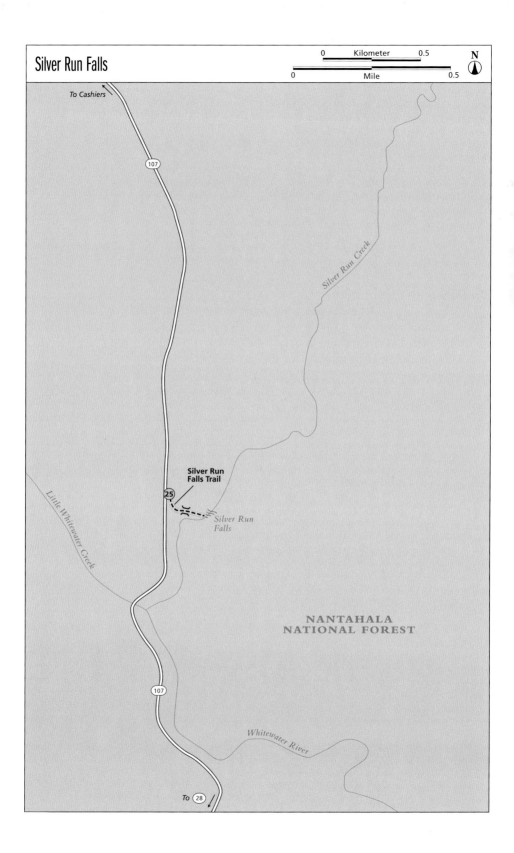

Silver Run Falls

To Cashiers

107

Silver Run Creek

Silver Run
Falls Trail

25

Silver Run
Falls

Little Whitewater Creek

NANTAHALA
NATIONAL FOREST

107

Whitewater River

To 28

0   Kilometer   0.5
0   Mile   0.5

N

A perfect swimming hole is formed at the base of Silver Run Falls.

Miles and Directions

0.0 From the trailhead, hike southeast back into the woods.

0.1 The trail quickly leads to the creek. Cross the creek on the footbridge and hike east a short distance further to where you see a side trail on your right leading south toward the falls.

0.2 Arrive at the base of Silver Run Falls (N35 03.981 / W83 03.935). Return the way you came.

0.4 Arrive back at the trailhead.

26 Hurricane Falls

Tranquility! This picture-perfect waterfall flows sweetly into Lake Glenville. The waterfall is located on private property but can be viewed from the roadside. The man-made lake is spring fed and sits near the top of the watershed, which gives it exceptionally clear water.

Height: 40 feet
Beauty rating: Excellent
Distance: 0.2 mile out and back
Difficulty: Easy
Trail surface: Paved public road
Approximate hiking time: 10 minutes

Blaze color: No blazes
County: Jackson
Land status: Private property
Maps: *DeLorme: North Carolina Atlas & Gazetteer:* Page 52 E2

Finding the trailhead: From the junction of NC 107 and US 64 in Cashiers, drive north on NC 107 for 1.8 miles. Turn left onto North Norton Road (SR 1145) and travel for 0.6 mile to a small pull-off on your right just after you cross the bridge.

From the junction of NC 107 and NC 281 in Tuckasegee, drive south on NC 107 for 12.7 miles. Turn right onto North Norton Road (SR 1145) and follow directions above.

GPS: N35 08.275 / W83 07.56

The Hike

From where you parked, carefully walk south along North Norton Road for less than 0.1 mile until you get a good view of Hurricane Falls at the southeast corner of the lake.

There has been an ongoing battle over the name of this lake since it was first formed during World War II. Known as the Thorpe Reservoir for many years, in 2002 its name was officially changed to Lake Glenville.

Hurricane Falls

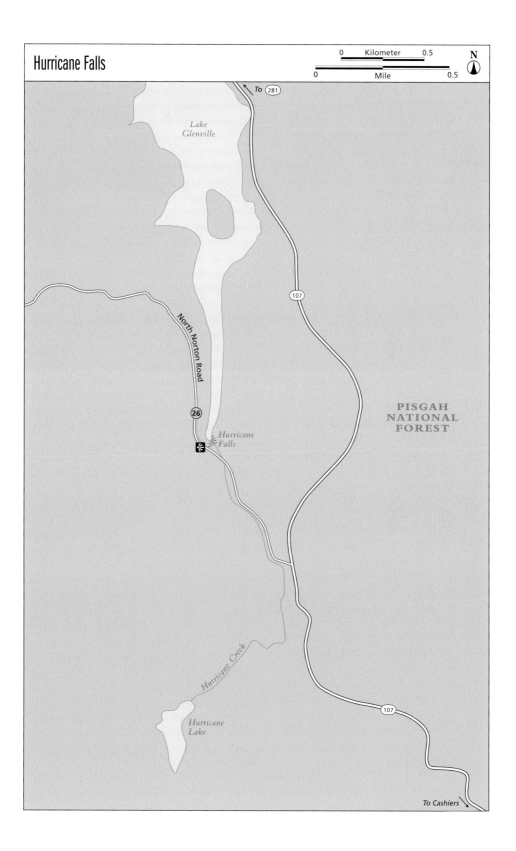

Hurricane Falls flows into the pristine water of Lake Glenville.

Miles and Directions

0.0 From the pullout, walk south on North Norton Road.

0.1 View Hurricane Falls from the roadside (N35 08.212 / W83 07.560). Return the way you came.

0.2 Arrive back at the parking area.

27 Grassy Creek Falls (Tuckasegee)

Soothing! The sound of Grassy Creek Falls soothes like stalks of wheatgrass blowing in the breeze. Grassy Creek Falls is actually located on Little Mill Creek. Although both creeks flow into the West Fork of the Tuckasegee River, Grassy Creek is actually one creek to the south of Little Mill Creek. It seems that the original mapmakers accidentally switched the names of these creeks, and no one ever bothered to rename the falls. So to this day, Grassy Creek Falls flows on Little Mill Creek.

See overview map on page iv.
Height: 100 feet
Beauty rating: Good
Distance: Roadside
Difficulty: Easy

Blaze color: No blazes
County: Jackson
Land status: Private property
Maps: DeLorme: North Carolina Atlas & Gazetteer: Page 52 D2

Finding the trailhead: From the junction of NC 107 and US 64 in Cashiers, drive north on NC 107 for 10.5 miles. You'll see Grassy Creek Falls on your left just after passing the covered bridge, also on your left.

From the junction of NC 107 and NC 281 in Tuckasegee, drive south on NC 107 for 4.0 miles. You'll see Grassy Creek Falls on your right just before you reach the covered bridge, also on your right.

GPS: N35 14.258 / W83 08.154

The Hike

View Grassy Creek Falls from the roadside. While there is a narrow path that goes down to the river at the base of the falls, there's no place to park; you would have to walk along NC 107 to get to it. For these reasons, I have included this as a roadside waterfall only. You are likely to get the best views of Grassy Creek Falls in wintertime, when the leaves have fallen and the view is not obscured by trees.

28 Rough Butt Creek Falls

Celebration! Like the sounds of a wolf pack howling in the night, Rough Butt Creek Falls surrounds you with the echoing sounds of celebration.

Height: 60 feet
Beauty rating: Excellent
Distance: 2.2 miles out and back
Difficulty: Moderate to strenuous
Trail surface: Wide, rocky road
Approximate hiking time: 1 hour, 10 minutes
Other trail users: Equestrians
Blaze color: No blazes

County: Jackson
Land status: National forest
Trail contact: Nantahala National Forest, Nantahala Ranger District; (828) 524-6441; www.fs.fed.us
Maps: *DeLorme: North Carolina Atlas & Gazetteer:* Page 52 C2-C3

Finding the trailhead: From the junction of NC 107 and NC 281 in Tuckasegee, drive north on NC 107 for 3.0 miles. Turn right onto the unmarked Caney Fork Road (SR 1737) (across from the gas station) and travel for 9.3 miles to where a gravel road forks off to the right. Go right here and continue approximately 0.1 mile; find a place to park along the gravel road across from the horse pasture. (**Note:** Do not block the road. This is a private drive. The owner has been kind enough to allow you to park here, so please respect the owner and his property!)

From the junction of NC 107 and NC 116 near Sylva, drive south on NC 107 for 7.0 miles. Turn left onto the unmarked Caney Fork Road (SR 1737) (across from the gas station) and follow the directions above.

GPS: N35 19.496 / W83 02.275

The Hike

Hike due east on the gravel road, past the home on your left and into the forest. Ford the creek and follow the rough, rocky road on a steady incline the entire way. When you come to a second creek, find a good place to cross. Once on the other side, look for an obscure trail on your right that heads up and southeast. Take this trail.

The remainder of the hike is a thick bushwhack that follows the creek upstream. You will pass several small cascades before arriving at the base of the much taller Rough Butt Creek Falls.

The waterfall is named for Rough Butt Bald, elevation 5,925 feet. Portions of the bald are registered North Carolina Heritage Areas. The bald is home to a red spruce–Fraser fir forest that does not typically occur this far south and is home to many rare animal species as well. Most notable of these are the federally endangered Carolina northern flying squirrel, the northern saw-whet owl, and the Appalachian yellow-bellied sapsucker.

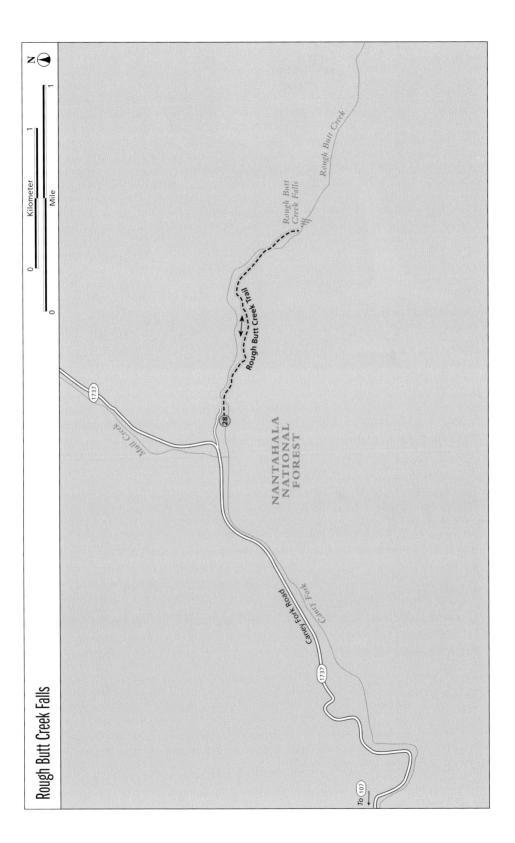

Rough Butt Creek Falls

Bring a towel; you have to ford the creek twice before you reach this little beauty—Rough Butt Creek Falls.

Special thanks go out to Mitch and Leonard on this one. These two gentlemen were kind enough to pull my vehicle out of a ditch, which enabled me to finish this and many other trails to come. Thank you, guys!

Miles and Directions

0.0 From where you parked, hike east on the gravel road.

0.1 Cross the creek; continue east on the old roadbed as it makes a steady incline.

0.8 Cross the creek a second time. About 50 feet after the crossing, look for an obscure trail that heads up and to your right (southeast). From here, bushwhack your way upstream past many small cascades.

1.1 Arrive at the base of Rough Butt Creek Falls (N35 19.199 / W83 01.403). Return the way you came.

2.2 Arrive back at the trailhead.

29 Toxaway Falls

Destiny! Every time I look upon Toxaway Falls, I am dumbfounded by its origins. This magnificent waterfall is fed by Lake Toxaway and passes through a small pipe on the north side of US 64. What comes out on the south side of US 64 (what you see in the photo) is the continuation of the Toxaway River.

See map on page 80.
Height: 150 feet
Beauty rating: Good
Distance: Roadside
Difficulty: Easy
Blaze color: No blazes
County: Transylvania

Land status: Private property
Trail contacts: Nantahala National Forest, Nantahala Ranger District; (828) 524-6441; www.fs.fed.us
Toxaway House Restaurant; (828) 966-9226
Maps: *DeLorme: North Carolina Atlas & Gazetteer:* Page 52 E3

Finding the trailhead: From the junction of US 64 and NC 281 north in Lake Toxaway, drive west on US 64 for 0.5 mile. Just after crossing the Bill McNeely Jr. Bridge, turn left into the parking lot for the Toxaway House restaurant.

From the junction of US 64 and NC 281 south in Lake Toxaway, drive east on US 64 for 2.1 miles. Just before crossing the Bill McNeely Jr. Bridge, turn right into the parking lot for the Toxaway House restaurant.

GPS: N35 07.331 / W82 55.927

The Hike

All the land surrounding the falls is private property, so the best way to get a good view of Toxaway Falls is from the parking lot of the Toxaway House restaurant. Better yet, visit the restaurant, which has a wonderful deck overlooking the falls. You can take in the sights and sounds of the falls while enjoying a fresh home-cooked meal.

Lake Toxaway, the largest private lake in North Carolina, is named for Chief Toxawah, whose name means "red bird" in Cherokee. The great chief is said to be buried on top of Indian Grave Ridge, which overlooks the present-day lake and falls.

The man-made lake was built in 1903, and the area was once famous for the Lake Toxaway Inn. This lavish hotel catered to the wealthy and saw the likes of Rockefeller, Edison, Ford, Firestone, Duke, and Vanderbilt. It flourished for years until 1916, when the dam burst and a great flood destroyed everything in its path, including the inn.

Toxaway Falls is surrounded by private property, but you can enjoy a view of the falls, and a meal, on the deck of the Toxaway House restaurant.

30 Waterfalls of the Horsepasture River: Rainbow, Turtleback, Drift, and Stairway Falls

Enchanting and astounding! You're in for an incredible treat here. One trail provides you with four different waterfalls of four different natures. I recommend spending an entire day picnicking, frolicking, and basking at these beauties.

Height: Rainbow Falls, 150 feet; Turtleback Falls, 20 feet; Drift Falls, 40 feet; Stairway Falls, 70 feet
Beauty rating: Very good for Drift and Turtleback Falls; excellent for Rainbow and Stairway Falls
Distance: 4.6 miles out and back (Stairway only, 2.6 miles; Rainbow only, 3.0 miles, Rainbow and Turtleback, 3.4 miles; Rainbow, Turtleback, and Drift, 4.0 miles)
Difficulty: Strenuous
Trail surface: Wide gravel and hard-packed dirt

Approximate hiking time: 3 hours
Blaze color: Orange circles
County: Transylvania
Land status: National forest; state park
Trail contacts: Pisgah National Forest, Pisgah Ranger District; (828) 877-3265; www.fs.fed .us (waterfall information)
   Gorges State Park; (828) 966-9099; www .ncsparks.net (trailhead information)
FYI: Hours of operation vary through the year; contact Gorges State Park for current info
Maps: *DeLorme: North Carolina Atlas & Gazetteer:* Page 52 E3

Finding the trailhead: From the junction of NC 281 south and US 64 in Lake Toxaway, drive south on NC 281 for 0.9 mile. Turn left into Gorges State Park and follow the park road for 1.6 miles to the Grassy Ridge parking area on the right.
   From the junction of NC 281 and the North Carolina–South Carolina state line, drive north on NC 281 for 7.7 miles. Turn right into Gorges State Park and follow the directions above.
   The trailhead is located at the southwest corner of the parking area. GPS: N35 05.314 / W82 57.124

The Hike

Although the Rainbow Falls Trail begins in Gorges State Park, after less than a mile the trail enters Pisgah National Forest, where three of the four waterfalls are located. Shortly after entering the national forest, you come to a side trail that leads to Stairway Falls. Be sure to make note of this trail so that you can visit Stairway on the way out. (*Option:* Of course you can turn around at any point to make a shorter hike—and see fewer falls. See Miles and Directions below.)
   The trail descends most of the way before climbing steeply and bringing you to a pristine

▶ Rainbows are formed by combining water and light. As the light is refracted through millions of water droplets, the full spectrum of color appears: red, orange, yellow, green, blue, indigo, and violet.

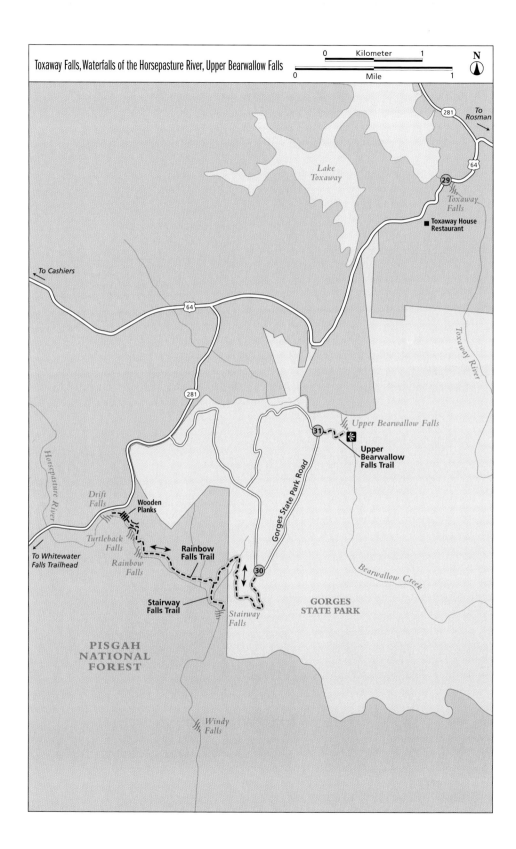

Toxaway Falls, Waterfalls of the Horsepasture River, Upper Bearwallow Falls

0   Kilometer   1

0   Mile   1

N

To
Rosman

Lake
Toxaway

Toxaway
Falls

Toxaway House
Restaurant

To Cashiers

Toxaway River

Upper Bearwallow Falls

Upper
Bearwallow
Falls Trail

Gorges State Park Road

Horsepasture River

Drift
Falls

Wooden
Planks

Turtleback
Falls

Rainbow
Falls Trail

Bearwallow Creek

To Whitewater
Falls Trailhead

Rainbow
Falls

Stairway
Falls Trail

GORGES
STATE PARK

Stairway
Falls

PISGAH
NATIONAL
FOREST

Windy
Falls

It's good luck to see a rainbow at Rainbow Falls.

overlook of Rainbow Falls. Thunderous, the waters here crash down with amazing intensity. If you're lucky, you might be greeted with a rainbow, created when sunlight hits the constant mist that blows off the face of the falls.

From Rainbow Falls follow the rugged trail upstream and uphill until you arrive at Turtleback Falls. This area is often occupied by swimmers, sunbathers, and people sliding down Turtleback Falls. Beware! The currents are very strong, and many people have been injured here. Several people have drowned, and others have plunged over Rainbow Falls to their death. Please enjoy the swift waters of Turtleback Falls from the bank.

A large sliding rock is created by Drift Falls.

From Turtleback Falls continue to follow the river upstream to Drift Falls. More like a massive water slide, this untouchable beauty is located on private property. Please respect the boundaries.

Now onto Stairway Falls. Backtrack to the side trail I mentioned earlier and follow it west–northwest, heading steeply down to a primitive campsite. From here head south, following the river downstream to the base of Stairway Falls. Stairway Falls climbs down the rocky ledge "steps" as it flows with purpose into the seemingly virgin river. If you visit this waterfall, you're likely to have it to yourself.

With each drop it makes, a "stairway" of water is formed by the rocky ledges of Stairway Falls.

A great battle over the fate of the Horsepasture River began in 1984 between a California-owned power company and local and state organizations. The power company had acquired a 6-mile stretch of the river, including the falls, and planned to divert the river to create hydroelectric power. This diversion of water would have had a negative effect on the falls and the river's entire ecosystem. After two years of litigation, the Horsepasture River gained national protection and was designated a Wild and Scenic River in 1986. A group called the Friends of the Horsepasture River, led by Bill Thomas, should be given recognition as the driving force behind this wonderful victory.

Miles and Directions

0.0 Start at the trailhead and hike southwest down the gravel path on a slow and steady descent.

0.3 Come to a T junction. Go right (northwest) and continue hiking downhill.

0.7 The trail flattens out taking you across a wet-weather tributary and continues west.

0.8 Arrive at a signpost that reads LEAVING GORGES STATE PARK, NC. This is the park boundary, and you now enter Pisgah National Forest. Continue hiking southwest and you soon see a side trail shooting off to your right (northwest). Bypass this and continue descending south-southeast.

1.0 Come to another side trail that shoots off to the left (south-southwest) from behind a sign reading RAINBOW FALLS →. This is the trail to Stairway Falls. Bypass this for now, and continue hiking west-northwest toward Rainbow Falls. (*Option:* Follow directions below from milepoint 3.0 and hike to Stairway Falls, which sits 0.3 mile away.)

1.1 After crossing a tributary, reach a large primitive campsite. Go straight across (west) the campsite and pick the trail up on the other side. From here the trail begins to climb steeply as it follows the river upstream. Bypass any side trails leading toward the river.

1.5 Arrive at the overlook for Rainbow Falls (N35 05.425 / W82 57.896). Continue to follow the rugged trail north and upstream. (***Option:*** Return to the trailhead for a 3.0-mile total hike.)

1.7 Arrive at the base of Turtleback Falls (N35 05.545 / W82 57.952). To get to Drift Falls, continue north and upstream. Cross the small footbridge and continue following the rocky path upstream (west). (***Option:*** Return to the trailhead for a 3.4-mile hike.)

1.8 Come to a fork with a narrow trail that goes straight ahead (north) and a rocky path heading up to the right (northeast). Go straight ahead (north), continuing to stay with the river.

1.9 Cross the wooden, plank bridge and continue straight ahead (west) until you come to a fence with a large PRIVATE PROPERTY sign. Go left (south) just before the fence, and follow the side trail toward the river.

2.0 Once at the river, you get a perfect view of Drift Falls (N35 05.623 / W82 58.121). From Drift Falls, backtrack 1.0 mile to the side trail that leads down to Stairway Falls.

3.0 Turn right (west-northwest) onto the side trail and follow it steeply downhill. (***Option:*** Skip Stairway Falls and return to the trailhead for a hike of 4.0 miles.)

3.1 Once at the bottom of the hill, the trail takes you into a large primitive campsite. Go straight (south) across the campsite, and pick up the obscure trail on the other side. Cross the wet-weather tributary and you soon arrive alongside the falls.

3.3 A side trail leads to the river at the base of Stairway Falls (N35 05.125 / W82 57.368). Return to the main trail, turn right (north-northeast) and retrace your steps to the trailhead.

4.6 Arrive back at the trailhead.

31 Upper Bearwallow Falls

Worthy! Although these falls are viewed from afar, you can feel their strength and power running through your veins.

See map on page 80.
Height: 80 feet
Beauty rating: Good
Distance: 0.6 mile out and back
Difficulty: Moderate to strenuous
Trail surface: Wide dirt path
Approximate hiking time: 30 minutes
Blaze color: Blue triangles
County: Transylvania
Land status: National forest; state park

Trail contacts: Pisgah National Forest, Pisgah Ranger District; (828) 877-3265; www.fs.fed .us (waterfall information)
    Gorges State Park; (828) 966-9099; www .ncsparks.net (trailhead information)
FYI: Hours of operation vary through the year; contact Gorges State Park for current info
Maps: *DeLorme: North Carolina Atlas & Gazetteer:* Page 52 E3

Finding the trailhead: From the junction of NC 281 south and US 64 in Lake Toxaway, drive south on NC 281 for 0.9 mile. Turn left into Gorges State Park and follow the signs to the picnic area, and travel for 2.7 miles to the large parking area on the left, following the signs to the picnic area.
    From the junction of NC 281 and the North Carolina–South Carolina state line, drive north on NC 281 for 7.7 miles. Turn right into Gorges State Park and follow the directions above.
    The trailhead is at the east side of the parking area near the large trail information sign. GPS: N35 06.084/W82 56.721

The Hike

This short but enjoyable hike takes you around a few switchbacks before leading to an observation deck overlooking Upper Bearwallow Falls.

The falls are located within Gorges State Park, North Carolina's only state park west of Asheville. Because Gorges State Park is so new, it's still in the planning and development phase. The park currently encompasses nearly 7,500 acres and offers stunning views of sheer rock walls and waterfalls plummeting through rugged river gorges. The "gorges" for which the park is named are formed by the abrupt change in elevation from the piedmont of South Carolina to the mountains of North Carolina. Conservation studies of this area began in the 1970s, and by 1982 the state had placed 275 acres on the North Carolina Registry of Natural Heritage Areas. Today the park contains nearly 125 rare plant and animal species and is home to twelve endangered species. Keep this in mind when you visit, and be sure to tread lightly.

I highly recommend that you also hike to the waterfalls of the Horsepasture River while visiting Gorges State Park.

Miles and Directions

0.0 From the trailhead hike east down the stone steps and across the main park road. From here follow the trail southeast, down and around several switchbacks.

0.3 Arrive at an observation deck overlooking Upper Bearwallow Falls (N35 06.072 / W82 56.573). Return the way you came.

0.6 Arrive back at the trailhead.

32 High Falls on the Thompson River

Shy but not Timid! High Falls on the Thompson River tries to hide from you, while its power reaches out, from just outside your grasp.

Height: 70 feet
Beauty rating: Good
Distance: 3.0 miles out and back
Difficulty: Moderate to strenuous
Trail surface: Overgrown, rocky trail
Approximate hiking time: 1 hour, 30 minutes
Other trail users: Equestrians

Blaze color: No blazes
County: Transylvania
Land status: National forest
Trail contact: Pisgah National Forest, Pisgah Ranger District; (828) 877-3265; www.fs.fed.us
Maps: *DeLorme: North Carolina Atlas & Gazet-teer:* Page 52 E3

Finding the trailhead: From the junction of NC 281 south and US 64 in Lake Toxaway, drive south on NC 281 for 3.6 miles. Turn left onto Brewer Road (CR 1189), and immediately find a place to park.

From the junction of NC 281 and the North Carolina–South Carolina state line, drive north on NC 281 for 5.0 miles. Turn right onto Brewer Road (CR 1189) and follow the directions above.

GPS: N35 04.679 / W82 59.618

The Hike

The trail begins beside NC 281 where it meets Brewer Road. You will see a small patch of pavement leading southwest and up to a gated dirt road. This overgrown path begins as a wide gravel road but soon narrows before making a slow descent into the forest. Be sure to stay on the main trail until you reach the second fork, bypassing any small trails that lead toward the sound of moving water.

As you hear the sound of the falls in the distance, the trail winds around. Pay close attention here to find the correct side trail to the base of the falls. Also be sure to follow the compass directions and distances provided below to make sure you take the right path, which takes you down to the river, just downstream from High Falls on the Thompson River.

The Thompson River was originally named the Jocassee River. The river and the lake that lies below it in South Carolina were both named for the Indian Princess Jocassee. Over time, as white settlers began to inhabit the area, the name was changed to the Thompson River in honor of the Reverend John Thompson.

The Reverend Thompson was a Presbyterian preacher who in 1752 was granted 627 acres, including some property along the river. His plan was to clear and cultivate the land over the next three years. Sadly, he died before his dreams came to fruition.

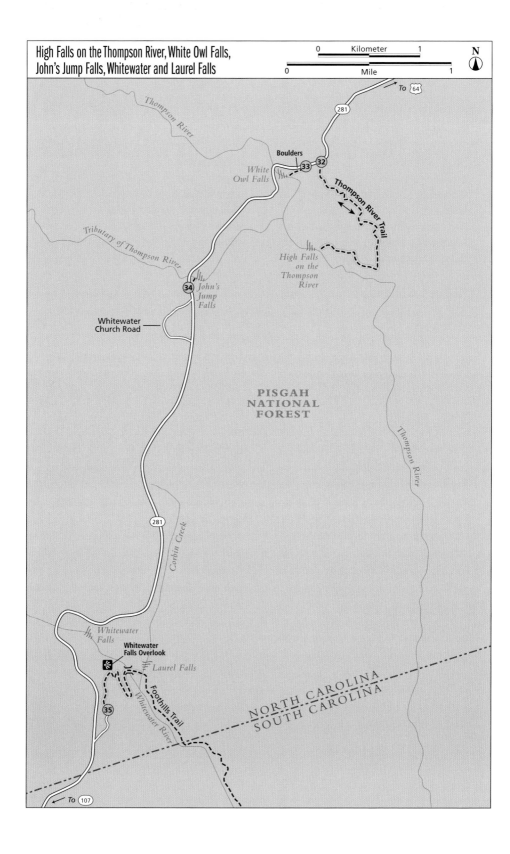

High Falls on the Thompson River, White Owl Falls, John's Jump Falls, Whitewater and Laurel Falls

0 Kilometer 1

0 Mile 1

N

Thompson River

281

To 64

Boulders

33 32

White Owl Falls

Thompson River Trail

Tributary of Thompson River

High Falls on the Thompson River

34 John's Jump Falls

Whitewater Church Road

PISGAH NATIONAL FOREST

Thompson River

281

Corbin Creek

Whitewater Falls

Whitewater Falls Overlook

Laurel Falls

Foothills Trail

35

Whitewater River

NORTH CAROLINA
SOUTH CAROLINA

To 107

Hidden away in a private cove, High Falls on the Thompson River is cradled by the rock around it.

A number of waterfalls flow along the Thompson River, including High Falls, White Owl Falls, and John's Jump. While visiting any of these falls, take note of the botanical diversity that occurs here. The Thompson River gorge is home to more than 500 species of vascular plants.

Miles and Directions

0.0 From the trailhead, hike southwest up the patch of pavement and toward the gate. Go around the gate and continue hiking uphill.

0.1 Come to a fork at the top of the hill. Go right (south-southeast) and follow the overgrown path on a slow descent.

0.9 Come to another fork with a narrow clay path shooting off to your right (south-southwest) through the pine trees and the main trail continuing straight ahead (south-southeast). Go right (south-southwest) on the narrow path, following it through an open area. The trail then leads you back into the forest.

1.3 As the main trail heads due north, you will see an obvious side trail heading due west and down toward the river. Go left (west) here and scramble your way down to the river.

1.4 Arrive at the river's edge; go right (northwest) and scramble steeply uphill before returning to the river's edge.

1.5 Arrive just downstream from High Falls on the Thompson River (N35 04.212 / W82 59.634). Return the way you came.

3.0 Arrive back at the trailhead.

33 White Owl Falls

Wisdom! White Owl Falls lies tucked away from the masses. Although hundreds pass by it every day, only a handful come to seek its knowledge.

See map on page 88.
Height: 20 feet
Beauty rating: Very good
Distance: 0.4 mile out and back
Difficulty: Strenuous
Trail surface: Narrow, overgrown dirt path
Approximate hiking time: 30 minutes

Blaze color: Red and orange duct tape
County: Transylvania
Land status: National forest
Trail contact: Pisgah National Forest, Pisgah Ranger District; (828) 877-3265; www.fs.fed.us
Maps: *DeLorme: North Carolina Atlas & Gazetteer:* Page 52 E3

Finding the trailhead: From the junction of NC 281 south and US 64 in Lake Toxaway, drive south on NC 281 for 3.55 miles to a small pull-off on the right.

From the junction of NC 281 and the North Carolina–South Carolina state line, drive north on NC 281 for 4.95 miles to a small pull-off on the left.

GPS: N35 04.642 / W82 59.755

The Hike

While this hike is short, it's not easy to follow. Begin by walking south on NC 281 for approximately 0.05 mile. You will see some faint utility lines crossing over the road and the beginning (north end) of the guardrail. This is the trailhead. Go around the guardrail, and hike southwest down a cement drainage. Once you reach the bottom of the drainage, the trail becomes very overgrown and a near bushwhack.

VENOMOUS VIPERS

Of the thirty-seven species of snakes found within North Carolina, only six are venomous. Of those six, only two are common in the western mountain region: the copperhead and the canebrake rattlesnake, also known as the timber rattler, which is equipped with a telltale rattle.

These venomous vipers can be identified by their large, diamond-shaped head, which has a pit on each side of it, located between the nostril and the eye. These pits are where they store their precious venom. These snakes also have two hollow fangs that act like hypodermic needles and allow them to inject their venom into prey.

If you get bitten by any snake, venomous or not, stay calm and immediately seek medical attention.

The white water of White Owl Falls is hidden in plain sight—to those who look.

Look for the red and orange duct tape wrapped around some saplings. The tape acts as trail blazes, flagging you in the right direction. When in doubt, follow the sound of the falls as you bushwhack your way to the base of White Owl Falls.

A word of warning: I personally saw a venomous copperhead snake in this area in 2010, so make sure to watch where you step.

This waterfall was named by a mill worker in the early 1900s. He worked near the falls by day and spent many a night hunting near them as well. He recalled that owls could be heard hooting so loudly near the falls that he could hear them over the flowing river. That combined with the white flowing water is how White Owl Falls came to be named.

Miles and Directions

0.0 Go around the guardrail and hike southwest down the cement drainage. At the bottom of the drainage, an obscure trail heads to the right (west).

0.1 Cross the boulders and continue to bushwhack toward the sound of the falls.

0.2 Arrive at the base of White Owl Falls (N35 04.589 / W82 59.831). Return the way you came.

0.4 Arrive back at the trailhead.

34 John's Jump Falls

Surreal! The way the milky white water makes its way aggressively over the rocky ledge seems almost surreal.

See map on page 88.
Height: 25 feet
Beauty rating: Very good
Distance: 0.2 mile out and back
Difficulty: Strenuous
Trail surface: Overgrown dirt path
Approximate hiking time: 15 minutes

Blaze color: No blazes
County: Transylvania
Land status: National forest
Trail contact: Pisgah National Forest, Pisgah Ranger District; (828) 877-3265; www.fs.fed.us
Maps: DeLorme: North Carolina Atlas & Gazetteer: Page 52 F3

Finding the trailhead: From the junction of NC 281 south and US 64 in Lake Toxaway, drive south on NC 281 for 4.9 miles to a pull-off on the left.

From the junction of NC 281 and the North Carolina–South Carolina state line, drive north on NC 281 for 3.7 miles to a pull-off on the right. (**Note:** The pull-off is just north of the northernmost intersection of Whitewater Church Road (SR 1188) and NC 281.)

GPS: N35 04.038 / W83 00.459

The Hike

The sounds of the falls are audible from the pull-off. An obscure trail heads north from the north end of the pull-off. Follow this trail into the woods and steeply down to the base of John's Jump Falls.

This waterfall is said to have been named by Chucky Joe Huger, an explorer and botanist who lived in this area in the 1920s. Chucky Joe frequently named natural features while exploring the land with hatchet in hand. One day while Chucky Joe was out in the woods with his friend John Hinkle, John jumped from a large boulder to get to the base of the falls. From that day on, the falls came to be known as John's Jump Falls.

Miles and Directions

0.0   From the trailhead, hike north and into the woods on the obscure trail.

0.1   Arrive at the base of John's Jump Falls (N35 04.071 / W83 00.431). Return the way you came.

0.2   Arrive back at the trailhead.

Rock cairns stand stacked at the base of John's Jump Falls.

35 Whitewater and Laurel Falls

Conquering! Like an avalanche thunderously crashing down the mountainside in a mass of white powder—such is the sound and sight of Whitewater Falls. Although Laurel Falls is also impressive in height, she's much tamer than her big brother, and only a small portion of her prowess is visible.

See map on page 88.

Height: Whitewater Falls, 411 feet; Laurel Falls, 400 feet

Beauty rating: Excellent for Whitewater Falls; good for Laurel Falls

Distance: 2.0 miles out and back (Whitewater Falls observation deck, 0.6 mile)

Difficulty: Moderate for Whitewater Falls; very strenuous for Laurel Falls

Trail surface: Whitewater, paved path and wooden staircase; Laurel, rugged trail

Approximate hiking time: 1 hour, 20 minutes

Blaze color: White

County: Transylvania and Jackson

Land status: National forest

Trail contact: Pisgah National Forest, Pisgah Ranger District; (828) 877-3265; www.fs.fed.us

FYI: The area is open from dawn to dusk year-round. Small day-use fee is payable at a self-serve kiosk in the parking lot.

Maps: *DeLorme: North Carolina Atlas & Gazetteer:* Page 52 F3

Finding the trailhead: From NC 281 south and US 64 in Lake Toxaway, drive south on NC 281 for 8.4 miles. Turn left at the WHITEWATER FALLS sign; the road leads you down to a large parking area.

From the junction of NC 281 and the North Carolina–South Carolina state line, drive north on NC 281 for 0.2 mile. Turn right at the WHITEWATER FALLS sign, and follow the directions above.

The trailhead is at the northwest corner of the parking area. GPS: N35 01.815 / W83 00.974

The Hike

The trail leads to both waterfalls. First you are greeted with wonderful views of Whitewater Falls from the observation deck. Then the trail leads you on a strenuous trek down many primitive steps and around a few switchbacks before finally coming out along the river's edge. Massive boulders fill this area, leaving you in awe of the power that Mother Nature wields.

Follow the boulders downstream a short distance, cross the bridge over the river, and make your way back into the forest. You soon arrive at a footbridge at the base of Laurel Falls. To get a better view of the falls, I recommend that you cross the footbridge and head upstream a bit.

At 411 feet, Whitewater Falls is touted as the highest waterfall east of the Mississippi River and, needless to say, the tallest in North Carolina as well. The area surrounding both of these falls is such a natural wonder that it has been designated as one of North Carolina's special Natural Heritage Areas. Please treat it with the respect it so fully deserves; "pack it in, pack it out." Trash cans and a primitive restroom are available in the parking area.

Whitewater Falls may very well be the king of the east.

Miles and Directions

0.0 Head uphill (northwest) from the parking area on the paved path.

0.2 Go right (east), and head down the stairs.

0.3 Arrive at an observation deck overlooking Whitewater Falls (N35 02.028 / W83 00.969). To go on to Laurel Falls, continue down the steep, primitive wooden steps. (*Option:* Return to the trailhead for a 0.6-mile out and back hike of about 30 minutes.)

0.4 Arrive at a fork with a trail to the right that leads south-southwest back to NC 281. Bear left (northeast) here, continuing down the many stone and wooden steps that lie ahead.

0.8 Cross the bridge over the Whitewater River and continue hiking east.

1.0 Arrive at the base of Laurel Falls (N35 02.012 / W83 00.766). Return the way you came.

2.0 Arrive back at the trailhead.

36 Granny Burrell and Frolictown Falls

Rustic! The rough and rocky face of Granny Burrell Falls shows the timeworn and weathered years that the name implies. This is more of a long rock slide than a waterfall, and there's a good chance you'll have it all to yourself. Enjoy the peace and solitude while you can before heading off the beaten path on your way to Frolictown Falls.

Height: Granny Burrell Falls, 20 feet (main drop); Frolictown Falls, 18 feet
Beauty rating: Good for Granny Burrell Falls; excellent for Frolictown Falls
Distance: 3.8 miles out and back (Granny Burrell Falls, 2.4 miles)
Difficulty: Moderate to strenuous
Trail surface: Wide gravel and sandy road; narrow, hard-packed dirt trail
Approximate hiking time: 2 hours, 15 minutes
Blaze color: No blazes

County: Jackson
Land status: National forest
Trail contact: Nantahala National Forest, Nantahala Ranger District; (828) 524-6441; www.fs.fed.us
FYI: Before you hike any of the trails in Panthertown Valley, I recommend purchasing the *Guide's Guide to Panthertown* by Burt Kornegay.
Maps: *DeLorme: North Carolina Atlas & Gazetteer:* Page 52 D2

Finding the trailhead: From the junction of US 64 and NC 281 south in Lake Toxaway, drive west on US 64 for 8.2 miles to Cedar Creek Road (SR 1120). Turn right onto Cedar Creek Road and travel 2.2 miles before turning right onto Breedlove Road (SR 1121) at the Panthertown Valley Access Site sign. Continue for 3.3 miles to where the road makes a hard bend to the left and becomes gravel. Follow the bumpy gravel road for 0.3 mile to where it ends at a gate.

From the junction of US 64 and NC 107 in Cashiers, drive east on US 64 for 1.9 miles to Cedar Creek Road (SR 1120). Turn left onto Cedar Creek Road and follow the directions above.

GPS: N35 10.071 / W83 02.394

The Hike

From the parking area you will see a gated road that leads straight ahead and down, the Blackrock Spur Trail (#447) to your left, and an open camping area to your right. Go straight ahead (south), around the gate, and follow the Panthertown Valley Trail (#474) downhill. As you make your descent into the valley, you will pass a side trail that leads to Wilderness Falls. Stay on the main trail, following it around a bend and down. As the trail descends, it offers stunning views of the bald-faced mountains all around you.

Pass another trail junction with the Deep Gap Trail (#449) before arriving at a four-way intersection with the North Road Trail (#453) and the Mac's Gap Trail (#482). Follow the Mac's Gap Trail south as you continue downhill.

Once you reach the valley floor, you soon pass by a primitive campsite and what appears to be an old homestead on your left. Soon after, you come to a fork. The trail

Granny Burrell and Frolictown Falls, Wilderness Falls

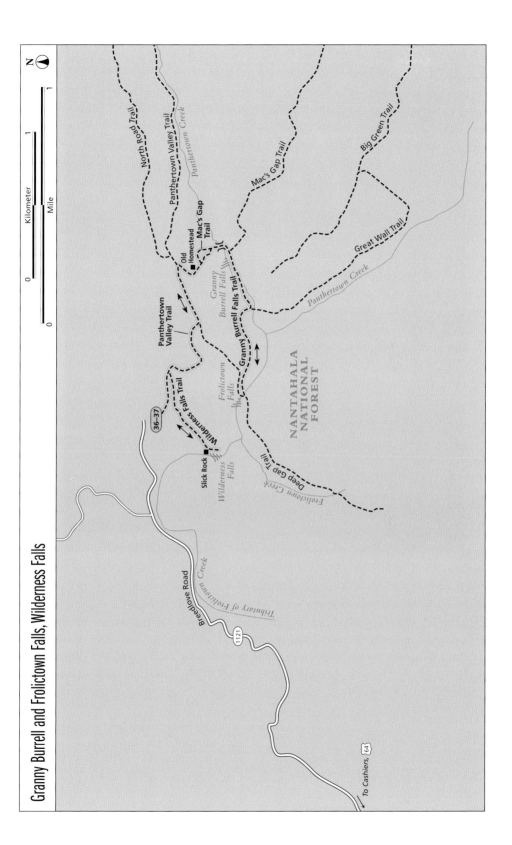

North Road Trail

Panthertown Valley Trail

Panthertown Creek

Mac's Gap Trail

Big Green Trail

Old Homestead

Mac's Gap Trail

Granny Burrell Falls

Great Wall Trail

Panthertown Valley Trail

Granny Burrell Falls Trail

Panthertown Creek

Frolictown Falls

NANTAHALA NATIONAL FOREST

Falls Trail

36–37

Wilderness Falls

Slick Rock

Wilderness Falls

Deep Gap Trail

Frolictown Creek

Breedlove Road

Tributary of Frolictown Creek

Frolictown Creek

1121

To Cashiers, 64

0   1   Kilometer   1

0   Mile   1

N

The simple face of Frolictown Falls awaits.

to the left heads northeast through some pine trees; the trail to the right heads southeast through a clearing. While I prefer the left-hand route, you can take either—the paths reunite less than 0.1 mile down the trail.

After the trails reunite, cross over Panthertown Creek before reaching the final trail junction. Follow the Granny Burrell Falls Trail (#486) upstream and soon arrive at Granny Burrell Falls. From Granny Burrell, continue following the overgrown trail upstream (southwest).

The trail takes you through a wonderful rhododendron tunnel, before bringing you to a T junction. Head right at the T junction, and immediately rock-hop across Panthertown Creek. After crossing the creek, you will come to a fork. Head left here. The trail climbs, bringing you through more rhododendron and mountain laurel.

MOUNTAIN LAUREL

Nature's genius is once again shown in the spring-loaded blooms of the mountain laurel. The stamens of the mountain laurel blossom have a special mechanism that flings pollen onto unsuspecting insects that come to drink of the blossom's sweet nectar.

With its striated bark and showy, star-shaped white to pale-pink blossoms, mountain laurel is one of the prettiest flowering shrubs in the western North Carolina mountains. But beware: Every part of this gorgeous shrub is poisonous.

The wide, sandy path leads to one last T junction. Go left here and follow the trail downhill. Just before crossing the creek again, a side trail leads you on a short, steep scramble to the base of Frolictown Falls.

Along with four other waterfalls, Granny Burrell and Frolictown Falls are located within the area known as Panthertown Valley, which is pronounced *painter-town*. Although the valley has changed hands many times over the years, it was given its name by early settlers who took up residence here.

At the dawn of the twentieth century, the valley was a far cry from what you see today. In fact, it was considered such a wild place that the settlers referred to it as a town of painters, by which they meant "panthers." Today the valley belongs to the USDA Forest Service and comprises 6,700 acres, with miles of well-maintained trails for your hiking and biking pleasure.

Credit must be given to Carlton McNeil, whose home once stood near the eastern trailhead. A trail blazer and builder, Carlton was the guardian of Panthertown Valley for many years. He passed away in 2007 at the age of eighty-six.

Thank you, USDA Forest Service!

Miles and Directions

0.0 Starting from the parking area, go around the gate and hike south on the Panthertown Valley Trail (#474).

0.3 As the wide, gravel main trail bends right (southwest), bypass the side trail to the right, which leads to Wilderness Falls, and continue descending into the valley.

0.6 The Deep Gap Trail (#449) comes in from the right (southwest). Bypass this, stay on the main trail and continue hiking east and downhill.

0.8 Come to a four-way intersection, with the Panthertown Valley Trail continuing straight (east) and down, the North Road Trail (#453) going left (northeast) and up, and the Mac's Gap Trail (#482) heading right (south) and down. Turn right onto the Mac's Gap Trail and continue hiking downhill.

1.0 Pass the remains of an old homestead before reaching a fork. The right fork leads (southeast) through a clearing; the left heads (northeast) through a lovely stand of pine trees. Choose whichever path you like; they reunite less than 0.1 mile down the trail.

1.1 After the trails reunite, cross over Panthertown Creek and then come to a fork. The Mac's Gap Trail continues straight ahead (south-southeast), and the Granny Burrell Falls Trail (#486) goes to the right (west). Bear right here and follow the Granny Burrell Falls Trail upstream.

1.2 Arrive in the middle of Granny Burrell Falls (N35 09.780 / W83 01.692). After enjoying yourself at Granny Burrell, continue upstream (southwest) on the overgrown trail. (*Option:* Return to the trailhead for a 2.4-mile out and back hike of an hour and a half.)

1.4 Come to a T junction with the Great Wall Trail (#489). Turn right (northeast) and immediately rock-hop across Panthertown Creek.

1.5 After crossing the creek, come to a fork. Bear left at the fork and hike northwest.

1.8 Come to another T junction at the Deep Gap Trail (#449). Go left here, following the trail northwest and back downhill.

1.9 Just before the trail crosses the creek again, you will see a side trail to the left (south-southeast). Take this trail on a short, steep scramble to the base of Frolictown Falls (N35 09.725 / W83 02.279). Return the way you came.

3.8 Arrive back at the trailhead.

37 Wilderness Falls

Diamond in the rough! Hiking through Panthertown Valley is always a treat, but when you round the bend and Wilderness Falls comes into view, you immediately know you've stumbled onto a real gem. Glistening in the sun, the beauty of this waterfall easily matches that of the finest of diamonds.

See map on page 99.
Height: 150 feet
Beauty rating: Excellent
Distance: 1.5 miles out and back
Difficulty: Moderate
Trail surface: Wide, gravel road and hard-packed dirt
Approximate hiking time: 45 minutes
Blaze color: No blazes
County: Jackson

Land status: National forest
Trail contact: Nantahala National Forest, Nantahala Ranger District; (828) 524-6441; www.fs.fed.us
FYI: Before you hike any of the trails in Panthertown Valley, I recommend purchasing the *Guide's Guide to Panthertown* by Burt Kornegay.
Maps: *DeLorme: North Carolina Atlas & Gazetteer:* Page 52 D2

Finding the trailhead: From the junction of US 64 and NC 281 south in Lake Toxaway, drive west on US 64 for 8.2 miles to Cedar Creek Road (SR 1120). Turn right onto Cedar Creek Road and continue for 2.2 miles before turning right onto Breedlove Road (SR 1121) at the PANTHERTOWN VALLEY ACCESS SITE sign. Continue for 3.3 miles to where the road makes a hard bend to the left and becomes gravel. Follow the bumpy gravel road for 0.3 mile to where it ends at a gate.

From the junction of US 64 and NC 107 in Cashiers, drive east on US 64 for 1.9 miles to Cedar Creek Road (SR 1120). Turn left onto Cedar Creek Road and follow the directions above.

GPS: N35 10.071 / W83 02.394

The Hike

From the parking area, you will see a gated road that leads straight ahead and down, the Blackrock Spur Trail (#447) to your left, and an open camping area to your right. Go straight ahead (south) and around the gate, following the Panthertown Valley Trail (#474) downhill. As you make your descent, you will see the Wilderness Falls Trail (#490) on your right (southwest) and heading downhill. Take this narrow, winding trail and after 0.4 mile you cross over some slickrock in an open area. Continue hiking south, straight down the rock, and soon pick up the dirt trail again. Follow this narrow trail as it leads steeply down to the creek at the base of Wilderness Falls.

As you round the bend and Wilderness Falls comes into view, you're in for a great surprise.

Miles and Directions

0.0   From the trailhead, go around the gate and hike downhill (south) on the wide gravel trail.

0.3   Come to the junction with Wilderness Falls Trail (#490) on your right (southwest). Go right here, following the narrow, winding trail southwest and downhill.

0.7   Cross over some slickrock in an open area. Head south, straight down the slickrock, and soon pick up a narrow dirt trail. Follow this trail steeply downhill toward the creek.

0.75 Arrive at the base of Wilderness Falls (N35 09.815 / W83 02.536). Return the way you came.

1.5   Arrive back at the trailhead.

38 Raven Rock Falls

Graceful! Raven Rock Falls represents grace itself as it plummets on a clean freefall from the top and then tickles the layered rocks below. The best part is that you're likely to have this one to yourself.

Height: 100 feet
Beauty rating: Excellent
Distance: 0.5 mile out and back
Difficulty: Easy to moderate
Trail surface: Narrow, hard-packed dirt
Approximate hiking time: 20 minutes
Blaze color: Yellow and blue

County: Transylvania
Land status: National forest
Trail contact: Nantahala National Forest, Nantahala Ranger District; (828) 524-6441; www.fs.fed.us
Maps: *DeLorme: North Carolina Atlas & Gazetteer:* Page 52 D3

Finding the trailhead: From the junction of NC 281 north and US 64 in Lake Toxaway, drive north on NC 281 for 0.8 mile to Cold Mountain Road (across from the fire station). Turn left onto Cold Mountain Road and travel for 4.5 miles. Find a place to pull off near telephone pole #61, which will be on your left. The trailhead is approximately 50 feet south of the telephone pole on the west side of the road. GPS: N35 09.566 / W82 58.794

The Hike

The narrow, overgrown path leads you down into the woods before bringing you to a small stream crossing in front of a lovely small waterfall. Rock-hop the stream and continue on the foot-worn path until you come to a primitive footbridge that goes behind another small waterfall. After crossing behind the falls, follow the tiny creek downstream. The path soon heads right, leading to the base of Raven Rock Falls.

Also known as Raven Falls, the waterfall is presumably named for nearby Ravenrock Mountain. At 4,321 feet and just a few miles away, the mountain stands tall while overseeing the falls.

Raven Rock Falls, Greenland Creek Falls, Schoolhouse and Warden's Falls

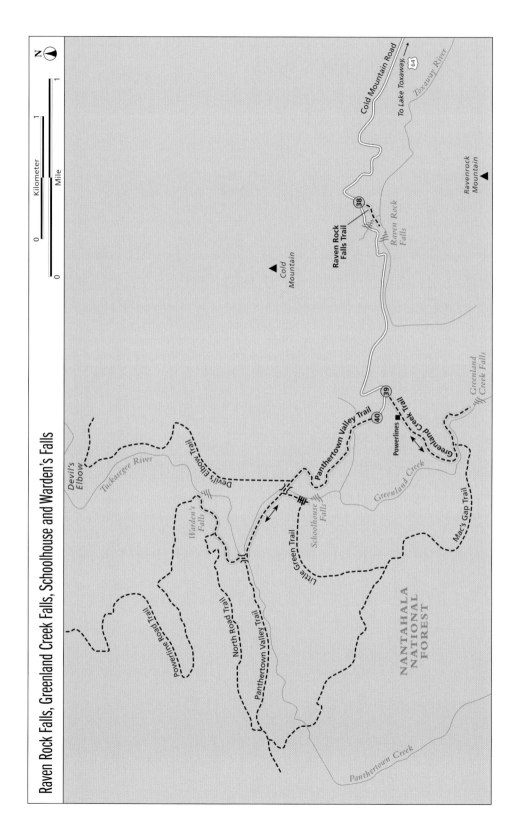

Raven Rock Falls makes a free fall before cascading down the rocks below.

Miles and Directions

0.0   From the trailhead follow the narrow, overgrown path southwest and down and into the woods. Quickly come to a fork with a yellow blaze with a "25" on a tree, a trail heading left (southeast), and a trail to the right (southwest). Go right here and follow the path southwest.

0.1   Rock-hop a tributary in front of a lovely, small waterfall. Continue west-southwest on the foot-worn path.

0.2   Cross a primitive footbridge and then head left (south). Follow the creek downstream a short distance; the trail then heads right (south-southwest).

0.25 Arrive at the base of Raven Rock Falls (N35 09.485 / W82 58.905). Return the way you came.

0.5   Arrive back at the trailhead.

39 Greenland Creek Falls

Sensational! An unexpected surprise awaits as you round the corner and are greeted with the beauty and might of Greenland Creek Falls. Deep within the valley, the inviting pools and multicolored rocks along the creek make this a sensational experience. Whether you're planning a picnic, taking a dip, or just passing by, you're sure to enjoy this waterfall.

See map on page 106.
Height: 50 feet
Beauty rating: Excellent
Distance: 2.0 miles out and back
Difficulty: Easy
Trail surface: Hard-packed dirt
Approximate hiking time: 1 hour
Other trail users: Mountain bikers, equestrians
Blaze color: No blazes
County: Jackson

Land status: National forest
Trail contact: Nantahala National Forest, Nantahala Ranger District; (828) 524-6441; www.fs.fed.us
FYI: Before you hike any of the trails in Panthertown Valley, I recommend purchasing the *Guide's Guide to Panthertown* by Burt Kornegay.
Maps: *DeLorme: North Carolina Atlas & Gazetteer:* Page 52 D3

Finding the trailhead: From the junction of NC 281 north and US 64 in Lake Toxaway, drive north on NC 281 for 0.8 mile to Cold Mountain Road (across from the fire station). Turn left onto Cold Mountain Road and travel for 5.7 miles to a fork in the road. (Cold Mountain Road becomes gravel after 2.4 miles.) Go left at the fork at the Panthertown Valley Recreation Site sign and continue for 0.1 mile. Turn right onto the unmarked dirt road and immediately park in the small pull-off on the left. The trailhead is on the left (west) side of the pull-off. GPS: N35 09.464 / W82 59.815

The Hike

Hike southwest and downhill on the Mac's Gap Trail (#482). The trail meanders through rhododendron thickets as you head deeper into the valley. After approximately 0.5 mile the trail passes and then joins with the Greenland Creek Trail (#488). Follow the conjoined trail for a short distance and the pathways soon go their separate ways. Continue to follow the Greenland Creek Trail upstream.

The trail slowly climbs as the creek beside you becomes more active. The narrow path winds through the thick forest and leads you to cross a tributary three times. The sound of the falls grows nearer as you come out alongside Greenland Creek. Continue hiking upstream as the lush forest offers fantastic views of the creek. Soon arrive at the base of mammoth Greenland Creek Falls.

This is one of six Panthertown Valley waterfalls I've included in this guide. While you're at the parking area for Greenland Creek, I highly recommend that you also visit Schoolhouse and Warden's Falls. The trailhead for these waterfalls is located at the far north end of the dirt road that you parked alongside. If you are partial to mountain biking, you could enjoy the falls and then continue exploring the many miles of multiuse trails that run throughout the valley.

Miles and Directions

0.0 From the trailhead, hike southwest on the Mac's Gap Trail (#482) as you make a slow descent.

0.2 The trail passes under some power lines. Continue hiking southwest as you make your way farther into the valley.

0.6 As the trail begins to bend left (southeast), you will see the Greenland Creek Trail (#488) shooting off to the right (west). Bypass this, and continue around the bend southeast on the Mac's Gap Trail. The Mac's Gap Trail soon unites with the Greenland Creek Trail. Continue hiking on the conjoined trails.

0.7 Arrive at a small opening in the forest where the Mac's Gap Trail heads right (south-southwest) toward the creek and the Greenland Creek Trail continues straight ahead (east). Go straight here, following the Greenland Creek Trail upstream.

0.8 Cross a tributary and continue hiking southwest on the narrow path.

0.9 Cross two more tributaries and continue south-southeast through the dense forest.

1.0 Arrive at the base of Greenland Creek Falls (N35 09.063 / W82 59.899). Return the way you came.

2.0 Arrive back at the trailhead.

40 Schoolhouse and Warden's Falls

Hypnotic! As you sit perched on the sandy beach at the base of the falls, you become entranced by the beauty that surrounds you. The sounds that greet you as the water falls gracefully into the inviting plunge pool are truly hypnotic.

See map on page 106.
Height: Schoolhouse Falls, 20 feet; Warden's Falls, 40 feet
Beauty rating: Excellent for Schoolhouse Falls; very good for Warden's Falls
Distance: 4.3 miles out and back (Schoolhouse Falls, 2.0 miles)
Difficulty: Easy to moderate for Schoolhouse Falls; moderate for Warden's Falls
Trail surface: Gravel road, hard-packed dirt, and wide sandy road
Approximate hiking time: 2 hours, 45 minutes

Blaze color: Red
County: Jackson
Land status: National forest
Trail contact: Nantahala National Forest, Nantahala Ranger District; (828) 524-6441; www.fs.fed.us
FYI: Before you hike any of the trails in Panthertown Valley, I recommend purchasing the *Guide's Guide to Panthertown* by Burt Kornegay.
Maps: *DeLorme: North Carolina Atlas & Gazetteer:* Page 52 D3

Finding the trailhead: From the junction of NC 281 north and US 64 in Lake Toxaway, drive north on NC 281 for 0.8 mile to Cold Mountain Road (across from fire station). Turn left onto Cold Mountain Road and travel for 5.7 miles to a fork in the road. (Cold Mountain Road becomes gravel after 2.4 miles.) Go left at the fork at the PANTHERTOWN VALLEY RECREATION SITE sign and continue for 0.1 mile. Turn right onto an unmarked dirt road and follow the road for 0.2 mile to its end. The trailhead is at the far north end of the dirt road where you parked. GPS: N35 09.478/W82 59.952

The Hike

From the end of the dirt road you will see a gated road for the Greenland Creek Trail (#488) straight ahead (northwest) and the Panthertown Valley Trail (#474) shooting off to your right (north). Take the Panthertown Valley Trail into the forest as it leads you down to a gravel road. Head left on the gravel road; and after 0.2 mile, a narrow footpath acts as a shortcut before bringing you back to the gravel road.

Follow the road downhill and bypass the Devil's Elbow Trail (#448) before crossing a bridge over the creek. Immediately after crossing the bridge, come to a T junction. The right leads toward Warden's Falls. For now, head left as you make your way toward Schoolhouse Falls. Remember this junction though; you'll be backtracking to here to get to Warden's Falls.

On the way to Schoolhouse Falls, you'll cross a wooden boardwalk as you follow the creek upstream. The trail then leads you down some wooden steps to a wonderful sandy beach at the base of Schoolhouse Falls. After enjoying the falls, backtrack to the T junction and continue straight ahead (northwest) as you follow the creek

Many years ago, a small schoolhouse sat near the brink of Schoolhouse Falls.

downstream and head deeper into the forest. The trail leads you over another wooden bridge before bringing you to another T junction. Turn right (northeast) and follow the Powerline Road Trail (#451) as the sandy path makes its way up and around a bend.

Ignore any side trails, and continue hiking until you come to a fork. Stay right here, and soon reach a side trail that leads steeply down to the Tuckasegee River and to the middle of Warden's Falls.

Symphonic! The sweetest of sounds can be heard here, formed by Mother Nature's very own orchestra. As you rest upon the rocks amidst the falls, a symphony of water plays in perfect harmony and elicits your every emotion. Please use caution while tapping your toes to the music though; the rocks here are very slippery.

Miles and Directions

0.0 Hike north from the trailhead on the Panthertown Valley Trail (#474) as it makes a slow descent.

0.2 Cross a small footbridge over the creek. Go left (northwest) on the gravel road and soon cross under some power lines.

0.3 Pass a trail information signpost as you continue to hike down the road and around a gate.

0.4 As the gravel road makes a sharp U-turn to the left (south), you will see a narrow footpath heading straight ahead (north-northwest) off of the road. Follow this footpath steeply downhill and to a T junction. Go left (southwest) at the T junction and continue following the narrow trail downhill.

0.5 Come to a fork with a narrow trail heading right (north) and the main trail heading left (west), leading to some wooden steps. Take the steps and end up back on the gravel road. Go right (northwest) on the road and continue your descent.

0.8 As you make your way downhill, pass the Devil's Elbow Trail (#448) on the right (northeast) as you continue to follow the Panthertown Valley Trail straight ahead (northwest).

0.9 Cross the wooden bridge over the creek and come to a T junction. The right leads northwest to Warden's Falls; the left heads southwest toward Schoolhouse Falls. Go left for now; you are now on the unmarked Little Green Trail (#485). Follow this trail southwest as you hike over the wooden boardwalk. (*Option:* Follow the directions from milepoint 1.2 and hike to Warden's Falls.)

1.0 Come to another fork where the Little Green Trail heads off to the right and another trail heads left and down some wooden steps. Go left (south) here and soon arrive at the base of Schoolhouse Falls (N35 09.799 / W83 00.405). Backtrack to the T junction. (*Option:* Return to the trailhead for a 2.0-mile hike of one hour.)

1.2 Arrive back at the T junction and hike straight ahead (northwest) as you follow the creek downstream on the way toward Warden's Falls.

1.7 Cross another bridge over the creek and immediately come to a T junction. The Panthertown Valley Trail heads left (west), and the Powerline Road Trail (#451) goes to the right (northeast). Go right here, following the sandy Powerline Road Trail as it heads uphill and around a bend. Ignore any side trails.

2.1 Come to the last fork in the trail, with the North Road Trail (#453) heading left (west) and bending around and the Powerline Road Trail leading straight ahead (northeast). Continue straight ahead on the Powerline Road Trail as it bends and climbs. Immediately after the trail bends left, you will see a side trail over your right shoulder (if you get to the power lines, you went too far). Take this side trail east; it immediately bends left (northeast) as it winds steeply down toward the Tuckasegee River.

2.3 Arrive in the middle of Warden's Falls (N35 10.320 / W83 00.383). Backtrack toward the trailhead.

4.3 Arrive back at the trailhead.

41 Paradise Falls

Exotic! Like the skin of a spotted leopard, these nearly untouchable falls are difficult to reach but offer great rewards to those who succeed.

Height: 100 feet
Beauty rating: Excellent
Distance: 1.0 mile out and back
Difficulty: Very strenuous
Trail surface: Hard-packed dirt
Approximate hiking time: 1 hour
Blaze color: No blazes

County: Jackson
Land status: National forest
Trail contact: Nantahala National Forest, Nantahala Ranger District; (828) 524-6441; www.fs.fed.us
Maps: *DeLorme: North Carolina Atlas & Gazetteer:* Page 52 D3

Finding the trailhead: From the junction of NC 281 north and US 64 in Lake Toxaway, drive north on NC 281 for 12.6 miles to a large pull-off on the left (just south of the Wolf Creek Baptist Church).

From the junction of NC 281 and NC 107 in Tuckasegee, drive south on NC 281 for approximately 12.4 miles to a large pull-off on the right (just south of the Wolf Creek Baptist Church).

The trailhead is at the far north end of the pull-off and approximately 20 feet from the road. GPS: N35 13.537/W83 00.221

The Hike

The narrow path is very overgrown and may be hard to see. Be sure to ignore the more obvious trail that heads down from the middle of the pull-off.

The narrow path soon widens, becoming a more reasonable trail. After hiking less than 0.25 mile, a side trail branches off the main path and leads you down to the creek. Wade across, and the trail then leads downstream to the brink of the falls. After passing the brink, the trail becomes a very steep and strenuous scramble down to the creek. The most amazing clean, green water awaits as an inviting swimming hole lures you in. To get the best view of this waterfall, you have to wade across the creek again and find a spot where you can enjoy the thrills Paradise Falls has to offer.

Paradise Falls became the inspiration for the independent film of the same name, which was produced and directed by Cullowhee native Nick Searcy. Although parts of the movie were filmed in North Carolina, no part of it was filmed at Paradise Falls. Searcy acted in the film as well, but is best known for roles he played in other blockbuster films such as *The Fugitive,* with Harrison Ford, and my personal favorite, *Fried Green Tomatoes.*

Paradise Falls

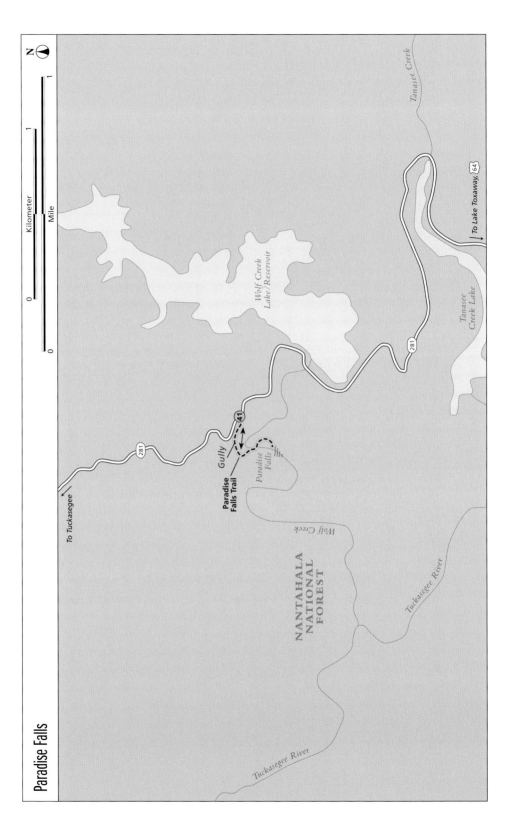

Paradise Falls really is paradise.

Miles and Directions

0.0   From the trailhead, hike northwest on the overgrown path as it heads downward.

0.1   Arrive at an area where it appears as though part of the mountain has fallen off to your left and had a mudslide forming a gully. Continue hiking west straight across the gully.

0.2   You see an obvious side trail that goes down and to your left (southeast) just before the main trail bends right (west-northwest). Take this side trail southeast toward the creek. In about 250 feet, wade across the creek, go right (south), and the trail begins to climb.

FRIED GREEN TOMATOES

This recipe was adapted from www.simplyrecipes.com. Enjoy!

3 medium-size firm green tomatoes

½ cup all-purpose flour

¼ cup milk

2 eggs, beaten

⅔ cup fine dry breadcrumbs

¼ cup olive oil

½ teaspoon salt

¼ teaspoon pepper

1. Cut unpeeled tomatoes into ½-inch slices; sprinkle with salt and pepper to taste. Let tomato slices stand for 15 minutes. Meanwhile, place the flour, milk, beaten eggs, and breadcrumbs in four shallow dishes.

2. Heat 2 tablespoons olive oil in a skillet over medium heat.

3. Dip the tomato slices in milk, then flour, then eggs, then breadcrumbs. Fry half the coated tomato slices for 4 to 6 minutes on each side, or until golden brown. As you cook the second half of the tomatoes, add olive oil as needed. Serve hot.

Serves 4

0.3 After climbing a short distance, you come to the brink of the falls. Continue to hike southeast past the brink.

0.4 The trail begins a very steep descent south to the creek.

0.5 Arrive at the creek at the base of Paradise Falls (N35 13.435 / W83 00.333). Return the way you came.

1.0 Arrive back at the trailhead.

42 French Broad, Mill Shoals, Rooster Tail, Lower Rooster Tail, and Bird Rock Falls

Astonishing! Five fantastic waterfalls on one short trail as the North Fork of the French Broad River passes by. The trail to access these wonderful waterfalls is located on private property and is owned by the Living Waters Ministry. The people at Living Waters have been gracious enough to allow the public to visit the falls, providing that you check in first and, as always, respect the property! Pack it in; pack it out.

Height: French Broad Falls, 15 feet; Mill Shoals Falls, 20 feet; Rooster Tail Falls, 15 feet; Lower Rooster Tail Falls, 6 feet; Bird Rock Falls, 15 feet
Beauty rating: Excellent for all
Distance: 0.4 mile out and back
Difficulty: Easy
Trail surface: Rooty dirt path
Approximate hiking time: 20 minutes

Blaze color: No blazes
County: Transylvania
Land status: Private property; accessible with permission
Trail contact: Living Waters Ministry; www .thereismoreministries.com
Maps: *DeLorme: North Carolina Atlas & Gazetteer:* Page 52 D4

Finding the trailhead: From the junction of NC 215 and US 64 near Rosman, drive north on NC 215 for 7.7 miles and turn left into the Living Waters Ministries. Park at the south end of the parking lot, and obtain permission at "Mary Beth's Kitchen" prior to hiking.

From the junction of NC 215 and the Blue Ridge Parkway near Milepost 425, drive south on NC 215 for 9.1 miles and turn right into the Living Waters Ministries. Follow directions above for parking and check-in.

GPS: N35 13.413 / W82 51.643

The Hike

After you've gained permission, walk to the far south end of the property, past the red "chalet." An obvious trail on the right heads steeply down and into the woods. Bypass this trail and take the next trail that heads northwest, making a less-steep descent toward the river. As soon as you reach the river, you are graced with both Mill Shoals Falls to the right and French Broad Falls (also known as Elysium Falls) directly in front of you.

The trail continues to follow the French Broad River downstream. Soon come to an overlook above the Rooster Tail. Continue downstream along the river's edge and find yourself beside Rooster Tail Falls, named for the "rooster tail" of water that shoots up from the falls. Just downstream from here sits Lower Rooster Tail Falls.

French Broad, Mill Shoals, Rooster Tail, Lower Rooster Tail, and Bird Rock Falls

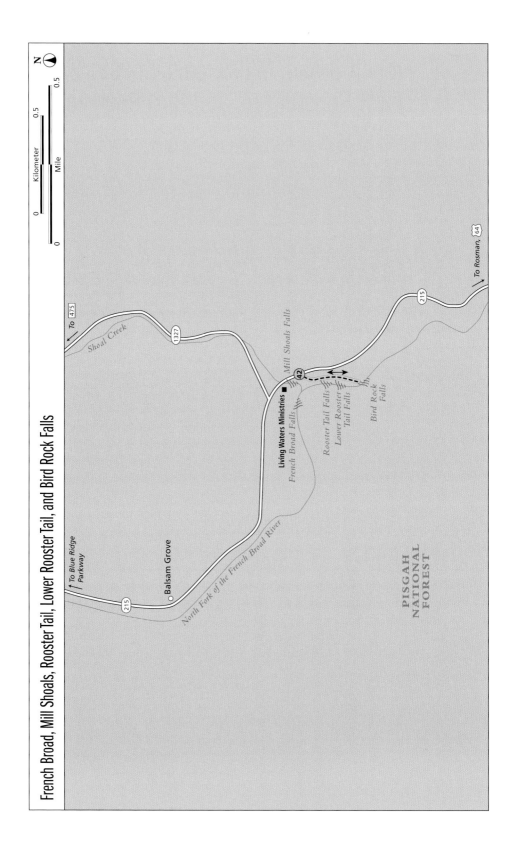

N

Kilometer
0   0.5

Mile
0   0.5

To 475

Shoal Creek

1327

Balsam Grove

215

To Blue Ridge Parkway

North Fork of the French Broad River

Living Waters Ministries

French Broad Falls

Mill Shoals Falls

42

Rooster Tail Falls

Lower Rooster Tail Falls

Bird Rock Falls

215

To Rosman, 64

PISGAH NATIONAL FOREST

French Broad Falls is also referred to as Elysium Falls.

Mill Shoals Falls sits beside the lovely red chalet.

The water shoots up in the air on the right side of the falls, giving Rooster Tail Falls its name.

Bird Rock Falls is often called Cathedral Falls.

Lower Rooster Tail comes to life.

Continue farther downstream to the brink of Bird Rock Falls (also known as Cathedral Falls). Please use caution while at the brink of this or any waterfall. From the brink, the trail leads down to the base of the falls. A monumental cliff towers above, dwarfing this small but lively waterfall. This cliffside area was once home to hundreds of purple martins. Now the walls seem barren, but as a result, a thunderous echo can be heard as Bird Rock Falls booms from below.

A special thanks to Earl Langford for all his knowledge and kindness in sharing these gems.

The French Broad River makes quite a first impression as it thunders through the property owned by the Living Waters Ministry. The river got its name when early settlers noticed that it turned to the west. The lands to the west were claimed by France, while those to the east belonged to England. Since the river headed into French territory, it came to be known as the French Broad River.

Miles and Directions

0.0   From the parking area, head south over the bridge and past the red "chalet." Follow the second narrow trail on your right northwest and down toward the river.

0.1   Arrive at the river at the base of French Broad Falls to the left and Mill Shoals Falls to your right (N35 13.427 / W82 51.671). Continue to follow the river downstream and soon come to a T junction at an overlook above Rooster Tail Falls. Go left (southeast) and continue downstream to a side trail that leads to the base of Rooster Tail Falls (N35 13.343 / W82 51.648). From Rooster Tail, continue downstream a bit farther and arrive at Lower Rooster Tail Falls (N35 13.325 / W82 51.648). Continue to follow the river downstream.

0.2   Come to the brink of Bird Rock Falls. From the brink head south and downstream and soon arrive at the base of Bird Rock Falls (N35 13.265 / W82 51.668). Return the way you came.

0.4   Arrive back at the trailhead.

43 Chestnut Falls

Staggering! This small but powerful waterfall is full of life and character. As it sits waiting within its own private cove, the energy created by Chestnut Falls is utterly enchanting.

Height: 25 feet
Beauty rating: Excellent
Distance: 1.8 miles out and back
Difficulty: Easy to moderate
Trail surface: Wide, grassy road
Approximate hiking time: 50 minutes
Blaze color: No blazes

County: Transylvania
Land status: National forest
Trail contact: Pisgah National Forest, Pisgah Ranger District; (828) 877-3265; www.fs.fed.us
Maps: *DeLorme: North Carolina Atlas & Gazetteer:* Page 52 C4

Finding the trailhead: From the junction of NC 215 and US 64 near Rosman, drive north on NC 215 for 10.3 miles. Turn right onto FR 140 and travel for 2.6 miles to a pull-off on the right just before the gated logging road (Kiasee Creek Road/FR 5031). Please do not block the gate.

From the junction of NC 215 and the Blue Ridge Parkway near Milepost 425, drive south on NC 215 for 6.5 miles. Turn left onto FR 140 and follow the directions above.

The trailhead is at the gate where you parked. GPS: N35 16.143/W82 53.497

The Hike

Go around the gate and hike northwest and uphill on the overgrown logging road. As you head deeper into the forest, the trail flattens and climbs, then flattens again, before making a slow descent to a fork in the road. From here a narrow trail shoots off the grassy road and leads you down to the creek and then upstream to the base of Chestnut Falls.

The headwaters of Chestnut Creek flow from Chestnut Bald. The bald, the creek, and the falls are all named for the great American chestnut tree (*Castanea dentate*). Once the most plentiful tree in the eastern forest, the mighty chestnut was a thriving force

Hearts-a-bustin' blooms in autumn.

throughout the Southern Appalachians. In the late 1800s, however, Asian chestnut trees carrying the fungus *Chryphonectria parasitica* were imported from Japan and China. This deadly fungus caused the great chestnut blight, which by the 1930s had killed off or infected almost every chestnut tree in the United States. Today, only small trees and hybrids remain of this once majestic species.

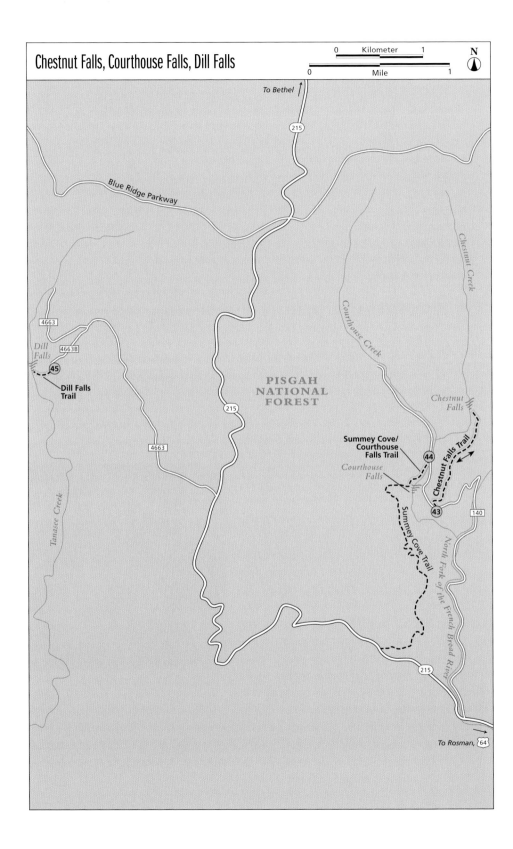

Chestnut Falls, Courthouse Falls, Dill Falls

0   Kilometer   1

0   Mile   1

N

To Bethel

215

Blue Ridge Parkway

Chestnut Creek

Courthouse Creek

4663

Dill
Falls

4663B

45

Dill Falls
Trail

Chestnut
Falls

PISGAH
NATIONAL
FOREST

215

4663

Summey Cove/
Courthouse
Falls Trail

Chestnut Falls Trail

44

Courthouse
Falls

Tanasee Creek

43

140

Summey Cove Trail

North Fork of the French Broad River

215

To Rosman, 64

Chestnut Falls sits tucked away in its own private cove.

Miles and Directions

0.0 From the trailhead hike northwest up the grassy forest road.

0.7 Come to a fork in the trail. Just before the fork, an obscure side trail on your left heads west and down into the woods. Follow this narrow trail, which immediately bends right (north) toward the creek.

0.8 Reach the creek; go right (north) and follow it upstream.

0.9 Arrive at the base of Chestnut Falls (N35 16.735 / W82 53.241). Return the way you came.

1.8 Arrive back at the trailhead.

44 Courthouse Falls

Intoxicating! Courthouse Falls is one of my favorites. It has a character of its own that cannot be described in words. Powerful yet tranquil, this waterfall is highly recommended.

See map on page 122.
Height: 45 feet
Beauty rating: Excellent
Distance: 0.8 mile out and back
Difficulty: Easy
Trail surface: Damp, rooty, rocky trail
Approximate hiking time: 20 minutes

Blaze color: Blue
County: Transylvania
Land status: National forest
Trail contact: Pisgah National Forest, Pisgah Ranger District; (828) 877-3265; www.fs.fed.us
Maps: DeLorme: North Carolina Atlas & Gazetteer: Page 52 C4

Finding the trailhead: From the junction of NC 215 and US 64 in Rosman, drive north on NC 215 for 10.3 miles to FR 140. Turn right onto FR 140 and travel for 3.0 miles to a pull-off on the right just after crossing the bridge.

From the junction of NC 215 and the Blue Ridge Parkway near Milepost 425, drive south on NC 215 for 6.5 miles to FR 140. Turn left onto FR 140 and follow the directions above.

The trailhead is southwest of the pull-off, right next to the bridge on the opposite side of the road. GPS: N35 16.439 / W82 53.537

The Hike

From the trailhead follow the Summey Cove Trail downstream alongside Courthouse Creek. As you make your way into the forest, you get a glimpse of the falls on your left.

Continue hiking until the trail begins to make a deep bend to the right. Just before this bend you will see a side trail that makes a sharp switchback down and to your left. This is the Courthouse Falls Trail. Follow this trail toward the creek, and soon arrive at the base of Courthouse Falls.

Courthouse Creek came to be named because it originates from the mountain that holds the geological formation known as Devil's Courthouse. Judaculla (English for the Cherokee Tsul'Kalu) kept court in the "courthouse" and was said to be a giant slant-eyed, seven-fingered devil. He could leap from mountain to mountain and cast thunderbolts down from the sky. Within his chambers, he would pass final judgment on the dead before they could move on to the spirit world. As a result, many consider the

▶ One of the area's most scenic viewpoints is located atop the Devil's Courthouse. On a clear day you can see four different states from the summit: North Carolina, South Carolina, Georgia, and Tennessee.

A perfect swimming hole waits at the base of Courthouse Falls.

waters of Courthouse Creek to be sacred. The Devil's Courthouse overlook is located between Mileposts 422 and 423 on the Blue Ridge Parkway.

Miles and Directions

0.0 From the Summey Cove Trailhead, hike southwest, following the creek downstream.

0.3 As the main trail begins to make a deep bend to the right (west), a side trail on your left heads southeast down to the creek. Take this trail toward the falls.

0.4 Arrive at the base of Courthouse Falls (N35 16.294 / W82 53.660). Return the way you came.

0.8 Arrive back at the trailhead.

45 Dill Falls

Extraordinary! Like the smell of sweet grass in the air, the fresh breeze from Dill Falls and the way the water dances in the creek arouse the most splendid sensations.

See map on page 122.
Height: 50 feet
Beauty rating: Very good
Distance: 0.4 mile out and back
Difficulty: Easy to moderate
Trail surface: Hard-packed dirt
Approximate hiking time: 20 minutes
Blaze color: No blazes

County: Jackson
Land status: National forest
Trail contact: Nantahala National Forest, Nantahala Ranger District; (828) 524-6441; www.fs.fed.us
Maps: *DeLorme: North Carolina Atlas & Gazetteer:* Page 52 C3

Finding the trailhead: From the junction of NC 215 and US 64 near Rosman, drive north on NC 215 for 14.2 miles to FR 4663, an unmarked gravel road between two houses. Turn left onto FR 4663 and travel for 0.5 mile to where a road forks off to the right. Continue straight ahead (north-northeast) at the fork and travel for another 1.3 miles to a second fork in the road where FR 4663B goes down and to the left. Go left onto FR 4663B and travel for 0.6 mile to where it ends at a three-way fork in the road. Park alongside the road at the fork.

From the junction of NC 215 and the Blue Ridge Parkway near Milepost 425, drive south on NC 215 for 2.6 miles to FR 4663, an unmarked gravel road between two old houses. Turn right onto FR 4663 and follow the directions above.

The trailhead is at the start of the center logging road. GPS: N35 16.966 / W82 56.460

The Hike

From where you parked at the three-way fork, hike south-southwest down the center logging road; follow the road to where it dead-ends at the creek. Once at the creek, look upstream and Dill Falls comes into view.

Dill Falls is located on Tanasee Creek, which flows from the 5,565-foot Tanasee Bald. According to folklore, Judaculla, a giant slant-eyed, seven-fingered devil, lives atop the bald and frolics on the ridge that also bears the Tanasee name.

Miles and Directions

0.0 From the trailhead hike south-southwest down the center logging road until you reach the creek.

0.2 Arrive at the creek just downstream from Dill Falls (N35 16.976 / W82 56.612). Return the way you came.

0.4 Arrive back at the trailhead.

To get the best views of Dill Falls, you may want to wade out into the creek.

46 Wildcat Falls and Falls on Flat Laurel Creek

Calming! When you reach the Falls on Flat Laurel Creek, you find a surprising calm in the air. The random pile of rock cairns left by contemplative campers, the diversity of the flora, and the views of the valley below all come together to create an ever-so-soothing atmosphere. Take your time, step away from the real world, and enjoy the stress relief that this waterfall has to offer. You'll find that Wildcat Falls is a minor perk as you make your way to the real show—Falls on Flat Laurel Creek.

Height: Wildcat Falls, 200 feet; Falls on Flat Laurel Creek, hundreds of feet
Beauty rating: Fair for Wildcat Falls; excellent for Falls on Flat Laurel Creek
Distance: 4.0 miles out and back (Wildcat Falls, 1.4 miles)
Difficulty: Easy
Trail surface: Hard-packed dirt with rocky sections

Approximate hiking time: 2 hours
Blaze color: Orange
County: Haywood
Land status: National forest
Trail contact: Pisgah National Forest, Pisgah Ranger District; (828) 877-3265; www.fs.fed.us
Maps: DeLorme: North Carolina Atlas & Gazetteer: Page 52 C4

Finding the trailhead: From the junction of NC 215 and the Blue Ridge Parkway near Milepost 425, drive north on NC 215 for 0.8 mile to a sharp, narrow right turn into the parking area for the Flat Laurel Creek Trail marked by a small tent-camping sign reading BR 1.

From the junction of NC 215 and US 276 near Waynesville, drive south on NC 215 for 16.7 miles to a sharp, narrow left turn into the parking area for the Flat Laurel Creek Trail marked by a small tent-camping sign reading BR 1.

The trailhead is northeast of the parking area. GPS: N35 18.486 / W82 54.527

The Hike

Hike straight back (east) from the trailhead and you will pass a small, primitive camping area before coming to a creek. Rock-hop across the creek and soon pass by a lovely small waterfall on your right. After enjoying this little beauty, continue hiking for another 0.5 mile before coming to a cement bridge over Wildcat Falls.

From Wildcat Falls the narrow path leads you farther into the forest while affording grand views of the surrounding wilderness. The dirt path remains easy to follow for the next 1.3 miles as it takes you around Little Sam Knob. Bypass the side trail on your left that heads up to a small primitive camping area and continue hiking until you come alongside the Falls on Flat Laurel Creek. Several paths lead steeply down to the creek amidst the falls. Choose the best route, and bask in the splendor of this beauty.

Make sure you bring lots of water on this hike. The trail is very dry, and you are exposed to the sun for most of the way.

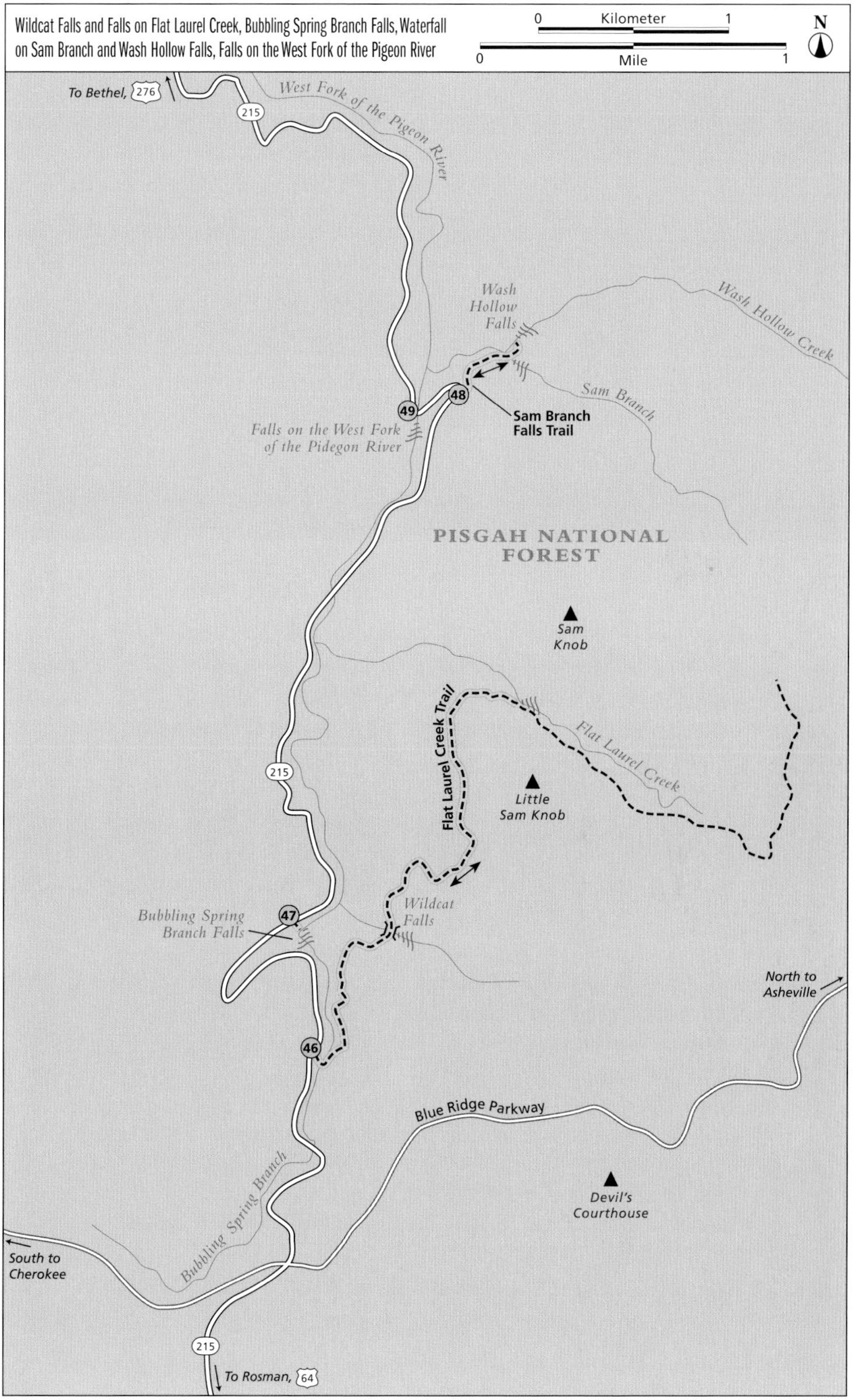

Wildcat Falls and Falls on Flat Laurel Creek, Bubbling Spring Branch Falls, Waterfall on Sam Branch and Wash Hollow Falls, Falls on the West Fork of the Pigeon River

0 ___ Kilometer ___ 1
0 ___ Mile ___ 1

N

To Bethel, 276

West Fork of the Pigeon River

215

Wash Hollow Creek

Wash Hollow Falls

49 48

Sam Branch

Sam Branch Falls Trail

Falls on the West Fork of the Pidegon River

PISGAH NATIONAL FOREST

▲ Sam Knob

Flat Laurel Creek Trail

Flat Laurel Creek

215

▲ Little Sam Knob

Bubbling Spring Branch Falls

47

Wildcat Falls

North to Asheville

46

Blue Ridge Parkway

▲ Devil's Courthouse

South to Cherokee

Bubbling Spring Branch

215

To Rosman, 64

Views of the Shining Rock Wilderness seem to go on forever.

This is one of the few places where I recommend heading to the brink of the falls. The creek upstream from the brink is brimming with character, and the views of the surrounding Shining Rock Wilderness are absolutely stunning.

Five mountain peaks in Shining Rock soar above the impressive height of 6,000 feet. The tallest of these is Grassy Cove Top, which stands at a proud 6,040 feet. Probably the most well known, however, is Cold Mountain. Made popular by the movie that shares its name, Cold Mountain can be viewed in the distance from an overlook on the Blue Ridge Parkway near Milepost 412. Rising to 6,030 feet, it is quite an impressive sight.

Miles and Directions

0.0 From the trailhead hike east past a primitive campsite. The trail then bends to the right (south) and leads you to the creek. Rock-hop across the creek and hike east-southeast as you head into the Shining Rock Wilderness.

0.2 Pass a lovely small waterfall on your right (east-southeast). Continue hiking around and to the left (north-northwest).

0.7 Arrive at a bridge over the creek at Wildcat Falls (N35 18.837 / W82 54.268). From here the narrow path bends left (north-northwest) and continues deeper into the forest, affording grand views of the surrounding wilderness. (*Option:* Return to the trailhead for a 1.4-mile out and back hike of 40 minutes.)

1.4 A narrow side trail heads up and to the left (north) to a primitive campsite. Bypass this trail and continue hiking north.

2.0 Arrive at the Falls on Flat Laurel Creek (N35 19.486 / W82 53.841). Return the way you came.

4.0 Arrive back at the trailhead.

47 Bubbling Spring Branch Falls

Quaint! With each drop it makes, a bubbling spring appears, inviting you to relax in the cool water. Bubbling Spring Branch Falls is easily viewed from the roadside, but you'll want to bring binoculars. Or, you can take a quick stroll down to the bank to get an even better view.

See map on page 129.
Height: 200 feet
Beauty rating: Excellent
Distance: Roadside or 0.2 mile out and back
Difficulty: Easy to moderate
Trail surface: Hard-packed dirt
Approximate hiking time: 15 minutes

Blaze color: No blazes
County: Haywood
Land status: National forest
Trail contact: Pisgah National Forest, Pisgah Ranger District; (828) 877-3265; www.fs.fed.us
Maps: DeLorme: North Carolina Atlas & Gazetteer: Page 52 C4

Finding the trailhead: From the junction of NC 215 and the Blue Ridge Parkway near Milepost 425, drive north on NC 215 for 1.8 miles to the third large gravel pull-off on the right.

From the junction of NC 215 and US 276 near Waynesville, drive south on NC 215 for approximately 15.7 miles to a large pull-off on the left.

The trailhead is located in the center of the pull-off. GPS: N35 18.865 / W82 54.616

The Hike

Bubbling Spring Branch Falls can be viewed from the pull-off by looking to the south. If you want to take a short hike down to the base of the falls, start at the trailhead and head south, steeply downhill, to the creek. Cross the creek and head upstream a short distance to the base of the Bubbling Spring Branch Falls.

The falls sits along the southern slope of the beautiful Balsam Mountains within the heart of the Shining Rock Wilderness. Shining Rock was named for the quartzite rock found upon the surrounding mountaintops. In years past, the rock would set off amazing colorful reflections from the sun's light. Now, however, as trees mature and vegetation grows, the colorful glimmers atop these balds are far less noticeable.

Miles and Directions

0.0 From the trailhead follow the path south and steeply downhill to the creek. Cross the creek and head right (south-southeast) and upstream.

0.1 Arrive at the base of Bubbling Spring Branch Falls (N35 18.838 / W82 54.591). Return the way you came.

0.2 Arrive back at the trailhead.

48 Waterfall on Sam Branch and Wash Hollow Falls

Gallant! Two fantastic falls greet you along this short and easy trail. The first is the gallant and gorgeous Waterfall on Sam Branch. Next along the path is Wash Hollow Falls—in a word, cleansing. As the name implies, this is nature's bathhouse, with perfect little bathing pools found all along the creek.

See map on page 129.

Height: Waterfall on Sam Branch, 60 feet; Wash Hollow Falls, 50 feet
Beauty rating: Very good
Distance: 0.6 mile out and back (Waterfall on Sam Branch, 0.4 mile)
Difficulty: Easy, with a short strenuous climb
Trail surface: Hard-packed dirt
Approximate hiking time: 25 minutes

Blaze color: No blazes
County: Haywood
Land status: National forest
Trail contact: Pisgah National Forest, Pisgah Ranger District; www.fs.fed.us; (828) 877-3265
Maps: *DeLorme: North Carolina Atlas & Gazetteer:* Page 52 B4

Finding the trailhead: From the junction of NC 215 and the Blue Ridge Parkway near Milepost 425, drive north on NC 215 for 3.9 miles to a small pull-off on the right as the road makes a left hairpin curve.

From the junction of NC 215 and US 276 near Waynesville, drive south on NC 215 for approximately 13.6 miles to a small pull-off on the left as the road makes a right hairpin curve.

The trailhead is located at the south end of the guardrail on the east side of the road. GPS: N35 20.371 / W82 54.057

The Hike

Walk south from the pull-off on SR 215 until you see a narrow trail heading east and steeply up into the woods. After making the steep climb, the trail becomes an easy stroll as it wraps around the mountainside and leads you to Waterfall on Sam Branch. Remnants of cables from when this was a thriving logging area can still be seen here. After enjoying Sam Branch, carefully cross the creek and continue hiking on the narrow trail until it dead-ends at the base of Wash Hollow Falls.

Sam Branch and nearby Sam Knob are both named for Edmund Sams, a Patriot captain during the Revolutionary War and a renowned "Indian fighter." One of the first settlers in the Asheville area, Sams is credited with establishing and operating the first ferry across the French Broad River. This was quite a feat, as there were no bridges across the river at the time. Sams later was elected as the first coroner of Buncombe County, and then went on to serve as a member of the county court.

Ursus americanus, *the American black bear, is unique to North America and can be found throughout the mountains of western North Carolina.*

Miles and Directions

0.0 From the trailhead hike east up the steep, narrow path until you reach a T junction at the top of the hill. Go left (north) at the T junction and follow the trail as it wraps around the mountainside.

0.2 Arrive at the middle of Waterfall on Sam Branch (N35 20.461 / W82 53.884). Carefully cross the creek and continue hiking northeast on the narrow trail. (*Option:* Return to the trailhead for a 0.4-mile hike.)

0.3 Arrive at Wash Hollow Falls (N35 20.492 / W82 53.862). Return the way you came.

0.6 Arrive back at the trailhead.

49 Falls on the West Fork of the Pigeon River

Picturesque! As though straight out of a fairy tale, the stone bridge that sits above the falls brings the forest and the falls together, creating a happy ending for all who visit.

See map on page 129.
Height: Several hundred feet
Beauty rating: Excellent
Distance: Roadside
Difficulty: Easy
Blaze color: No blazes

County: Haywood
Land status: National forest
Trail contact: Pisgah National Forest, Pisgah Ranger District; (828) 877-3265; www.fs.fed.us
Maps: *DeLorme: North Carolina Atlas & Gazetteer:* Page 52 B4

Finding the trailhead: From the junction of NC 215 and the Blue Ridge Parkway near Milepost 425, drive north on NC 215 for 4.3 miles to a pull-off on the left, immediately after crossing the bridge.

From the junction of NC 215 and US 276 near Waynesville, drive south on NC 215 for 13.2 miles to a pull-off on the right, just before crossing the bridge.

GPS: N35 20.292 / W82 54.200

The Hike

Although the upper portion of this waterfall is easily viewed from the roadside, a steep scramble down the bank will give you a great view of the falls from under the bridge, as seen in the photo.

The West Fork of the Pigeon River flows under what is known to locals as the High Arch Bridge. This stone masterpiece was one of the many wonders built by the Civilian Conservation Corps in 1937. It lies along the Forest Heritage National Scenic Byway, a 79-mile auto loop that follows NC 215 and also includes portions of US 64 and US 276. If you have some time to spare, enjoy this beautiful drive through the heart of the Pisgah National Forest.

This "High Arch Bridge" was built by the Civilian Conservation Corps.

50 Lower Falls on Little Beartrap Branch

Fickle! This waterfall has been known to boom like thunder. Yet at other times of the year, it's a mere trickle. Keep this in mind when you plan your visit. If water levels are low, skip this one and continue up the road to the Falls on Middle Prong—a real beauty any time of year.

Height: 100 feet
Beauty rating: Fair
Distance: From gate, 2.2 miles out and back; from trailhead, 0.2 mile out and back
Difficulty: Easy to moderate
Trail surface: Gravel road and hard-packed dirt
Approximate hiking time: 1 hour

Blaze color: No blazes
County: Haywood
Land status: National forest
Trail contact: Pisgah National Forest, Pisgah Ranger District; (828) 877-3265; www.fs.fed.us
Maps: *DeLorme: North Carolina Atlas & Gazetteer:* Page 52 B3

Finding the trailhead: From NC 215 and the Blue Ridge Parkway near Milepost 425, drive north on NC 215 for 8.4 miles and turn left onto FR 97 (Lickstone Road). (The turn is immediately after crossing the bridge over Middle Prong and just before the Pisgah Sunburst Campground.) Continue on FR 97 for 0.25 mile to a gate with a sign reading To Haywood Gap. If the gate is locked, park here, but please do not block the gate. If the gate is open, continue for another 1.0 mile to a pull-off on the left where the road makes its first hard switchback to the right.

From the junction of NC 215 and US 276 near Waynesville, drive south on NC 215 for 9.1 miles and turn right onto FR 97 (Lickstone Road). (The turn is just after the Pisgah Sunburst Campground and immediately before crossing the bridge over Middle Prong.) After turning onto FR 97, follow the directions above.

GPS: N35 22.176 / W82 56.380

The Hike

I've been told that the gate for FR 97 is open at different times of the year; however, in the many times I've hiked here, I've never seen this gate open. Therefore, I am providing trail directions as though you must park at the locked gate. If you're lucky enough to find the gate open, drive rather than hike the first 1.0 mile up the gravel road.

From the gate, hike southwest and up FR 97 as it begins to rise and follows Middle Prong from high above. Stay on the forest road for approximately 1.0 mile until you come to the first hard switchback to the right. A narrow trail heads straight ahead (southwest) from the switchback and into the woods. Take this narrow, overgrown path as it leads you up and alongside Little Beartrap Branch before bringing you to the middle of Lower Falls on Little Beartrap Branch.

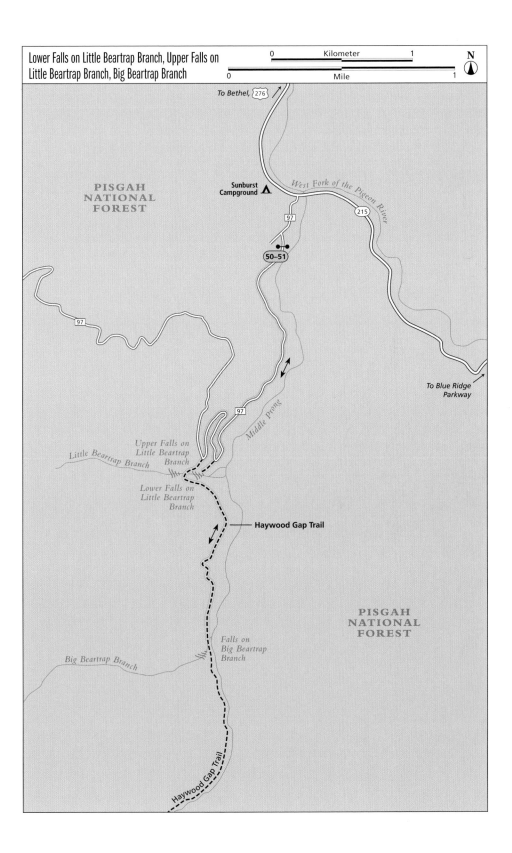

Lower Falls on Little Beartrap Branch, Upper Falls on
Little Beartrap Branch, Big Beartrap Branch

0   Kilometer   1

0   Mile   1

N

To Bethel, 276

PISGAH
NATIONAL
FOREST

Sunburst
Campground

West Fork of the Pigeon River

97

215

50–51

*To Blue Ridge
Parkway*

97

97

Middle Prong

Upper Falls on
Little Beartrap
Branch

Little Beartrap Branch

Lower Falls on
Little Beartrap
Branch

Haywood Gap Trail

PISGAH
NATIONAL
FOREST

*Falls on
Big Beartrap
Branch*

Big Beartrap Branch

Haywood Gap Trail

The Middle Prong Wilderness is known for its rugged isolation. If you choose to day hike here and are looking for a base camp, the Sunburst Campground sits just outside the wilderness. What Middle Prong offers in privacy, though, the campground completely lacks. Sunburst is limited to ten campsites, but they are planted right atop one other, and there is no forest cover to offer privacy.

Special thanks to Terrie and Bob Galeotti for sharing this waterfall with us all.

Miles and Directions

0.0 From the gate hike southwest and uphill on gravel FR 97.

1.0 Come to the first hard switchback to the right (northwest) on the gravel road, where a narrow trail heads straight ahead (southwest) into the woods. Follow this trail into the forest.

1.1 Arrive in the middle of Lower Falls on Little Beartrap Branch (N35 21.361 / W82 56.773). Return the way you came.

2.2 Arrive back at the trailhead.

51 Upper Falls on Little Beartrap Branch and Falls on Big Beartrap Branch

Priceless! While the Upper Falls on Little Beartrap Branch are pleasant, as you meander through the forest toward Middle Prong, you have no idea of the treasure that awaits you. After making your final descent, Falls on Big Beartrap Branch come into view, and the sensations that follow are priceless.

See map on page 137.
Height: Little Beartrap, 200 feet; Big Beartrap, 15 feet
Beauty rating: Good for Little Beartrap; excellent for Big Beartrap
Distance: From gate, 5.0 miles out and back (Little Beartrap, 3.2 miles); from Haywood Gap Trailhead, 2.0 miles out and back (Little Beartrap, 0.2 mile)
Difficulty: Easy to moderate

Trail surface: Gravel road and hard-packed dirt
Approximate hiking time: 2 hours, 30 minutes
Blaze color: No blazes
County: Haywood
Land status: National forest
Trail contact: Pisgah National Forest, Pisgah Ranger District; (828) 877-3265; www.fs.fed.us
Maps: DeLorme: North Carolina Atlas & Gazetteer: Page 52 B3

Finding the trailhead: From the junction of NC 215 and the Blue Ridge Parkway near Milepost 425, drive north on NC 215 for 8.4 miles and turn left onto FR 97 (Lickstone Road). (The turn is immediately after crossing the bridge over Middle Prong and just before the Pisgah Sunburst Campground.) Travel for 0.25 mile to a gate with a sign reading To Haywood Gap. If the gate is locked, park here. If the gate is open, continue driving for another 1.5 miles to a pull-off on the left where the road makes its second hard switchback to the right.

From NC 215 and US 276 near Waynesville, drive south on NC 215 for 9.1 miles and turn right onto FR 97. (The turn is just after the Pisgah Sunburst Campground and immediately before crossing the bridge over Middle Prong.) After turning onto FR 97, follow the directions above.

GPS: N35 22.176 / W82 56.380

The Hike

I've been told that the gate for FR 97 is open at different times of the year; however, in the many times I've hiked here, I've never seen this gate open. Therefore I am providing trail directions as though you must park at the locked gate. If you're lucky enough to find the gate open, drive rather than hike the first 1.5 miles up the gravel road.

Hike southwest on FR 97, which continues to rise as it follows Middle Prong from high above. Stay on the forest road for approximately 1.5 miles until you've reached the second hard switchback to the right. At this switchback, a narrow trail

Falls on Big Beartrap Branch is a wonderful treat within the Middle Prong Wilderness.

heads straight ahead (south-southwest) into the woods. This is the Haywood Gap Trail. Follow this trail for 0.1 mile to reach the Upper Falls on Little Beartrap Branch.

Continue south past the falls as the trail slowly climbs, remaining high above Middle Prong. Along the way you will cross several wet-weather tributaries before making a final rocky descent to the creek at the base of Falls on Big Beartrap Branch. (**Note:** Although you are likely to have FR 97 to yourself, if the gate is closed, the extra 3.0-mile round-trip on the gravel forest road can make for a pretty boring hike.)

Designated in 1984, the 7,900-acre Middle Prong Wilderness is best known for its vast plant and animal diversity. The wilderness serves as a black bear sanctuary and is home to many other mammals, including the ever-elusive bobcat. Ornithologists consider this area prime for birding as well, so you may want to bring binoculars along on this hike.

The nearby Sunburst Campground was the site of the original mill for the Champion Lumber Company back in 1911. The lumber company played a large role in forming the "balds" you now see throughout the Middle Prong Wilderness and neighboring Shining Rock Wilderness.

Miles and Directions

0.0   From the gate hike southwest and uphill on gravel FR 97.

1.5   Come to the second hard switchback to the right (north) on the gravel road. The narrow Haywood Gap Trail (FR 97H) heads straight ahead (south-southwest) into the woods. Follow this trail into the forest.

1.6   Arrive at the base of Upper Falls on Little Beartrap Branch (N35 21.357 / W82 56.820). Continue south, heading deeper into the forest on the Haywood Gap Trail. (***Option:*** Return to the trailhead for a 3.2-mile hike.)

2.5   Arrive at the creek at the base of Falls on Big Beartrap Branch (N35 20.733 / W82 56.708). Return the way you came.

5.0   Arrive back at the trailhead.

52 Second Falls at Graveyard Fields

Serenading! Like the sweet sound of the angels singing, Second Falls serenades you in the most perfect way.

Height: 60 feet

Beauty rating: Excellent

Distance: 0.6 mile out and back

Difficulty: Easy to moderate

Trail surface: Paved path, hard-packed dirt, and wooden stairway

Approximate hiking time: 40 minutes

Blaze color: Blue

County: Haywood

Land status: National forest

Trail contact: Pisgah National Forest, Pisgah Ranger District; (828) 877-3265; www.fs.fed.us

Maps: *DeLorme: North Carolina Atlas & Gazetteer:* Page 52 C4

Finding the trailhead: From the junction of the Blue Ridge Parkway (BRP) and US 276, drive south on the BRP for 6.9 miles to an overlook on the right signed for GRAVEYARD FIELDS.

From the junction of the BRP and NC 215, drive north on the BRP for 6.3 miles to an overlook on the left signed for GRAVEYARD FIELDS.

The overlook is between Mileposts 418 and 419 on the Blue Ridge Parkway. The trailhead and trail map are located at the northeast end of the parking lot. GPS: N35 19.226 / W82 50.818

The Hike

Head down the stone steps and follow the paved path downhill to the creek. Cross the bridge and immediately come to a fork. The left leads southwest toward Upper Falls; the right leads to Second Falls. Go right, following the obvious blue-blazed trail northeast and downstream. Soon arrive at the many stairs that lead down to the base of Second Falls (also known as Lower Falls).

The only morbid tale of Graveyard Fields is that of the land itself. During the logging boom of the early 1900s, this area was clear-cut, leaving nothing but hundreds of moss-covered stumps resembling gravestones. A devastating fire in 1925 and another in 1940 destroyed any remaining growth and rendered the soil sterile, leaving it barren for years to come. While the area may seem destitute at times, the undergrowth still puts on quite a show in autumn, complementing the beauty of this waterfall in a most superb way.

Miles and Directions

0.0 From the trailhead head north down the stone steps and paved path.

0.2 Cross the bridge over Yellowstone Prong; turn right (northeast) and immediately come to a fork. Bear right at the fork (northeast) and follow the blue-blazed trail downstream.

0.3 Hike southeast down the wooden steps, which lead to the base of Second Falls (N35 19.340 / W82 50.783). Return the way you came.

0.6 Arrive back at the trailhead.

Second Falls at Graveyard Fields, Upper Falls at Graveyard Fields, Skinny Dip Hole

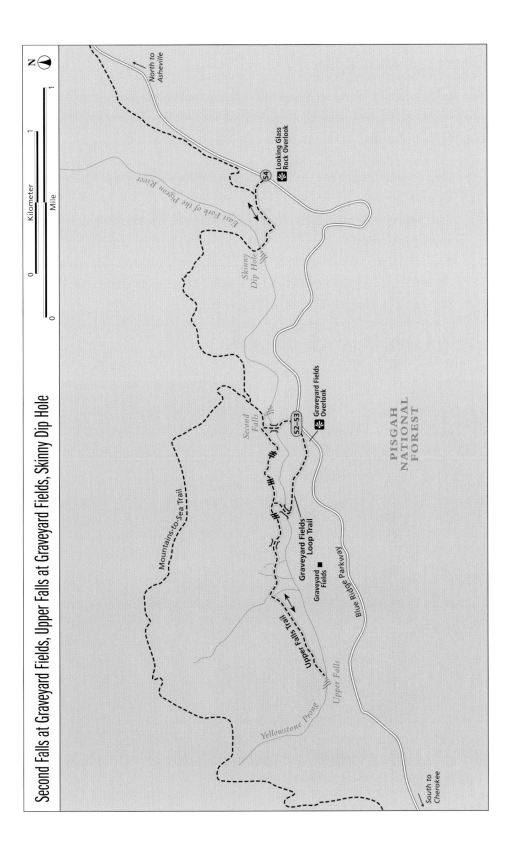

FOREST FIRE PREVENTION

More than 75 percent of forest fires in the United States in the twentieth century were attributed to human activity. While some were accidents and some intentional, others were due to sheer negligence. Here are a few things you can do to help prevent forest fires:

- Build a smaller campfire and sit close to it, as opposed to building a large bonfire and sitting far away.
- Never leave a campfire unattended, and always make sure that it is completely out before vacating your campsite.
- Be mindful of your car's exhaust pipe. The exhaust can reach temperatures in excess of 900 degrees, and exhaust can easily ignite dry brush if it blows on the brush for too long.
- Don't toss cigarette butts (lit or not) on the ground.

As Smokey Bear says, "Only *you* can prevent forest fires."

Some hikers take a break at Second Falls.

53 Upper Falls at Graveyard Fields

Open and airy! The sanctuary-like setting of Upper Falls at Graveyard Fields calms and gives peace with its slow and soothing flow. Upper Falls offers amazing views of the surrounding mountains and the "graveyard" fields below. You even get a glimpse of the Blue Ridge Parkway in the distance where this wonderful hike began.

See map on page 143.
Height: 50 feet
Beauty rating: Good
Distance: 3.0 miles out and back
Difficulty: Easy to moderate
Trail surface: Paved path and hard-packed dirt; rocky sections
Approximate hiking time: 1 hour, 15 minutes

Blaze color: Blue (at beginning of trail only)
County: Haywood
Land status: National forest
Trail contact: Pisgah National Forest, Pisgah Ranger District; (828) 877-3265; www.fs.fed.us
Maps: *DeLorme: North Carolina Atlas & Gazetteer:* Page 52 C4

Finding the trailhead: From the junction of the Blue Ridge Parkway (BRP) and US 276, drive south on the BRP for 6.9 miles to an overlook on the right signed for the GRAVEYARD FIELDS.

From the junction of the BRP and NC 215, drive north on the BRP for 6.3 miles to an overlook on the left signed for GRAVEYARD FIELDS.

The overlook is between milepost 418 and 419 on the Blue Ridge Parkway. The trailhead and trail map are located at the northeast end of the parking lot. GPS: N35 19.226 / W82 50.818

The Hike

Head down the stone steps and follow the paved path downhill to the creek. Cross the bridge and immediately come to a fork. The right leads northeast toward Second Falls; the left takes you to Upper Falls. Go left and follow the trail over a boardwalk.

As you make your way through the Graveyard Fields, an abundance of wildflowers greet you in season. Bypass the Graveyard Ridge Connector Trail and continue along the Upper Falls Trail. As you pass through the valley, you will cross two more make-shift boardwalks and come to follow the mild flow of Yellowstone Prong upstream.

The trail soon begins a subtle climb as you rock-hop across a couple tributaries and pass through a wonderful rhododendron tunnel. As you make your final ascent on the rocky path, you will come to an obscure fork at some boulders. Either route takes you to the falls. The right-hand path has you climbing up some stone "steps" before the trail shows itself again and leads you to the creek at the base of the falls. The left leads down to the creek. Once at the creek, cross it *carefully* and head upstream on the rock face until you reach the base of Upper Falls.

Be sure to bring lots of water on this hike. The tree cover is very sparse as you make your way through the Graveyard Fields.

Upper Falls at the Graveyard Fields offers amazing views of the valley below.

This is a trail for all seasons. A large variety of wildflowers are abundant through-out spring and summer, and the colors of the changing leaves in fall are unmatched by any other.

Miles and Directions

0.0 From the trailhead head north down the stone steps and paved path.

0.2 Cross the bridge over Yellowstone Prong. Turn right (northeast) and immediately come to a fork. Bear left (southwest) at the fork and pass several game trails as the main Upper Falls trail follows a primitive wooden fenceline.

0.3 Hike west over the wooden boardwalk.

0.4 Come to a fork with a trail that heads down to the left (south) and a trail that goes right (north) and up. Go right and immediately come to another fork with the Graveyard Ridge Connector Trail to the right (north) and the Upper Falls Trail to the left (northwest). Go left here, following the trail as it bends southwest and heads back toward the creek.

0.5 Cross a second boardwalk and continue southwest.

0.6 Come to a third fork. The trail to the left leads south-southwest, crosses over the creek, and is an alternate route back to the parking area. Take the trail to the right and continue north-northwest toward Upper Falls.

0.7 Cross another boardwalk and head left (south-southwest) as the creek comes into view. Follow the creek upstream on the narrow dirt path. Cross another wooden footbridge and follow the trail northwest as it begins a subtle climb.

0.9 Rock-hop two tributaries and hike west through a rhododendron tunnel, soon reaching the creek. Head west and follow the mild flow upstream.

1.0 Cross the creek and hike southwest.

1.2 Begin your final ascent on the rocky path heading west toward the falls.

1.4 Come to some boulders. You can either go left (south-southwest), which takes you to the lower portion of the falls, or go right and follow the narrow rocky path to where it ends at the falls. The left-hand trail takes you out on the rocky face of the lower portion of the falls. *Carefully* head upstream on the rock face toward the falls.

1.5 Arrive at the base of Upper Falls (N35 19.086 / W82 51.987). Return the way you came. (***Option:*** At 2.4 miles [back at 0.6 above], turn right (south-southwest) at the junction and cross the creek for a change of scenery on your way back to the trailhead. See below.)

3.0 Arrive back at the trailhead.

Option: On your way back to the trailhead, you can take an alternate route rather than totally retracing your path. Backtrack to the third fork at milepoint 0.6 in the Miles and Directions above, where the trail leads to a bridge over the creek. Cross the bridge and follow the trail as it heads downstream. This route travels through long tunnels of rhododendron before leading you up the stone steps at the southwest end of the parking area. This route is a shadier alternative that also offers a bit of variety in the terrain.

54 Skinny Dip Hole

Enticing! This cool and refreshing pool lures you into its inviting arms to refresh your soul and soothe your body on a hot, sunny day. Locals often leap from the boulders beside the falls into the chilly waters at the base. I've occasionally taken the leap myself.

See map on page 143.
Height: 30 feet
Beauty rating: Excellent
Distance: 1.0 mile out and back
Difficulty: Easy
Trail surface: Hard-packed dirt; rooty sections
Approximate hiking time: 30 minutes
Blaze color: Blue and white

County: Haywood
Land status: National forest
Trail contact: Pisgah National Forest, Pisgah Ranger District; (828) 877-3265; www.fs.fed.us
Maps: *DeLorme: North Carolina Atlas & Gazetteer:* Page 52 C4

Finding the trailhead: From the junction of the Blue Ridge Parkway (BRP) and US 276, drive south on the BRP for 5.1 miles to the overlook on your left for Looking Glass Rock.

From the junction of the BRP and NC 215, drive north on the BRP for 8.1 miles to the overlook on your right for Looking Glass Rock.

The overlook is located at Milepost 417 on the Blue Ridge Parkway.

GPS: N35 19.335 / W82 49.682

The Hike

The trail begins on the west side of the road, across the street from the overlook and just to the left of Milepost 417. Follow this path northwest, straight back into the woods to where it ends at a T junction at the Mountains-to-Sea Trail. Just before the T junction, be sure to take note of the amazing "trail tree" on the east side of the trail.

Head left on the Mountains-to-Sea Trail and follow it on a slow descent deeper into the forest. Bypass any side trails, and continue following the white blazes. The trail crosses a wooden footbridge before heading down to the creek at Skinny Dip Hole.

Special thanks go out to Earl Langford for sharing this one with us all.

The falls are located along the famed Mountains-to-Sea Trail—a 1,000-mile trail that literally makes its way from the mountains to the sea. It starts at Clingmans Dome in the Great Smoky Mountains and travels all the way to the Atlantic Ocean at Jockey Ridge on North Carolina's Outer Banks. The modern-day trail was started in 1973 but is said to follow the original path taken by Native Americans hundreds of years ago.

TRAIL TREES

Nearly 200 years ago, Native American Indians inhabited the North Carolina mountains around us. They lived off the land, and times were simpler. There were no hiking guidebooks or trail blazes to guide them, no topographic maps or GPS units to navigate by. And yet they still found their way through the rugged mountains—in part because of what are known as "trail trees."

Trail trees, usually white oak, are trees that have grown abnormally and seem to be pointing in a certain direction. Found along trails, they either indicate a direction of travel or something else of significance, such as a campsite or water source. The trees are not just freaks of nature. They were altered by the Indians and made to point a specific way as a navigational tool.

In the eastern United States, more than 1,600 of these trail trees have been documented by the Mountain Stewards as part of the Trail Tree Project. For more information on the Mountain Stewards' collection of trail trees, visit their website at www.mountainstewards.org.

Miles and Directions

0.0 From where you parked, *carefully* cross the Blue Ridge Parkway and hike northwest into the forest.

0.1 Come to a T junction in the trail at the Mountains-to-Sea Trail. Go left (west) here, head up the steps, and follow the white-blazed trail.

0.4 Cross the wooden footbridge and continue hiking northwest.

0.5 Take the steps down to a wooden footbridge over the creek at the base of Skinny Dip Hole (N35 19.343 / W82 50.022). Return the way you came.

1.0 Arrive back at the trailhead.

A "trail tree" points the way.

55 Eastatoe Falls

Fluent! As the Middle Fork of the French Broad River flows to create Eastatoe Falls, it flows with complete certainty, never once pausing to take a glimpse at the beauty around it.

Height: 60 feet
Beauty rating: Excellent
Distance: 0.2 mile out and back
Difficulty: Easy
Trail surface: Grass and narrow dirt path
Approximate hiking time: 15 minutes
Blaze color: No blazes

County: Transylvania
Land status: Private property
Trail contacts: Mountain Meadow Guest Cottage; (828) 862-3396; www.citcom .net/~mtmeadowgc/mtnmdwtour.htm
Maps: *DeLorme: North Carolina Atlas & Gazetteer:* Page 52 E4 and 53 E5

Finding the trailhead: From the junction of US 178 and US 64 in Rosman, drive south on US 178 for 3.4 miles. When traveling south through the town of Rosman, be sure to stay left at the fork where US 178 meets Main Street. Turn right at the easy-to-miss MOUNTAIN MEADOW sign and cross the small bridge. Park in front of the guest cottage on your left.

From the junction of US 178 and the North Carolina–South Carolina state line, drive north on US 178 for 3.0 miles. Turn left at the easy-to-miss MOUNTAIN MEADOW sign and follow the directions above.

GPS: N35 06.714 / W82 48.961

The Hike

From where you parked, head up the hill and follow the grass southwest along the tree line. The grassy field then leads to a narrow path back into the woods, to the boulder-filled base of Eastatoe Falls.

This waterfall is located on private property, but the owners of the Mountain Meadow Guest Cottage are kind enough to share this wonderful treasure with us. Please respect their property. If you're looking for a place to stay while visiting the area, consider staying at the guest cottage. The accommodations are quite nice, and you can have your very own waterfall—even if it is just temporary.

Eastatoe is the Cherokee word for the Carolina parakeet (*Conuropsis carolinensis*). There was even an Eastatoe tribe known as the "Green Bird People." The parakeet, which once flourished in western North Carolina, was the only parrot species native to the eastern United States. Its range covered as far north as the Ohio Valley and extended south to the Gulf of Mexico. The bird has been extinct since 1918, when the last one died in captivity, but its name lives on in Eastatoe Falls.

Eastatoe Falls

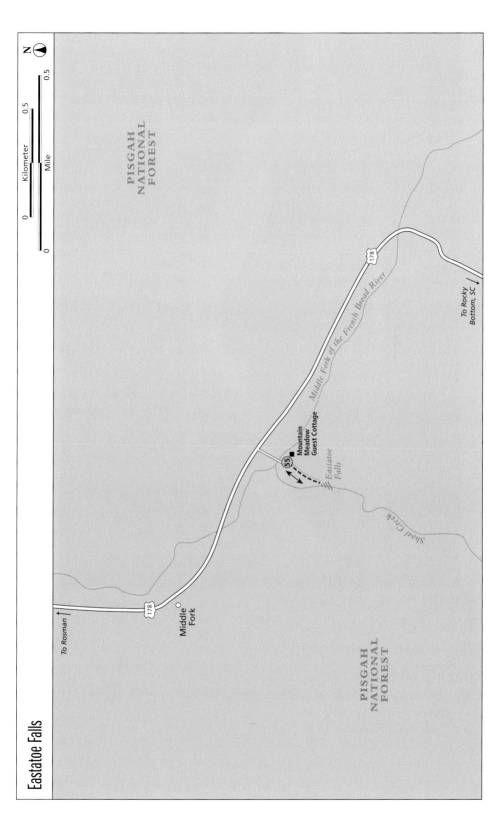

Eastatoe Falls towers over the creek below.

Miles and Directions

0.0 From the trailhead hike southwest along the tree line.

0.1 Arrive at the base of Eastatoe Falls (N35 06.639 / W82 49.018). Return the way you came.

0.2 Arrive back at the trailhead.

56 Cathey's Creek Falls

Glorious! Like a voice from the heavens, Cathey's Creek Falls serenades you with one of nature's most wonderful songs. Perch along the banks and enjoy the show.

Height: 75 feet
Beauty rating: Excellent
Distance: 0.2 mile out and back
Difficulty: Easy
Trail surface: Hard-packed dirt
Approximate hiking time: 10 minutes
Blaze color: No blazes

County: Transylvania
Land status: National forest
Trail contact: Pisgah National Forest, Pisgah Ranger District; (828) 877-3265; www.fs.fed.us
Maps: *DeLorme: North Carolina Atlas & Gazetteer:* Page 53 D5

Finding the trailhead: From the junction of US 64 and SR 215 in Rosman, drive east on US 64 for 5.4 miles. Turn left onto Cathey's Creek Road (SR 1401) at the KUYKENDALL CAMP sign and immediately turn left onto SR 1338. Continue on SR 1338 for 3.1 miles to a small pull-off on your right.

From the junction of US 64 and US 276 south in Brevard, drive west on US 64 for 3.4 miles. Turn right onto Cathey's Creek Road (SR 1401) at the KUYKENDALL CAMP sign and follow the directions above. (**Note:** SR 1338 becomes unpaved FR 471.)

GPS: N35 13.531 / W82 48.151

The Hike

From the pull-off, a narrow trail leads steeply down to the middle section of Cathey's Creek Falls. This section of the waterfall is approximately 75 feet tall; however, the entire falls are said to drop several hundred feet. This underrated waterfall is well worth a visit, even if you have to go out of your way.

The creek and waterfall were named for Captain George Cathey, a Revolutionary War veteran who worked his way up the ranks. Volunteering and entering as a private in 1776, he later reenlisted as a lieutenant and reached the rank of captain before retiring. As was common in those times, Captain Cathey was given land as a reward for his time in the service. The land he received was alongside Cathey's Creek, and included Cathey's Creek Falls.

Cathey's Creek Falls

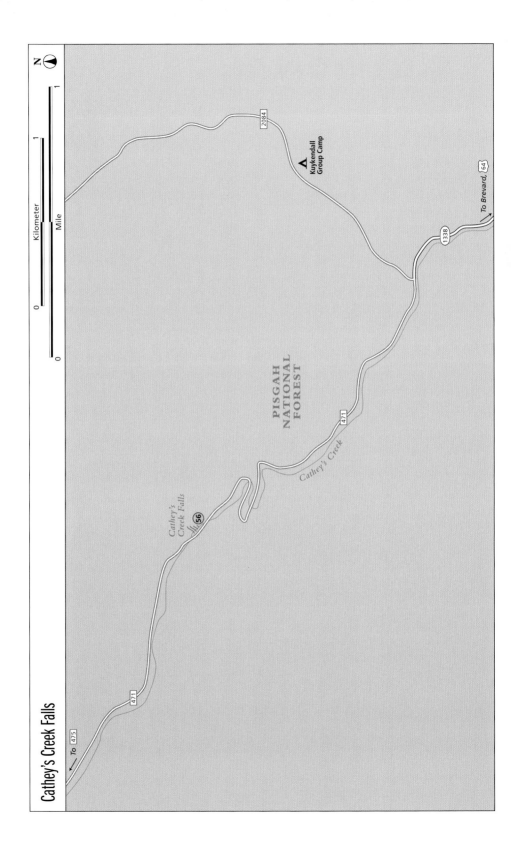

A short steep path leads to the base of majestic Cathey's Creek Falls.

Miles and Directions

0.0 From the trailhead a narrow path leads you north, steeply down to the creek.

0.1 Arrive at Cathey's Creek Falls (N35 13.559 / W82 48.146). Return the way you came.

0.2 Arrive back at the trailhead.

57 Waterfall on Avery Creek and Twin Falls

Dazzling! First you are treated with the small, but lovely Waterfall on Avery Creek. Next, as you hike from trail to trail, you finally arrive at Twin Falls. Like two sisters in the wild, they flow separately yet unite to form one trusting bond as they meet at the creek. This is the nature of Twin Falls: two tall but passive waterfalls a few hundred feet apart, that in turn, flow to create one creek.

Height: Waterfall on Avery Creek, 20 feet; both Twin Falls 100 feet

Beauty rating: Good

Distance: 4.0 miles out and back (Waterfall on Avery Creek, 1.0 mile)

Difficulty: Easy to moderate

Trail surface: Hard-packed dirt with rocky sections; often wet.

Approximate hiking time: 2 hours

Other trail users: Mountain bikers, equestrians

Blaze color: Blue and orange

County: Transylvania

Land status: National forest

Trail contact: Pisgah National Forest, Pisgah Ranger District; (828) 877-3265; www.fs.fed.us

Maps: *DeLorme: North Carolina Atlas & Gazetteer:* Page 53 C5

Finding the trailhead: From the junction of US 276 north and US 64 in Brevard, drive north on US 276 for 2.1 miles. Turn right onto FR 477 at the Riding Stables sign and travel for 2.3 miles to a small pull-off on the right.

From the junction of US 276 and the Blue Ridge Parkway near Milepost 412, drive south on US 276 for 12.6 miles. Turn left onto FR 477 at the Riding Stables sign and follow the directions above. (**Note:** When coming from the north, you will pass one entrance to FR 477 at 4.0 miles. Continue past it to the second entrance as listed above.)

The Avery Creek Trailhead is directly in front of the pull-off. GPS: N35 18.891 / W82 44.955

The Hike

This one's a bit tricky. So many trails converge in this area, so please follow the Miles and Directions closely. In particular, pay close attention to the blaze color, which will change several times throughout the hike.

The trail follows the creek upstream almost the entire way, leading you over many footbridges before leading you to Twin Falls. Used by hikers, mountain bikers, and horseback riders, this area sees quite a bit of traffic on a daily basis. Perhaps the heavy traffic is why this area tends to stay wet throughout the year.

The left twin flows from the headwaters of Avery Creek; the right is on an unnamed tributary.

While there were many Avery family members of note in the mid to late 1700s, it seems that Avery Creek was named for William Waightstill Avery. Avery served in the North Carolina House of Commons and later became Speaker in the North Carolina Senate in 1856.

Waterfall on Avery Creek is a nice treat along the way to Twin Falls.

There is an amusing story regarding Avery and president-to-be Andrew Jackson. In the early years, when they were both practicing law, Avery and Jackson came to have words. Avery accused Jackson of knowing nothing about the law, and after a few heated turns of the tongue, Jackson challenged Avery to a duel. Naturally Avery accepted, and the duel was set, with pistols as the weapon of choice. Being rational men, they realized that neither wished to be shot. They made a gentleman's arrangement, and when they drew their pistols, both men fired into the air and walked away unscathed.

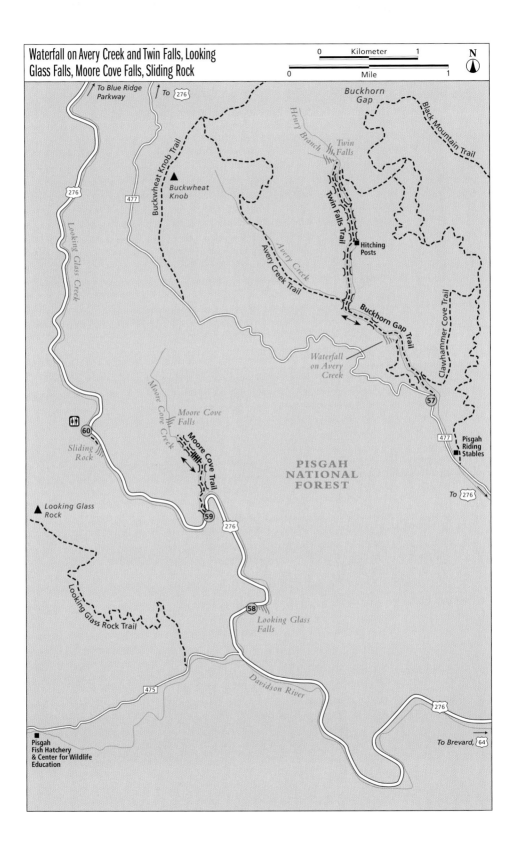

Waterfall on Avery Creek and Twin Falls, Looking Glass Falls, Moore Cove Falls, Sliding Rock

0 Kilometer 1

0 Mile 1

N

To Blue Ridge Parkway

To 276

Buckhorn Gap

Henry Branch

Twin Falls

Black Mountain Trail

276

477

Buckwheat Knob Trail

Buckwheat Knob

Twin Falls Trail

Looking Glass Creek

Avery Creek

Hitching Posts

Avery Creek Trail

Buckhorn Gap Trail

Clawhammer Cove Trail

Waterfall on Avery Creek

Moore Cove Creek

Moore Cove Falls

57

Moore Cove Trail

60

Sliding Rock

PISGAH NATIONAL FOREST

477

Pisgah Riding Stables

Looking Glass Rock

To 276

59

276

Looking Glass Rock Trail

58

Looking Glass Falls

Davidson River

475

276

Pisgah Fish Hatchery & Center for Wildlife Education

To Brevard, 64

The left twin of Twin Falls flows a few hundred feet away from the right twin.

Miles and Directions

0.0 From the trailhead in front of the pull-off, hike north-northeast down into the woods and alongside the creek.

0.2 Cross the first footbridge and immediately come to a T junction. Go left (north) at the T junction, staying on the blue-blazed Avery Creek Trail.

0.5 Arrive alongside the Waterfall on Avery Creek (N35 19.210 / W82 45.174). Follow the creek upstream and cross back-to-back log bridges. (**Option:** Return to the trailhead for a 1.0-mile out and back.)

0.7 Cross a second footbridge and go right (north), staying with the blue blazes.

0.9 The trail dead-ends at a T junction. Turn right (north) at the T junction. This is where the Avery Creek Trail joins the Buckhorn Gap Trail, and you are now being led by both blue and orange blazes.

1.0 Cross a third footbridge and go left (northwest) before coming to a fork in the trail where the Avery Creek and Buckhorn Gap Trails split. Bear right (southeast) on the orange-blazed Buckhorn Gap Trail, cross the footbridge, and continue upstream (north).

1.2 Come to another fork at a creek crossing. Head to the right (upstream); another footbridge awaits just a short distance away. Cross it and go right (north).

1.3 Cross two back-to-back log bridges and head left (north), still following the orange-blazed Buckhorn Gap Trail.

1.4 Head up a hill and pass some horse hitching posts. After descending the hill, come to another fork at a horse ford. Go right here, cross the footbridge, and continue to the right (north-northeast).

1.5 Cross yet another footbridge and go left (north-northwest).

1.6 Cross yet another footbridge and continue upstream (north-northeast) before finally arriving at the Twin Falls Trailhead. Go left (north-northwest) here, now following the blue blazes. Cross another footbridge, then head right (north) and up the steps.

1.7 Cross a log bridge over the creek and continue straight ahead (north).

1.8 After crossing a second log bridge, you will see a waterfall in the distance and a trail shooting left (west) toward it. Ignore that trail, and stay on the main trail heading straight (north-northeast).

1.9 Come to a flat area with narrow trails heading down and to the right (southeast and east). Bypass them and instead go left (north) and up the hill to arrive at the base of the Left Twin of Twin Falls (N35 20.161 / W82 45.604). Continue hiking east past the Left Twin.

2.0 Arrive at the Right Twin of Twin Falls (N35 20.163 / W82 45.579). Return the way you came.

4.0 Arrive back at the trailhead.

58 Looking Glass Falls

Artful! The smooth, free-flowing waters of Looking Glass Falls create a tornado-like effect at the base. This is one of nature's masterpieces, within the ranks of Monet and da Vinci. This work of nature's art is also one of the most accessible and frequently visited waterfalls in the area.

See map on page 158.
Height: 65 feet
Beauty rating: Excellent
Distance: Roadside
Difficulty: Easy
Blaze color: No blazes

County: Transylvania
Land status: National forest
Trail contact: Pisgah National Forest, Pisgah Ranger District; (828) 877-3265; www.fs.fed.us
Maps: *DeLorme: North Carolina Atlas & Gazetteer:* Page 53 C5

Finding the trailhead: From the junction of US 276 north and US 64 in Brevard, drive north on US 276 for 5.4 miles to the parking area along the roadside on the right.

From the junction of US 276 and the Blue Ridge Parkway near Milepost 412, drive south on US 276 for 9.2 miles to the parking area along the roadside on the left.

GPS: N35 17.768 / W82 46.151

The Hike

Looking Glass Falls can be viewed from the roadside, or you can take the stone steps down to the base.

Both the creek and falls are named for the nearby granite monolith known as Looking Glass Rock, which stands over 1,700 feet tall. This pluton was named for its appearance in wintertime. As rainwater freezes on the face of the rock, the rock reflects the sunlight like a giant mirror. The Cherokee called it "the devil's looking glass," perhaps for Judaculla, whose "courthouse" (Devil's Courthouse) is located between Mileposts 422 and 423 on the Blue Ridge Parkway. Looking Glass Rock is best viewed from the Parkway overlook at Milepost 417 or from the top of John Rock—another wonderful hike within the Pisgah National Forest.

The very popular Looking Glass Falls is visible from the roadside.

59 Moore Cove Falls

Incomparable! Echoes of the wild can be heard sweetly singing to you from the cave formed behind the fabulous free fall of Moore Cove Falls.

See map on page 158.
Height: 50 feet
Beauty rating: Very good
Distance: 1.2 miles out and back
Difficulty: Moderate
Trail surface: Hard-packed dirt
Approximate hiking time: 40 minutes

Blaze color: Yellow
County: Transylvania
Land status: National forest
Trail contact: Pisgah National Forest, Pisgah Ranger District; (828) 877-3265; www.fs.fed.us
Maps: *DeLorme: North Carolina Atlas & Gazetteer:* Page 53 C5

Finding the trailhead: From the junction of US 276 north and US 64 in Brevard, drive north on US 276 for 6.6 miles to a large pull-off on the right (just before crossing the bridge).
From the junction of US 276 and the Blue Ridge Parkway near Milepost 412, drive south on US 276 for 8.2 miles to a pull-off on the left (just after crossing the bridge).
GPS: N35 18.294 / W82 46.466

The Hike

From the parking area, walk toward the bridge on US 276 and see a wooden footbridge over the creek to your right. Cross the bridge and follow the trail on its rapid ascent into the forest. Bypass the side trail down some steps to your right and continue uphill on the easily followed trail as it winds through the woods. As you make your way through Moore Cove, you will cross several footbridges before arriving at the base of Moore Cove Falls. This unique waterfall flows from an overhanging rock, forming a cavelike area that allows you to walk behind the falls. Echoes of the pounding water resonate from the rocky walls, enhancing the experience even more.

Moore Cove was named in honor of Adam Q. Moore, although he owned the land surrounding the falls for a mere three years. In the late 1870s Moore was quite a prominent figure in this area. He was not only a local justice of the peace, but also a U.S. Commissioner.

Moore sold the land to George W. Vanderbilt in 1891 for only $155, thus contributing to the subsequent formation of the Pisgah National Forest.

Miles and Directions

0.0 Cross the footbridge and head right (northwest) as the trail begins its rapid ascent into the forest. Bypass the side trail down some steps on your right, and continue to follow the yellow-blazed trail uphill.

0.1 Cross a wooden footbridge and continue northwest.

0.4 Cross another footbridge and head left (northwest). The trail now traverses back-to-back wooden boardwalks. Continue hiking northwest deeper into the forest.

0.5 Cross a footbridge and head right, then cross another and head left as you follow the creek upstream (northwest).

0.6 Arrive at the base of Moore Cove Falls (N35 18.696 / W82 46.665). Return the way you came.

1.2 Arrive back at the trailhead.

60 Sliding Rock

Good clean mountain fun! Sliding Rock is one of the most popular recreational sites in the area. The cool mountain water gushes over the smooth rock surface at an estimated rate of 11,000 gallons per minute. As the name suggests, visitors can actually slide down the icy waterslide and plunge into the pool below.

See map on page 158.
Height: 60 feet
Beauty rating: Good
Distance: 0.2 mile out and back
Difficulty: Easy
Trail surface: Paved path
Approximate hiking time: 10 minutes
Blaze color: No blazes
County: Transylvania

Land status: National forest
Trail contacts: Pisgah National Forest, Pisgah Ranger District; (828) 877-3265; www.fs.fed.us USDA Forest Service; (828) 877-3265
FYI: A small day-use fee is charged per person from Memorial Day to mid-Aug
Maps: *DeLorme: North Carolina Atlas & Gazetteer:* Page 53 C5

Finding the trailhead: From the junction of US 276 north and US 64 in Brevard, drive north on US 276 for 7.7 miles; turn left into the parking lot for Sliding Rock.

From the junction of US 276 and the Blue Ridge Parkway near Milepost 412, drive south on US 276 for 7.1 miles; turn right into the parking lot for Sliding Rock.

The trailhead is located at the southeast end of the parking lot. GPS: N35 18.705 / W82 47.258

The Hike

A short, paved path leads to an observation deck at the brink and then continues to the base of Sliding Rock.

Although Sliding Rock isn't very eye appealing, it sure is entertaining to watch people slide down—even more so to take the plunge yourself. Be forewarned though: The water is very cold, and the bumpy slide to the base may leave you a bit bruised on the backside.

There is a nominal fee (per person) to park and visit Sliding Rock in season, and a lifeguard is on duty from Memorial Day through mid–August. The restrooms / changing rooms are unlocked during the peak summer months.

A young man enjoys the chilling water at Sliding Rock.

Miles and Directions

0.0   Hike southeast on the paved path, and soon arrive at the brink of the falls.

0.1   Arrive at the base of Sliding Rock (N35 18.664 / W82 47.183). Return the way you came.

0.2   Arrive back at the trailhead.

61 Cedar Rock Creek Falls and Falls on Grogan Creek

Invigorating! What a thrill is to be had here. You get two great waterfalls along the same trail and the delightful pleasure of the forest's cover to caress your senses.

Height: Cedar Rock Creek Falls, 25 feet; Falls on Grogan Creek, 25 feet
Beauty rating: Excellent for Cedar Rock Creek Falls; good for Falls on Grogan Creek
Distance: 4.0 miles out and back (Cedar Rock Creek Falls, 1.6 miles)
Difficulty: Easy to moderate
Trail surface: Hard-packed dirt with rooty sections

Approximate hiking time: 1 hour, 30 minutes
Blaze color: Orange and blue
County: Transylvania
Land status: National forest
Trail contact: Pisgah National Forest, Pisgah Ranger District; (828) 877-3265; www.fs.fed.us
Maps: DeLorme: North Carolina Atlas & Gazetteer: Page 53 C5

Finding the trailhead: From the junction of US 276 north and US 64 in Brevard, drive north on US 276 for 5.2 miles and turn left onto FR 475 at the PISGAH FISH HATCHERY sign. Travel for 1.4 miles to a left turn onto FR 475C into the parking area for the Pisgah Center for Wildlife Education and Fish Hatchery. Drive over the bridge to the parking lot on the left.

From the junction of US 276 and the Blue Ridge Parkway near Milepost 412, drive south on US 276 for 9.6 miles. Turn right onto FR 475 at the PISGAH FISH HATCHERY sign and follow the directions above.

The trailhead is at the southwest end of the parking lot, to the left of the fish hatchery. GPS: N35 17.021 / W82 47.519

The Hike

From the trailhead, a gated forest road (FR 475C) heads back into the forest. Hike around the gate, cross the bridge, and then immediately go right onto the Cat Gap Loop Trail. This trail takes you alongside the Pisgah Wildlife Center property before crossing a gravel service road. The trail rises and flattens for 0.5 mile until the sound of the falls becomes clear and you soon arrive at Cedar Rock Creek Falls.

Continue hiking on the Cat Gap Loop Trail and soon come to a junction with the Butter Gap Trail. Turn right and follow the Butter Gap Trail for about 0.5 mile to a fork at the Long Branch Trail. Stay with the blue-blazed Butter Gap Trail for another 0.5 mile until the brink of the falls becomes visible from the trail. Once at the brink, a steep path leads down to the base of the Falls on Grogan Creek.

There are miles and miles of trails to explore as you make your way to Falls on Grogan Creek.

Cedar Rock Mountain, for which the creek is named, and nearby John Rock have both earned the designation of North Carolina Natural Heritage Areas. I highly recommend exploring all the trails within this delightful area, especially John Rock. With many diverse natural communities and a wide array of species, you're sure to enjoy it. I'd also pop into the Pisgah Fish Hatchery and Center for Wildlife Education. Operated by the North Carolina Wildlife Resource Commission, this coldwater hatchery raises approximately half a million trout a year to be released in western North Carolina streams.

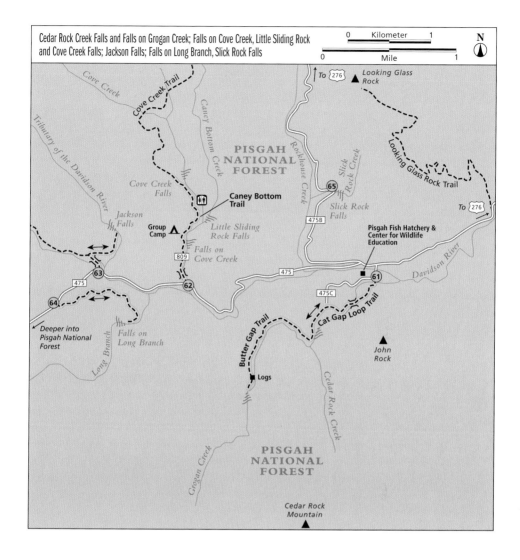

Cedar Rock Creek Falls and Falls on Grogan Creek; Falls on Cove Creek, Little Sliding Rock and Cove Creek Falls; Jackson Falls; Falls on Long Branch, Slick Rock Falls

Miles and Directions

0.0 From the trailhead, hike around the gate and head south over the bridge.

0.1 Go right (west) onto the Cat Gap Loop Trail and follow it alongside the chain-link fence.

0.3 Cross a tributary, and then cross a footbridge over Cedar Rock Creek. The trail then brings you to a gravel road. Go straight across, continuing to follow the Cat Gap Loop Trail north and uphill.

0.7 Bypass the obvious side trail on the left that leads south to a primitive campsite; continue hiking west-southwest.

Cedar Rock Creek Falls is the first of two fabulous waterfalls along the same trail.

0.8   A second obvious side trail to the left leads southeast to a primitive campsite and to the base of Cedar Rock Creek Falls (N35 16.663 / W82 48.000). After visiting the falls, continue hiking southwest on the Cat Gap Loop Trail deeper into the forest. (***Option:*** Return to the trailhead for a 1.6-mile hike of about 40 minutes.)

1.0   Come to a trail junction with the blue-blazed Butter Gap Trail. Go right (west) onto the Butter Gap Trail and immediately cross an open area. Continue hiking northwest back into the woods, following the passive flow of Grogan Creek.

1.5   Arrive at a fork with the red-blazed Long Branch Trail heading to the right (west-northwest) and the Butter Gap Trail continuing to the left (south). Go left here, staying with the blue blazes.

1.9   Cross the logs laid in the trail, and follow the trail around the bend to the right (west) as the sound of the falls becomes clearer.

2.0   Arrive at the brink of the falls. A steep, obscure trail on your left leads northeast down to the base of Grogan Creek Falls (N35 16.319 / W82 48.523). Return the way you came.

4.0   Arrive back at the trailhead.

62 Falls on Cove Creek, Little Sliding Rock, and Cove Creek Falls

Divine! Just like the leaves on a tree tremble in autumn before making their final fall to Earth, the cool waters of Cove Creek pause as though in thought before spilling over the stony slopes that make up Cove Creek Falls. Character exudes from all of these waterfalls.

See map on page 169.

Height: Falls on Cove Creek, 35 feet; Little Sliding Rock, 10 feet; Cove Creek Falls, 65 feet

Beauty rating: Very good for Falls on Cove Creek and Little Sliding Rock; excellent for Cove Creek Falls

Distance: 2.4 miles out and back (Falls on Cove Creek, 0.6 mile; Little Sliding Rock, 1.2 miles)

Difficulty: Easy to moderate

Trail surface: Gravel road; hard-packed dirt

Approximate hiking time: 1 hour

Blaze color: Blue

County: Transylvania

Land status: National forest

Trail contact: Pisgah National Forest, Pisgah Ranger District; (828) 877-3265; www.fs.fed.us

Maps: *DeLorme: North Carolina Atlas & Gazetteer:* Page 52 C4 and 53 C5

Finding the trailhead: From the junction of US 276 north and US 64 in Brevard, drive north on US 276 for 5.2 miles. Turn left onto FR 475 at the Pisgah Fish Hatchery sign and travel for 3.1 miles to a small parking area on the left, across from the Cove Creek Group Camp.

From the junction of US 276 and the Blue Ridge Parkway near Milepost 412, drive south on US 276 for 9.6 miles. Turn right onto FR 475 at the Pisgah Fish Hatchery sign and follow the directions above.

The trailhead is located across the road and north-northwest from the parking area. GPS: N35 16.994 / W82 49.025

The Hike

Go around the gate at the entrance to the Cove Creek Group Camp and hike up the wide gravel road. The road takes you uphill and across Cove Creek before reaching the first of three wonderful waterfalls. The Eden-like Falls on Cove Creek contain several pools, just waiting for someone to sit, relax, and ponder the beauty of the surrounding forest.

Continue hiking uphill on the gravel road and soon come to the lower of two group camping areas at a large open grassy field. There are restrooms to the left at the far east end of the field. Follow the gravel road toward the restrooms. Before the gravel road heads back into the woods, you will see a dirt trail heading north past the restrooms and up into the woods. This is the trail to Cove Creek Falls. But before you head that way, first go right (east) toward the creek.

Once at the creek, arrive at the base of Little Sliding Rock, where Caney Bottom Creek flows into Cove Creek. I wouldn't advise actually sliding on this rock. The water is a bit shallow, and you're bound to bruise your bum if you try.

After enjoying Little Sliding Rock, head back to the trail toward Cove Creek Falls and soon access the blue-blazed Caney Bottom Trail. After 0.2 mile come to a fork with the yellow-blazed Cove Creek Trail. Head right and continue following the Caney Bottom Trail downhill to a large primitive campsite alongside Cove Creek. An obscure trail follows the creek upstream to another fork. Go right here and soon arrive at the base of Cove Creek Falls.

Lying in the heart of the Pisgah National Forest, you're in for a real treat. There is so much to explore and so much life within this forest. Miles and miles of trails surround you. Whether you're hiking, mountain biking, fishing, or perhaps just sitting a spell, Pisgah is the perfect place to do it all.

Little Sliding Rock can be found near the Cove Creek group camping area in the heart of the Pisgah National Forest.

This is one example of the many colorful species of mushroom to be found in North Carolina's mountains.

Miles and Directions

0.0 From the trailhead hike north on the gravel road toward the Cove Creek group camping area.

0.1 Take the side trail on your right (northeast) upstream to a footbridge over Cove Creek. Cross the bridge and continue hiking north on the gravel road.

0.3 See and hear the falls on your right. Follow one of the side trails northeast, down to the base of Falls on Cove Creek (N35 17.225 / W82 49.043). Continue hiking north and uphill on the gravel road. (*Option:* Return to the trailhead for a short 0.6-mile hike of 20 minutes.)

0.5 Come to the large open grassy field, which is the group camp area. Go right (east) and continue hiking past the field on the gravel road.

0.6 Before the gravel road heads back into the woods, head right (east) toward the creek. Climb over the small fence and arrive at the base of Little Sliding Rock (N35 17.347 / W82 48.977). Backtrack to the gravel road and cross it, now heading north on the small dirt path at the far east end of the grassy field. Hike past the restrooms and into the forest. (*Option:* Return to the trailhead on a 1.2-mile out and back hike of 30 minutes.)

0.7 Arrive at a T junction. Go right and follow the blue-blazed Caney Bottom Trail northeast.

0.9 Come to a fork, with the yellow-blazed Cove Creek Trail to the left and heading up and the blue-blazed Caney Bottom Trail to the right and down. Go right here (north), following the Caney Bottom Trail downhill and toward the creek.

1.0 Arrive at a large primitive campsite next to the creek. Go left (northwest) and pick up the obscure trail at the far end of the campsite. Continue hiking upstream (northwest).

1.1 Come to another fork. Go right (northeast) and follow the trail down toward the creek.

1.2 Arrive at the base of Cove Creek Falls (N35 17.626 / W82 49.046). Return the way you came.

2.4 Arrive back at the trailhead.

63 Jackson Falls

Magnificent! Like the stone faces on Easter Island, the distinctive face of Jackson Falls smiles upon you. This rocky-front fall is unlike any other I've seen in this area. Although the flow is not massive, the falls are unique and worth the short hike.

See map on page 169.
Height: 150 feet
Beauty rating: Very good
Distance: 0.8 mile out and back
Difficulty: Easy
Trail surface: Gravel road
Approximate hiking time: 30 minutes

Blaze color: No blazes
County: Transylvania
Land status: National forest
Trail contact: Pisgah National Forest, Pisgah Ranger District; (828) 877-3265; www.fs.fed.us
Maps: DeLorme: North Carolina Atlas & Gazetteer: Page 52 C4

Finding the trailhead: From the junction of US 276 north and US 64 in Brevard, drive north on US 276 for 5.2 miles. Turn left onto FR 475 at the PISGAH FISH HATCHERY sign and travel for 3.8 miles to a large parking area on the right.

From the junction of US 276 and the Blue Ridge Parkway near Milepost 412, drive south on US 276 for 9.6 miles. Turn right onto FR 475 at the PISGAH FISH HATCHERY sign and follow the directions above.

The trailhead is at the north end of the parking area. GPS: N35 17.092 / W82 49.723

The Hike

From the trailhead go around the gate and hike up the wide gravel road on the Daniel Ridge Loop Trail. The trail takes you across the Davidson River before reaching a fork. Head right at the fork and continue to follow the gravel road until you arrive at Jackson Falls on your left. For an up close and personal experience, backtrack about 100 feet and take the narrow side trail that leads alongside Jackson Falls.

Jackson Falls is also known as Toms Spring Falls and Daniel Ridge Falls. Toms Spring is said to be named for Tom Daves, who prospected the area in the early 1900s. The falls were called Daniel Ridge for years, but since Daniel Ridge is located about 2 miles from the falls, the USDA Forest Service adopted the name Jackson Falls in honor of Ray Jackson, who is said to have found the falls while cutting a logging road in the area in 1970.

Miles and Directions

0.0   From the trailhead go around the gate and hike northwest up the gravel road. Cross the bridge over the Davidson River and continue hiking northwest.

The stony face of Jackson Falls waits to greet you.

0.1 Come to a fork in the trail. Go right (north-northeast) as the road narrows and begins to climb.

0.3 Bypass the Daniel Ridge Trail on your left (southwest) and continue straight ahead (northeast) on the gravel road.

0.4 Arrive at Jackson Falls (N35 17.318 / W82 49.586). Return the way you came.

0.8 Arrive back at the trailhead.

64 Falls on Long Branch (Brevard)

Reflective! As the shining sun beats upon the rocky face of the Falls on Long Branch, it sends bright, reflective rays that warm you from within.

See map on page 169.
Height: 15 feet
Beauty rating: Very good
Distance: 1.8 miles out and back
Difficulty: Easy until the bushwhack, then moderate to strenuous
Trail surface: Wide, overgrown, gravel forest road

Approximate hiking time: 45 minutes
Blaze color: No blazes
County: Transylvania
Land status: Pisgah National Forest, Pisgah Ranger District; (828) 877-3265; www.fs.fed.us
Maps: *DeLorme: North Carolina Atlas & Gazetteer:* Page 52 C4

Finding the trailhead: From the junction of US 276 north and US 64 in Brevard, drive north on US 276 for 5.2 miles. Turn left onto FR 475 at the Pisgah Fish Hatchery sign and travel for 4.3 miles to a parking area on the left in front of the gated Searcy Creek Road (FR 5095). Please do not block the gate.

From the junction of US 276 and the Blue Ridge Parkway near Milepost 412, drive south on US 276 for 9.6 miles. Turn right onto FR 475 at the Pisgah Fish Hatchery sign and follow the directions above.

GPS: N35 16.845 / W82 50.048

The Hike

The trail to Long Branch Falls is not the most scenic. Although the waterfall is pretty, the scenery along the overgrown gravel forest road is not. On top of that, the final bushwhack to the falls is quite a challenge. With this in mind, I would save this waterfall till after you've seen the rest.

The not so aptly named Long Branch does not seem to be any longer than the other creeks that freely flow into the Davidson River. As the river flows through the heart of the Pisgah National Forest, it is too shallow for kayaking, but is very popular with tubers in the summer months. (There's a tube rental stand near the pillared entrance into the forest.) Along with tubing, this forest offers miles of mountain bike and hiking trails, a horseback riding stable, trout fishing, a very busy campground, and many primitive campsites scattered throughout the forest.

Miles and Directions

0.0 From the trailhead, go around the gate and hike southeast up the gravel forest road.

0.8 The creek cascades down on your right. Just before the creek, an obscure trail heads up into the woods on your right (southwest). Follow this trail, bushwhacking your way upstream.

0.9 Arrive at Falls on Long Branch (N35 16.745 / W82 49.476). Return the way you came.

1.8 Arrive back at the trailhead.

65 Slick Rock Falls

Subtle! Although this waterfall sits within the heart of waterfall country, Slick Rock Falls remains tucked away from the masses. You'd think this short, easily accessible trail would entice more people, but the passive flow of the falls tends to not keep your attention for very long.

See map on page 169.
Height: 30 feet
Beauty rating: Good
Distance: 0.2 mile out and back
Difficulty: Easy
Trail surface: Hard-packed dirt
Approximate hiking time: 10 minutes

Blaze color: Yellow
County: Transylvania
Land status: National forest
Trail contact: Pisgah National Forest, Pisgah Ranger District; (828) 877-3265; www.fs.fed.us
Maps: DeLorme: North Carolina Atlas & Gazetteer: Page 53 C4

Finding the trailhead: From the junction of US 276 north and US 64 in Brevard, drive north on US 276 for 5.2 miles. Turn left onto FR 475 at the Pisgah Fish Hatchery sign and travel for 1.3 miles to FR 475B (Headwaters Road). Turn right onto FR 475B and continue for 1.1 miles to a small pull-off on your right where the road makes a sharp bend to the left.

From the junction of US 276 and the Blue Ridge Parkway near Milepost 412, drive south on US 276 for 9.6 miles. Turn right onto FR 475 at the Pisgah Fish Hatchery sign and follow the directions above.

GPS: N35 17.599 / W82 47.877

The Hike

Head up the stone steps from the parking area and follow the yellow blazes to a side trail that leads to the base of Slick Rock Falls.

The overhanging bluff at the brink of the aptly-named falls is covered with algae, moss, and lichens. I've heard people speak of seeing the occasional deer carcass found at the base of the falls and am very thankful that I've never seen it myself. Sadly though, just a few years ago there was a human fatality at Slick Rock Falls. I again implore you to use caution at all waterfalls.

Miles and Directions

0.0 From the trailhead, head up the stone steps and hike northeast. A side trail forks off to the the right (southeast) toward the falls. Follow the side trail.

0.1 Arrive alongside Slick Rock Falls (N35 17.594 / W82 47.855). Return the way you came.

0.2 Arrive back at the trailhead.

66 Waterfall on Log Hollow Branch and Falls on Tributary of Big Bearpen Branch

Enriching! The Waterfall on Log Hollow Branch breathes new life into your soul. As you make the final turn to head toward the falls, you are greeted with a very pleasant surprise. Sit a spell, enjoy the experience, and you'll soon find your spirit uplifted and heart beating freely. While Log Hollow Branch is splendid anytime of the year, Big Bearpen Branch tends to be very overgrown, so you may want to save this part of the hike for winter time, when the leaves have fallen and you can get a better view of the falls.

Height: Waterfall on Log Hollow, 50 feet; Falls on Tributary of Big Bearpen Branch, 100 feet
Beauty rating: Very good for Log Hollow Branch; fair for Big Bearpen Branch
Distance: 2.0 miles out and back (Log Hollow Branch, 1.0 mile)
Difficulty: Easy
Trail surface: Gravel forest road

Approximate hiking time: 1 hour
Blaze color: Blue (scantily placed)
County: Transylvania
Land status: Pisgah National Forest, Pisgah Ranger District; (828) 877-3265; www.fs.fed.us
Maps: DeLorme: North Carolina Atlas & Gazetteer: Page 53 C5

Finding the trailhead: From the junction of US 276 north and US 64 in Brevard, drive north on US 276 for 5.2 miles. Turn left onto FR 475 at the Pisgah Fish Hatchery sign and travel for 1.3 miles to FR 475B (Headwaters Road). Turn right onto FR 475B and continue for 5.0 miles to a pull-off on the left next to gated FR 5043 (Log Hollow Road) at the Pisgah Forest Management signpost. Please don't block the gate.

From the junction of US 276 and the Blue Ridge Parkway near Milepost 412, drive south on US 276 for 4.7 miles. Turn right onto FR 475B (Headwaters Road)and travel for 1.6 miles to a pull-off on the right next to gated FR 5043 (Log Hollow Road) at the Pisgah Forest Management signpost.
GPS: N35 19.587 / W82 48.121

The Hike

The trail begins by heading around the gate and following Log Hollow Road (FR 5043) west back into the forest. Follow the rocky forest road and cross two bridges before a side trail leads you directly to the base of the Waterfall on Log Hollow Branch. After enjoying this one, get back on the forest road and continue hiking southeast. A large variety of butterflies and moths seem to accompany you on this portion of the hike until you arrive at the Falls on Tributary of Big Bearpen Branch. This waterfall tends to be overgrown, and it flows underneath the forest road. These things detract

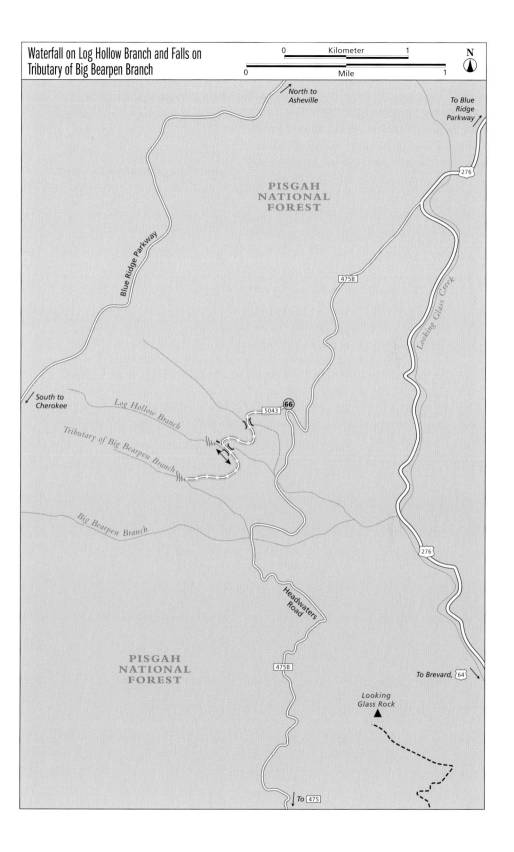

Waterfall on Log Hollow Branch and Falls on
Tributary of Big Bearpen Branch

0   Kilometer   1

0   Mile   1

N

*North to
Asheville*

*To Blue
Ridge
Parkway*

276

PISGAH
NATIONAL
FOREST

475B

Looking Glass Creek

Blue Ridge Parkway

*South to
Cherokee*

Log Hollow Branch

5043

66

Tributary of Big Bearpen Branch

Big Bearpen Branch

276

Headwaters
Road

PISGAH
NATIONAL
FOREST

475B

To Brevard, 64

*Looking
Glass Rock*

To 475

from its beauty, so you may want to save this one until you can get a winter view.

At 5,033 feet, Seniard Mountain is the trail's western terminus and forms the western border of Log Hollow. A designated North Carolina Natural Heritage Area, the mountain is home to high-quality forest and cliff communities, including extensive areas of chestnut-oak forest.

> Butterflies are often seen gathering on piles of dung. While this phenomenon is strange to us, these elegant insects are actually enjoying some fine dining. They are feeding on dissolved mineral salts, which can be found on the feces.

To see the full expanse of Log Hollow, visit the Log Hollow Overlook on the Blue Ridge Parkway, located between Mileposts 416 and 417.

Miles and Directions

0.0   From the trailhead, hike around the gate and follow Log Hollow Road west into the forest.

0.1   Cross the clearing and continue hiking west.

0.2   Cross a wooden footbridge; continue southeast on the rocky forest road as it narrows.

0.5   Cross a second timeworn bridge and immediately after, you'll see an obvious side trail on your right. Take this side trail west to the base of the Waterfall on Log Hollow Branch (N35 19.436 / W82 48.457). Backtrack to the main trail and turn right as you continue southeast, deeper into the forest. (*Option:* Return to the trailhead for a 1.0-mile hike of 30 minutes.)

1.0   Arrive at the Falls on Tributary of Big Bearpen Branch (N35 19.274 / W82 48.636). Return the way you came.

2.0   Arrive back at the trailhead.

67 High Falls on the Mills River

Inspiring! Just as each stone in the river has a story to tell, High Falls tells its own tale with every ripple it makes. This one is loaded with strength and beauty.

Height: 20 feet
Beauty rating: Excellent
Distance: 4.0 miles out and back
Difficulty: Easy to moderate
Trail surface: First mile, rocky; second mile, overgrown and rooty
Approximate hiking time: 2 hours
Other trail users: Mountain bikers, equestrians

Blaze color: No blazes
County: Transylvania
Land status: National forest
Trail contact: Pisgah National Forest, Pisgah Ranger District; (828) 877-3265; www.fs.fed.us
Maps: *DeLorme: North Carolina Atlas & Gazetteer:* Page 53 B5

Finding the trailhead: From the junction of US 276 north and US 64 in Brevard, drive north on US 276 for 11.5 miles. Turn right onto FR 1206 (Yellow Gap Road) and travel for 3.25 miles to FR 476 (Wolf Ford Road). Turn right onto FR 476 and continue for 1.3 miles to where it dead-ends.

From the junction of US 276 and the Blue Ridge Parkway near Milepost 412, drive south on US 276 for 3.2 miles. Turn left onto FR 1206 and follow the directions above.

The trailhead is at the gated logging road at the south end of parking area. GPS: N35 21.986 / W82 44.314

The Hike

Follow the old logging road alongside the river for close to 1.0 mile before straying from the official Mills River Trail at your first fork. From here the trail becomes an overgrown, narrow path, so you may want to wear long pants or gaiters for this hike.

Continue to follow the river downstream until you arrive at the river's edge and the trail seems to disappear. This is where a towel comes in handy, since you have to wade across the river. After crossing the river, head downstream past some small but lovely cascades before arriving at the base of High Falls on the Mills River.

Although it once was home to many mills, both grist and saw, throughout the years, that is not how the Mills River got its name. The river was actually named for Major William Mills, a loyalist during the Revolutionary War, who named the river for himself. Major Mills eventually changed his allegiance from England and became a Patriot. As a result, in 1787 he was awarded 640 acres of land along both the north and south forks of the river. It has been known as the Mills River ever since, and the surrounding community is among the oldest in the area.

> Gristmill versus sawmill: Gristmills are used to grind grain into flour or meal. Sawmills are used to transform timber from logs into usable boards.

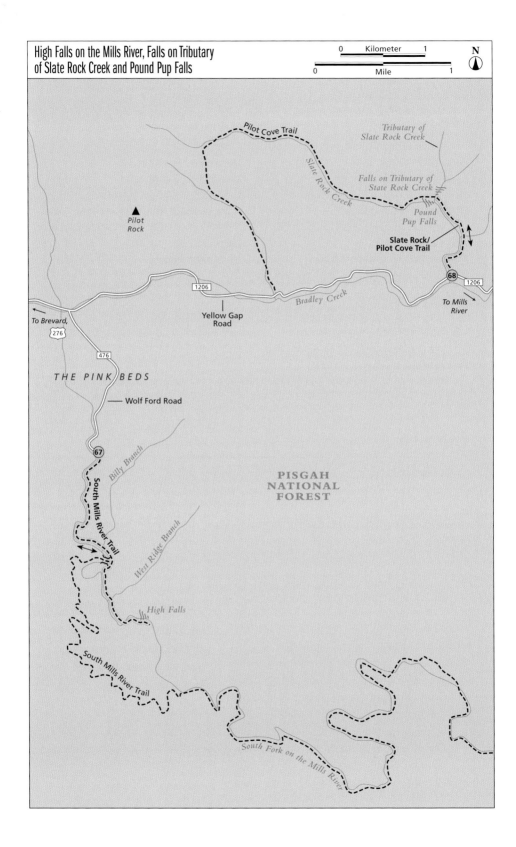

High Falls on the Mills River, Falls on Tributary
of Slate Rock Creek and Pound Pup Falls

0   Kilometer   1

0   Mile   1

N

Pilot Cove Trail

Tributary of
Slate Rock Creek

Slate Rock Creek

Falls on Tributary of
Slate Rock Creek

Pilot
Rock

Pound
Pup Falls

Slate Rock/
Pilot Cove Trail

68

1206

1206

Bradley Creek

To Mills
River

To Brevard,

276

Yellow Gap
Road

476

THE PINK BEDS

Wolf Ford Road

67

Billy Branch

South Mills River Trail

PISGAH
NATIONAL
FOREST

West Ridge Branch

High Falls

South Mills River Trail

South Fork on the Mills River

High Falls on the Mills River is one of the many wonderful sights along the South Fork of the Mills River.

Miles and Directions

0.0 Go around the gate and hike south on the old logging road, following the river downstream.

0.9 Come to a fork with a cement bridge to your right (south) and a narrow trail to your left heading northeast alongside a small tributary. Go left here and follow the tributary upstream.

1.0 Cross the tributary and then head right (south-southwest), back toward the river. Continue to follow the river downstream from high above.

1.2 Come to another fork with an obscure trail on your right (north-northwest) leading down to the water. Bear left here (west-southwest), heading uphill to a small primitive campsite next to a tributary.

1.5 Cross the tributary and continue hiking south on the overgrown path.

1.8 The trail seems to end at the river's edge next to some large flat rocks. Carefully wade across the river and pick up the trail at the far (east) end of the sandy beach.

1.9 As the trail begins to bend right (south), you will see the brink of the falls. A short distance farther, a side trail on the left leads north-northeast toward the base of the falls.

2.0 Arrive at the base of High Falls on the Mills River (N35 20.944 / W82 43.920). Return the way you came.

4.0 Arrive back at the trailhead.

68 Falls on Tributary of Slate Rock Creek and Pound Pup Falls

Angelic! This small but pristine waterfall passes through a narrow, rocky chute as it flows toward Slate Rock Creek. Although it is located right off the trail, I always enjoy this little beauty before making my way to the perfect swimming hole created by Pound Pup Falls.

See map on page 182.
Height: Falls on Tributary of Slate Rock Creek, 15 feet; Pound Pup Falls, 30 feet
Beauty rating: Very good
Distance: 1.6 miles out and back (Tributary of Slate Rock Creek, 1.4 miles)
Difficulty: Easy
Trail surface: Rocky path
Approximate hiking time: 45 minutes

Other trail users: Mountain bikers
Blaze color: Blue
County: Henderson
Land status: National forest
Trail contact: Pisgah National Forest, Pisgah Ranger District; (828) 877-3265; www.fs.fed.us
Maps: *DeLorme: North Carolina Atlas & Gazetteer:* Page 53 B6

Finding the trailhead: From the junction of US 276 north and US 64 in Brevard, drive north on US 276 for 11.5 miles. Turn right onto FR 1206 (Yellow Gap Road) and travel for 6.9 miles to a small parking area on the left.

From the junction of US 276 and the Blue Ridge Parkway near Milepost 412, drive south on US 276 for 3.2 miles. Turn left onto FR 1206 (Yellow Gap Road) and follow the directions above.

As you travel on FR 1206, you will pass a western trailhead for Pilot Cove at 5.2 miles. Be sure to continue to the eastern trailhead for the Pilot Cove/Slate Rock Trail. The trailhead is located at north end of the parking area. GPS: N35 23.126 / W82 41.530

The Hike

The easily followed Pilot Cove/Slate Rock Trail follows Slate Rock Creek all the way into Pilot Cove as it flows down from Slate Rock Ridge. As you enjoy the creekside hiking, continue upstream until you cross your second tributary at the base of the Falls on Tributary of Slate Rock Creek. Continue upstream a short distance to reach the much larger and livelier Pound Pup Falls.

Known primarily among mountain bikers, the Pilot Cove area has abundant mosses, ferns, and wildflowers, which makes it perfect for hiking as well. Designated as a North Carolina Natural Heritage Area, Pilot Cove is home to many diverse natural communities and contains several large granite outcrops. These outcrops may be why I am told that Pilot Cove is also home to many rattlesnakes.

▶ **Rattlesnakes tend to travel in pairs during their mating season—spring and early summer.**

A non-venomous snake rests trailside.

Miles and Directions

0.0 From the trailhead, hike north, straight back into the woods.

0.25 Come to a fork with a narrow trail continuing straight ahead and a trail leading up some steps to the right. Go right (north-northwest) and up the steps.

0.4 Rock-hop a small tributary.

0.6 Take the steps down and then head right (north).

0.7 Arrive at a second tributary at the base of the Falls on Tributary of Slate Rock Creek (N35 23.597 / W82 41.649). (***Option:*** Turn around here for a 1.4-mile hike.) Follow Slate Rock Creek upstream another 100 feet.

0.75 Carefully take the side trail on your left (south) on a steep, muddy scramble to the creek.

0.8 Arrive at the base of Pound Pup Falls (N35 23.589 / W82 41.665). Return the way you came.

1.6 Arrive back at the trailhead.

69 Laughing Falls

Aloof! I call this one Laughing Falls because it laughs at your inability to get a clear view. Unless you're willing to wade in the cold creek, you're not going to get a very good view from any angle. Keep this in mind before you visit.

Height: 70 feet
Beauty rating: Good
Distance: 0.6 mile out and back
Difficulty: Moderate
Trail surface: Narrow dirt path
Approximate hiking time: 30 minutes
Blaze color: No blazes

County: Transylvania
Land status: National forest
Trail contact: Pisgah National Forest, Pisgah Ranger District; (828) 877-3265; www.fs.fed.us
Maps: *DeLorme: North Carolina Atlas & Gazetteer:* Page 53 C6

Finding the trailhead: From the junction of NC 280 and US 64 in Brevard, drive east on NC 280 for 0.7 mile. Turn left onto Old NC 280 (SR 1361) and travel for 0.1 mile to Turkey Creek Road (SR 1360). Turn left onto Turkey Creek Road and continue for 0.6 mile to where it dead-ends. Be sure not to block the gates. GPS: N35 17.518/W82 41.956

The Hike

Hike down the gated forest road to the right and almost immediately come to a creek. After crossing the creek, the overgrown trail follows it upstream for less than 0.25 mile before you catch a glimpse of Laughing Falls in the distance. Unfortunately there is no way to get a good vantage point without getting wet.

Located within the town of Pisgah Forest, this waterfall was said to be named by the Cherokee for its "laughing waters." With so many other wonderful waterfalls within the nearby Pisgah National Forest, I would wait to visit this one until after you've seen the rest.

Miles and Directions

0.0 Hike north down the gated forest road on the right and quickly reach a creek. Cross the creek and immediately come to a fork. Go left (northwest) and follow the overgrown "road" uphill and upstream.

0.2 Take the wide, obvious side trail heading south-southwest down to the creek.

0.3 Arrive downstream of Laughing Falls (N35 17.700/W82 42.096). Return the way you came.

0.6 Arrive back at the trailhead.

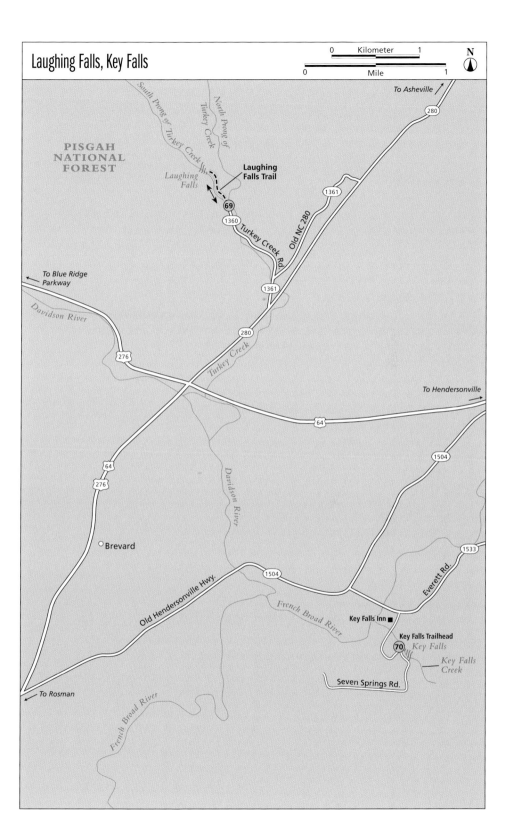

Laughing Falls, Key Falls

0 — Kilometer — 1
0 — Mile — 1

N

PISGAH
NATIONAL
FOREST

South Prong of Turkey Creek

North Prong of Turkey Creek

To Asheville

280

Laughing
Falls

Laughing
Falls Trail

1361

69

1360

Turkey Creek Rd.

Old NC 280

To Blue Ridge
Parkway

Davidson River

1361

280

Turkey Creek

276

To Hendersonville

64

1504

Davidson River

64

276

1533

Brevard

1504

Everett Rd.

Old Hendersonville Hwy.

French Broad River

Key Falls Inn ■

Key Falls Trailhead

70

Key Falls

Key Falls
Creek

Seven Springs Rd.

To Rosman

French Broad River

70 Key Falls

Pure! Like a puppy chasing its tail, this waterfall seems to be trying to catch up to itself. With a small volume of water flow, it's not that impressive, but what does catch the eye are the many stair "steps" the water tumbles over on its way to the base.

See map on page 187.
Height: 80 feet
Beauty rating: Fair
Distance: Roadside
Difficulty: Easy
Blaze color: No blazes

County: Transylvania
Land status: Private property
Trail contact: Key Falls Inn; (828) 884-7559; www.keyfallsinn.com
Maps: *DeLorme: North Carolina Atlas & Gazetteer:* Page 53 C6

Finding the trailhead: From the junction of US 64 and US 276 south in Brevard, drive east on US 64 for 0.8 mile to a road that forks off to the right. Go right here onto Old H-Ville Highway (SR 1504), just past the Ingles grocery store, and travel for 2.6 miles to Everett Road (SR 1533). Turn right onto Everett Road and continue for 0.3 mile to a right turn onto an unmarked dirt road at the Seven Springs sign. Turn here and follow this road for 0.2 mile to view Key Falls on your left.

From the junction of US 64 and US 276 north in Brevard, drive east on US 64 for 3.6 miles. Turn right onto Crab Creek Road (SR 1525) and immediately take your first right onto Old H-Ville Highway (SR 1504). Follow Old H-Ville Highway for 3.0 miles. Turn left onto Everett Road (SR 1533) and follow the directions above.

GPS: N35 14.880 / W82 40.635

The Hike

Key Falls can be viewed from the roadside.

The falls are located on the property of Key Falls Inn, a Victorian farmhouse that was built sometime between 1860 and 1868. Prior to becoming an inn, the building was known as the Patton House, home to Charles Patton. Patton was one of the main committee members who laid out the original plans for the town of Brevard, North Carolina.

With stunning mountain views and its own babbling brook, this bed-and-breakfast is a great place for a relaxing retreat. If you prefer more privacy, the innkeepers also have a rental cabin that's just a short walk away from the falls.

71 Glen Cannon Falls

Eloquent! As though it was placed on the golf course after the fact, Glen Cannon Falls completes the surroundings in which it sits with utter perfection.

See overview map on page iv.
Height: 30 feet
Beauty rating: Excellent
Distance: Roadside
Difficulty: Easy
Blaze color: No blazes
County: Transylvania

Land status: Private property
Trail contact: Glen Cannon Country Club; (828) 884-9160 or (828) 883-8175; www.glencannoncc.com
Maps: *DeLorme: North Carolina Atlas & Gazetteer:* Page 53 D6

Finding the trailhead: From the junction of US 276 south and US 64 in Brevard, drive south on US 276 for 2.0 miles. Turn left onto Wilson Road (SR 1540) and travel for 2.2 miles to Glen Cannon Drive (SR 1580). Turn right onto Glen Cannon Drive and continue for 0.7 mile to a gorgeous roadside view of the falls on your right.

From the junction of US 64 and US 276 north in Brevard, drive west on US 64 for 0.1 mile. Turn left onto Ecusta Road and follow it to where it ends at a stoplight at the unsigned Old H-Ville Highway. Turn right onto Old H-Ville Highway and then immediately left onto Wilson Road (SR 1540). Continue for 1.4 miles to a left turn onto Glen Cannon Drive (SR 1580) and follow the directions above.

GPS: N35 13.777 / W82 41.695

The Hike

Glen Cannon Falls can be viewed from the roadside and forms the backdrop of the second hole on the Glen Cannon Golf Course. If you want to catch a close-up view of these falls, you'll have to play a round of golf—at least the front nine. Contact the Glen Cannon Country Club for your tee time.

The glen and falls were named for Albert Cannon, a former North Carolina commissioner of agriculture. In the 1800s Cannon oversaw the clearing of the land within this area, including the falls that now carry his name.

Glen Cannon Falls overlooks the second hole on the Glen Cannon Golf Course.

72 Connestee Falls

Fantastic! For such a short hike, this one really packs a punch. Although the observation deck keeps you at a distance, the power and beauty of this waterfall make it worth a visit.

Height: 110 feet	**County:** Transylvania
Beauty rating: Very good	**Land status:** County park
Distance: 0.1 mile out and back	**Trail contact:** Connestee Falls Park; (828)
Difficulty: Easy	884-3156; http://rec.transylvaniacounty.org/
Trail surface: Paved path	connfallspark.htm
Approximate hiking time: 5 minutes	**Maps:** *DeLorme: North Carolina Atlas & Gazetteer:* Page 53 D5
Blaze color: No blazes	

Finding the trailhead: From the junction of US 276 south and US 64 in Brevard, drive south on US 276 for 5.7 miles. Turn right into the parking area at the sign for THE FALLS.

From the junction of US 276 and the North Carolina–South Carolina state line, drive north on US 276 for 6.6 miles. Turn left into the parking area at the sign for THE FALLS.

Park at the far right (southwest) end of the parking lot. The trailhead is located at the southwest corner of the parking area. GPS: N35 09.884 / W82 43.849

The Hike

A very short and obvious path leads south to an observation deck overlooking Connestee Falls.

Connestee Falls was named for the Cherokee Indian maiden known as Princess Connestee. Her tribe had captured an Englishman, and Connestee was responsible for nursing him back to health. The two fell deeply in love, and her tribe eventually came to accept him. They were wed by the tribal shaman, but soon after the wedding, her English lover returned to his people, abandoning Connestee and her tribe. The heartbroken Connestee leapt to her death from the crest of a waterfall. Whether it was this exact waterfall she leapt from is open to question.

Connestee Falls

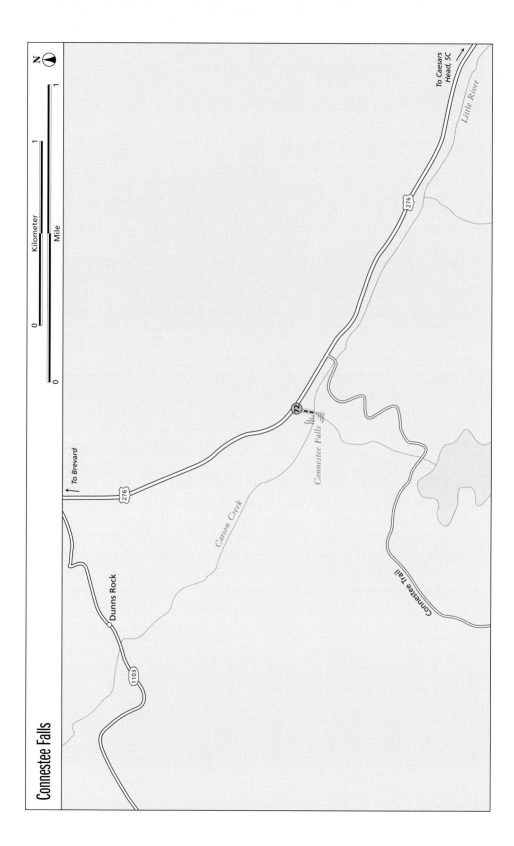

Two waterfalls come together to create Connestee Falls.

Miles and Directions

0.0 From the trailhead, follow the very short path south toward the falls.

0.05 Arrive at the overlook for Connestee Falls (N35 09.857 / W82 43.846). Return the way you came.

0.1 Arrive back at the trailhead.

73 Bridal Veil Falls in DuPont State Forest

Impeccable! Not only is the flow flawless but also each stone is set as though placed there by the hand of God. Like a gift from nature, the large, flat boulders that surround this beauty invite you to lounge about and soak in the sun's rays. Although you'll be hiking on gravel roads for most of this "trail," the final reward is well worth the less-wooded hike.

Height: 60 feet
Beauty rating: Very good
Distance: 4.2 miles out and back
Difficulty: Moderate
Trail surface: Wide gravel road
Approximate hiking time: 2 hours
Other trail users: Mountain bikers, equestrians

Blaze color: No blazes
County: Transylvania
Land status: State forest
Trail contact: DuPont State Forest; (828) 877-6527; www.dupontforest.com
Maps: *DeLorme: North Carolina Atlas & Gazetteer:* Page 53 D6

Finding the trailhead: From the junction of US 276 south and US 64 in Brevard, drive south on US 276 for 10.8 miles. Turn left onto Cascade Lake Road (SR 1536) at the DuPont State Forest sign and travel for less than 0.1 mile. Turn right onto Reasonover Road (SR 1560) and continue for 2.7 miles. Turn left at the sign for the Fawn Lake Access Area and head up the hill. The parking area is immediately on your left.

From the junction of US 64 and US 276 north in Brevard, drive east on US 64 for 3.6 miles. Turn right onto Crab Creek Road (SR 1127) at the sign for DuPont State Forest and travel for 4.2 miles. Turn right onto DuPont Road (SR 1259) at the sign for DuPont State Forest and continue for 5.3 miles to where it ends at Cascade Lake Road (note that DuPont Road becomes Staton Road along the way). Turn left onto Cascade Lake Road and travel for 2.3 miles before turning left onto Reasonover Road. After turning onto Reasonover Road, follow the directions above.

The trailhead is located at the northeast end of the parking area. GPS: N35 09.661 / W82 36.242

The Hike

From the trailhead, go around the gate and follow the wide gravel Reasonover Creek Trail a short distance to a T junction. Head left and follow the gravel Conservation Road for over 1.0 mile. Along the way you will bypass several other "trails" before coming to and crossing a small landing strip/runway.

Soon after passing the landing strip, the trail returns to the cover of the forest and makes its way downhill. When you reach the bottom, abandon Conservation Road and begin hiking west-northwest on Bridal Veil Falls Road. After passing some lovely horse pastures and an old barn, the road dead-ends at a turnaround.

From the turnaround, a narrow footpath leads straight back into the woods to an observation deck overlooking the falls. The trail then continues a short distance to the base of Bridal Veil Falls.

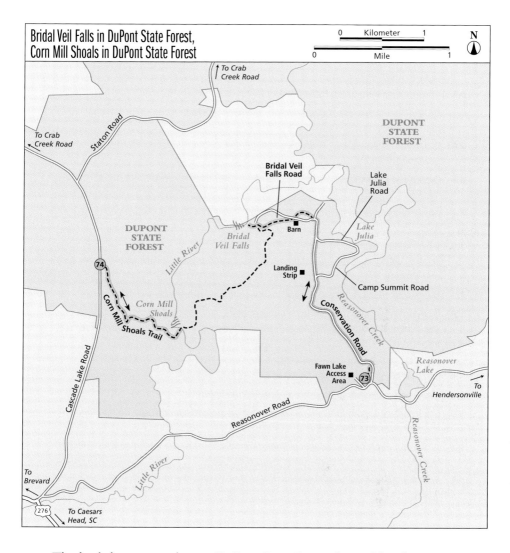

0   Kilometer   1

0   Mile   1

N

To Crab
Creek Road

To Crab
Creek Road

Staton Road

DUPONT
STATE
FOREST

Bridal Veil
Falls Road

Lake
Julia
Road

DUPONT
STATE
FOREST

Little River

Bridal
Veil Falls

Barn

Lake
Julia

74

Landing
Strip

Camp Summit Road

Corn Mill
Shoals

Reasonover Creek

Conservation Road

Corn Mill Shoals Trail

Cascade Lake Road

Fawn Lake
Access
Area

73

Reasonover
Lake

To
Hendersonville

Reasonover Road

Reasonover Creek

To
Brevard

Little River

276

To Caesars
Head, SC

The land that now makes up DuPont State Forest changed hands many times before finally becoming public. It was named for the original owner, the DuPont Company, which operated a plant here, but offered no public access. In 1996 DuPont began to sell off the land. Some went to the state of North Carolina and some to Sterling Diagnostics.

Sterling held the land for just a few years before selling to a private developer, Jim Anthony. Anthony was responsible for building many of the roads within the forest and for building the beautiful covered bridge over the top of High Falls. At the end of 2000, the State of North Carolina acquired the land and DuPont State Forest became the property of the citizens of North Carolina.

The forest is very popular among mountain bikers and hikers. The Little River is a favorite among the paddling community for both kayaks and canoes.

Miles and Directions

0.0 From the trailhead, go around the gate and head right (northeast) on the gravel Reasonover Creek Trail.

0.1 Go left (northwest) at the T junction and follow Conservation Road as it begins to climb.

0.3 Bypass the Scarlet Oak Trail on your left (southwest) and continue straight ahead (north-northwest).

0.6 Bypass the Shortcut Trail, which goes straight ahead (north), and go left (west), staying on Conservation Road.

0.7 Bypass Fawn Lake Road on the left and keep right (north-northeast), staying on Conservation Road.

0.9 Cross the small landing strip, and then hike parallel with it as you head north on the gravel road.

1.0 Bypass Camp Summit Road on the right (northwest) and continue straight ahead (north). The trail soon leaves the side of the landing strip and heads downhill, back into the shade of the forest.

1.3 Bypass Lake Julia Road on the right (east); continue hiking north and downhill.

1.4 Bypass the turn into the vehicle compound on the left and the Shelter Rock Trail on the left. Continue hiking straight ahead (north-northeast) and you soon come to a three-way intersection. The route to the right is gravel and heads uphill (northeast). To the left is the Barn Trail, which goes down (northwest). Take the center gravel road, which leads you north.

1.5 Arrive at another fork. Go left here and follow Bridal Veil Falls Road west-northwest.

1.6 Hike west-southwest past the horse pastures and barn.

1.9 The gravel road dead-ends at a turnaround. Hike straight ahead (west) on the narrow footpath back into the woods.

2.0 Arrive at an observation deck overlooking the falls. You can see the full picture of Bridal Veil Falls from here. Continue hiking toward the creek.

2.1 Arrive at the base of Bridal Veil Falls (N35 10.641 / W82 37.146). Return the way you came.

4.2 Arrive back at the trailhead.

74 Corn Mill Shoals in DuPont State Forest

Comforting! As you sit alongside the banks of the Little River, you are instantly comforted by the peaceful passing of the water's flow—so gentle that it soothes your every sense.

See map on page 195.
Height: 10 feet
Beauty rating: Good
Distance: 2.0 miles out and back
Difficulty: Easy
Trail surface: Wide gravel and sandy road
Approximate hiking time: 1 hour
Other trail users: Mountain bikers, equestrians

Blaze color: No blazes
County: Transylvania
Land status: State forest
Trail contact: DuPont State Forest; (828) 877-6527; www.dupontforest.com
Maps: *DeLorme: North Carolina Atlas & Gazetteer:* Page 53 D6

Finding the trailhead: From the junction of US 276 south and US 64 in Brevard, drive south on US 276 for 10.8 miles. Turn left onto Cascade Lake Road (SR 1536) at the sign for DuPont State Forest and travel for less than 1.75 miles to a large parking area on the left.

From the junction of US 64 and US 276 north in Brevard, drive east on US 64 for 3.6 miles. Turn right onto Crab Creek Road (SR 1127) at the sign for DuPont State Forest and travel for 4.2 miles. Turn right onto DuPont Road (SR 1259) at the sign for DuPont State Forest and continue for 5.3 miles to its end at Cascade Lake Road (note that DuPont Road becomes Staton Road along the way). Go left onto Cascade Lake Road and travel for 0.6 mile to a large parking area on your right.

The trailhead is located on the east side of the road, across the street from the parking area. GPS: N35 10.373 / W82 38.315

The Hike

The trail follows the wide gravel Corn Mill Shoals "Road" as it heads east into DuPont State Forest. You will pass the Longside and Big Rock Trails as the wide gravel and sandy road slowly rises and falls on your peaceful journey through the forest.

Bypass the Burnt Mountain Trail and you soon come to a fork. Continue on the Corn Mill Shoals Trail at this well-marked fork and the next until the trail seems to dead-end near the river. Head to the left (north) and immediately reach the Little River alongside Corn Mill Shoals.

This is an ideal place for a picnic; however, I recommend heading downstream a bit. The entire area, and this trail in particular, is a mountain bike mecca. The Corn Mill Shoals Trail is an entry point into the forest and leads to miles of other popular mountain bike trails, some of which you passed on the way to the falls. It's quite common to see mountain bikers carrying their bikes across the brink of the falls before they remount and continue hammering up the trail.

Hiking with a dog can be fun, but keep your furry friend on a leash for everyone's sake.

Miles and Directions

0.0 From the trailhead, follow wide, gravel Corn Mill Shoals "Road" east to a gate. Go around the gate and continue on the wide gravel and sandy road as it winds through the forest.

0.7 Arrive at a fork, with the Little River Trail to the left (southeast) and the Corn Mill Shoals Trail to the right (south). Head right and continue hiking south.

0.9 Come to a second fork, with the Burnt Mountain Trail going up and to the right (east) and the Corn Mill Shoals Trail heading down and to the left (northeast). Go left and continue to follow the Corn Mill Shoals Trail.

1.0 The trail seems to dead-end. Head left (north) and immediately arrive alongside Corn Mill Shoals (N35 09.993 / W82 37.679). Return the way you came.

2.0 Arrive back at the trailhead.

75 Hooker Falls in DuPont State Forest

Smooth and soft! Like a choreographed dance, the flow of Hooker Falls drops evenly into the plunge pool below. Although this waterfall is untouchable, you can gaze upon its beauty from the sandy beach downstream. Highly traveled, yes, but despite the traffic, it's a wonderful place to visit.

See map on page 201.

Height: 13 feet

Beauty rating: Excellent

Distance: 0.8 mile out and back

Difficulty: Easy

Trail surface: Wide gravel road

Approximate hiking time: 40 minutes

Blaze color: No blazes

County: Transylvania

Land status: State forest

Trail contact: DuPont State Forest; (828) 877-6527; www.dupontforest.com

Maps: DeLorme: North Carolina Atlas & Gazetteer: Page 53 D6

Finding the trailhead: From the junction of US 276 south and US 64 in Brevard, drive south on US 276 for 10.8 miles. Turn left onto Cascade Lake Road (SR 1536) at the DuPont State Forest sign and travel for 2.4 miles to Staton Road (SR 1591). Turn right onto Staton Road and continue for 2.3 miles before turning left into the large parking area signed for Hooker Falls Access Area.

From the junction of US 64 and US 276 north in Brevard, drive east on US 64 for 3.6 miles. Turn right onto Crab Creek Road (SR 1127) at the sign for DuPont State Forest and travel for 4.2 miles to a right turn onto DuPont Road (SR 1259) at the sign for DuPont State Forest. Continue for 3.0 miles before turning right into the large parking area signed for Hooker Falls Access Area.

Along the way, DuPont Road changes names and becomes Staton Road. The trailhead is located at the chained-off gravel road, at the far south end of the parking area. GPS: N35 12.168/W82 37.163

The Hike

The Hooker Falls Trail follows the Little River downstream the entire way. It first leads to an observation deck alongside the falls before continuing downhill, around a switchback, and to a wonderful sandy beach across from Hooker Falls.

While upstream from the falls is very popular with kayakers, canoeists tend to enjoy the calmer waters that wait downstream.

Miles and Directions

0.0 From the trailhead, go around the chain and hike southwest on the gravel road. Quickly come to a fork; go left (south) and follow Hooker Falls "Road" downstream.

0.3 Arrive at the observation deck next to the falls. Continue straight ahead (north-northwest), downhill and around a switchback.

0.4 Arrive at the sandy beach across from Hooker Falls (N35 12.129/W82 37.423). Return the way you came.

0.8 Arrive back at the trailhead.

76 Triple, High, and Grassy Creek Falls in DuPont State Forest

Grandiose! Located within DuPont State Forest, this one trail pleasures you with three, that's right, three waterfalls, the first two of which are most excellent.

Height: Triple Falls, 120 feet; High Falls, 150 feet; Grassy Creek Falls, 35 feet
Beauty rating: Excellent for Triple and High Falls; good for Grassy Creek Falls
Distance: 4.8 miles out and back (Triple Falls, 1.0 mile; High Falls, 2.4 miles)
Difficulty: Moderate
Trail surface: Wide gravel and sandy road
Approximate hiking time: 2 hours, 20 minutes

Other trail users: Mountain bikers, equestrians
Blaze color: No blazes
County: Transylvania
Land status: State forest
Trail contact: DuPont State Forest; (828) 877-6527; www.dupontforest.com
Maps: DeLorme: North Carolina Atlas & Gazetteer: Page 53 D6

Finding the trailhead: From the junction of US 276 south and US 64 in Brevard, drive south on US 276 for 10.8 miles. Turn left onto Cascade Lake Road (SR 1536) at the sign for DuPont State Forest and travel 2.4 miles to Staton Road (SR 1591). Turn right onto Staton Road and continue for 2.3 miles before turning left into the large parking area signed for Hooker Falls Access Area.

From the junction of US 64 and US 276 north in Brevard, drive east on US 64 for 3.6 miles. Turn right onto Crab Creek Road (SR 1127) at the sign for DuPont State Forest and travel for 4.2 miles to a right turn onto DuPont Road (SR 1259) at the sign for DuPont State Forest. Continue for 3.0 miles before turning right into the large parking area signed for Hooker Falls Access Area.

The trailhead is located at the southeast corner of the parking area. GPS: N35 12.161 / W82 37.146

The Hike

The wonderful thing about this trail is that it leads to three fabulous waterfalls. As a matter of fact, fabulous is an understatement with regards to Triple and High Falls. The downside is that the trail tends to be overpopulated, and although you follow the river for portions of it, you spend most of the time hiking on a wide gravel or dirt road. With these pros and cons in mind, I say "Go for it"!

The experience that awaits you on this trail is amazing. First you are treated to Triple Falls, which, in a word, is magical. As the name implies, this one drops in sections, creating the illusion of three waterfalls in one. If you'd like a more personal experience, you can take the many stairs that lead down to the middle of Triple Falls.

Next you come to an overlook with a phenomenal view of High Falls. Exhilarating! With a picturesque covered bridge at the brink, this mighty 150-foot waterfall

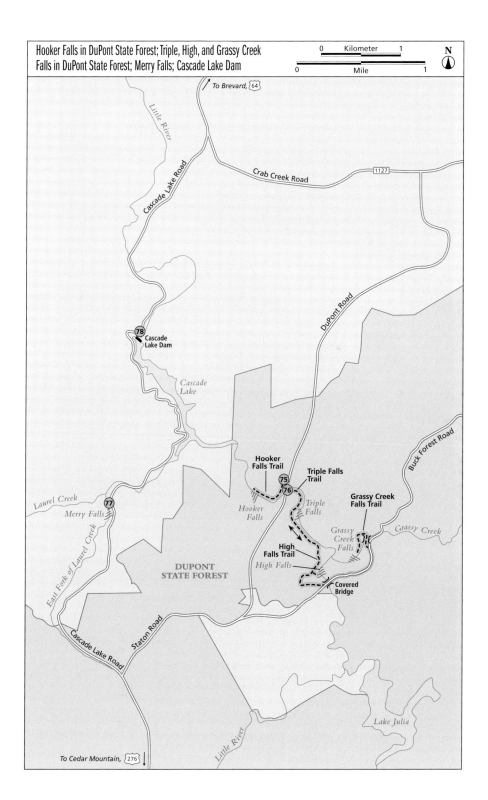

Hooker Falls in DuPont State Forest; Triple, High, and Grassy Creek
Falls in DuPont State Forest; Merry Falls; Cascade Lake Dam

0   Kilometer   1

0   Mile   1

N

To Brevard, 64

Little River

Cascade Lake Road

Crab Creek Road

1127

DuPont Road

78 Cascade
Lake Dam

Cascade
Lake

Laurel Creek

Buck Forest Road

Hooker
Falls Trail

Triple Falls
Trail

77

Merry Falls

75
76

Hooker
Falls

Triple
Falls

Grassy Creek
Falls Trail

Grassy Creek

East Fork of Laurel Creek

Grassy
Creek
Falls

High
Falls Trail

High Falls

DUPONT
STATE FOREST

Covered
Bridge

Cascade Lake Road

Staton Road

Little River

Lake Julia

To Cedar Mountain, 276

Three distinct sections make up Triple Falls.

gives a thrill and a chill. For a more exhilarating experience, you can take a side trail down to the waterfall's base and really feel its power.

The final treat along this trail is the relaxing waterslide that creates Grassy Creek Falls. While Grassy Creek Falls is not as impressive as the others, you are likely to have it all to yourself, which adds to its beauty. Also, as you hike from High Falls to Grassy Creek Falls, you have the pleasure of crossing the covered bridge and viewing the Little River from the brink of High Falls.

A lovely covered bridge sits atop High Falls.

When you come to see these three, I recommend that you also visit Hooker Falls, which shares the same parking area. If you enjoy mountain biking or horseback riding, DuPont State Forest is loaded with miles of trails to enjoy, no matter what your mode of travel.

Detailed maps can be purchased at several local outfitters, including The Hub, located at the corner of US 64 and US 276 north. They not only sell maps but also have a large variety of gear for all your outdoor needs—not to mention a bicycle shop and a tavern. What a treat!

Miles and Directions

0.0 From the trailhead, head up the steps and carefully cross the road and the bridge.

0.1 Take the steps that head down (east) and back into forest. At the bottom of the steps, head left (north) and immediately come to a T junction at the river. Go right (east) here onto the Triple Falls Trail, following the Little River upstream.

0.5 The trail begins to climb steeply before reaching the Triple Falls overlook. Continue southwest past the overlook and you will see some steps that head left (south-southeast) toward Triple Falls.

0.6 Arrive in the middle section of Triple Falls (N35 11.971/W82 37.036). Backtrack to the main trail and continue hiking southwest until you come to a T junction. Go left (south-southwest) at the T junction and continue uphill. (*Option:* Return to the trailhead for a 1.2-mile hike of 40 minutes.)

0.7 Come to a fork in the trail. Go left (south-southeast) onto the High Falls Trail and soon pass the brink of Triple Falls as you follow the lazy river upstream.

1.0 A second fork awaits. Go right (southwest) here and head uphill, away from the river.

1.2 Arrive at an overlook for High Falls. Continue past the overlook and you will see a trail to your left with some stone steps. This trail leads south to the base of High Falls.

1.3 Arrive at the base of High Falls (N35 11.581/W82 36.871). To get to Grassy Creek Falls, backtrack to the main trail and continue hiking uphill (southwest). (*Option:* Return to the trailhead for a 2.6-mile hike of 1 hour, 20 minutes.)

1.4 Once atop the hill, come to a T junction. Go left here and continue hiking southwest.

1.5 Come to a fork; go left (southeast) onto the Covered Bridge Trail.

1.6 Arrive at a T junction at Buck Forest Road. Go left (northeast) onto Buck Forest Road; immediately cross the covered bridge before following Buck Forest Road downhill.

2.1 Cross the small bridge heading north and immediately come to a fork. Go left (west) onto the Lake Imaging Trail. Follow this trail, bypassing the first dirt side trail on your left.

2.2 A wide dirt trail on your left heads straight back (south) into the woods. This is the Grassy Creek Falls Trail. Follow this trail all the way to the creek, bypassing any side trails.

2.3 The trail leads to the brink of the falls. Head downstream (southwest); several small side trails lead steeply down to the creek to view the falls.

2.4 Arrive at the base of Grassy Creek Falls (N35 11.713/W82 36.520). Return the way you came.

4.8 Arrive back at the trailhead.

Option: You can also park at the High Falls access area, which is located off Staton Road about 1.0 mile south of the Hooker Falls parking area. From the High Falls access area, hike less than 0.5 mile on Buck Forest Road, which takes you directly to the covered bridge above High Falls.

77 Merry Falls

Lush! The rocky ledges that make up Merry Falls are lush with moss and alive with character. Although you can't linger here, it's a lovely place to stop and visit, however brief it may be.

See map on page 201.
Height: 25 feet
Beauty rating: Excellent
Distance: Roadside
Difficulty: Easy

Blaze color: No blazes
County: Transylvania
Land status: Private property
Maps: *DeLorme: North Carolina Atlas & Gazetteer:* Page 53 D6

Finding the trailhead: From the junction of US 276 south and US 64 in Brevard, drive south on US 276 for 10.8 miles. Turn left onto Cascade Lake Road (SR 1536) at the sign for DuPont State Forest and travel for 4.4 miles to view Merry Falls on your left.

From the junction of US 276 north and US 64 in Brevard, drive east on US 64 for 3.6 miles. Turn right onto Crab Creek Road (SR 1127) at the sign for DuPont State Forest and travel for 2.3 miles to a right turn onto Cascade Lake Road (SR 1536). Follow Cascade Lake Road for 1.2 miles to a fork where the formerly paved road heads off to the left and becomes gravel (the paved road bends right and becomes Hart Road). Go left, onto the now gravel Cascade Lake Road and travel for 3.1 miles to view Merry Falls on your right.

GPS: N35 12.040 / W82 38.618

The Hike

Merry Falls is viewed from the roadside. The waterfall is located on private property, so don't leave the road or you will be trespassing.

If you're heading to the falls from the north, you get to appreciate the beautiful Little River Valley as you pass through. Since you can't spend the day enjoying Merry Falls, I recommend that you make a quick stop here and then visit nearby Cascade Lake Dam. Continue on from there and spend the rest of the day enjoying the many wonderful waterfalls to be found within DuPont State Forest.

Merry Falls is located on private property, so please don't linger.

78 Cascade Lake Dam

Thunderous! The passive Cascade Lake crashes over the dam with massive power and might. This unexpected gift is like thunder sent from above, causing all who pass to stop in awe.

See map on page 201.
Height: 100 feet
Beauty rating: Very good
Distance: Roadside or 0.1 mile out and back
Difficulty: Easy
Trail surface: Steep gravel
Approximate hiking time: 10 minutes
Blaze color: No blazes
County: Transylvania
Land status: National forest

Trail contacts: Pisgah National Forest, Pisgah Ranger District; (828) 877-3265; www.fs.fed.us
FYI: For info on camping and use of the lake, contact Cascade Lake Recreation Area; (828) 877-4475; www.cascadelakerecreation area.com; campground reservations: (828) 877-6625
Maps: DeLorme: North Carolina Atlas & Gazetteer: Page 53 D6

Finding the trailhead: From the junction of US 276 south and US 64 in Brevard, drive south on US 276 for 10.8 miles. Turn left onto Cascade Lake Road (SR 1536) at the sign for DuPont State Forest and travel for 6.8 miles to a small pull-off on the left.

From the junction of US 64 and US 276 north in Brevard, drive east on US 64 for 3.6 miles. Turn right onto Crab Creek Road (SR 1127) at the sign for DuPont State Forest and travel for 2.3 miles to a right turn onto Cascade Lake Road (SR 1536). Follow Cascade Lake Road for 1.2 miles to a fork where the paved Cascade Lake Road heads off to the left and becomes gravel (the paved road bends to the right and becomes Hart Road). Go left onto the now gravel Cascade Lake Road and travel for 0.7 mile to a small pull-off on the right.

GPS: N35 13.162 / W82 38.383

The Hike

Although the falls are visible from the road, a short, steep scramble south will give you an even better view of Cascade Lake Dam.

The Little River flows north through DuPont State Forest to form Cascade Lake. It then booms powerfully over the dam before continuing through the peaceful Little River Valley on its way to the French Broad River.

If you want to enjoy the lake to the fullest, Cascade Lake Campground offers boating, fishing, camping, and hiking and has its own private beach along the lake's edge. Although it's privately owned, the campground is currently run by the USDA Forest Service.

The Little River thunders over the Cascade Lake Dam.

Miles and Directions

0.0 From the pull-off, scramble south down the bank.

0.05 Arrive alongside Cascade Lake Dam (N35 13.157 / W82 38.378). Return the way you came.

0.1 Arrive back at the trailhead.

79 Wintergreen Falls in DuPont State Forest

Personality! Wintergreen Falls seems happy to see you as it smiles brightly within the forest. Compared to other waterfalls located within DuPont State Forest, this one is far less traveled. You could get lucky and have this one to yourself.

Height: 18 feet
Beauty rating: Excellent
Distance: 2.8 miles out and back
Difficulty: Moderate
Trail surface: Wide, sandy and gravel trail
Approximate hiking time: 1 hour, 20 minutes
Other trail users: Mountain bikers, equestrians

Blaze color: No blazes
County: Transylvania
Land status: State forest
Trail contact: DuPont State Forest; (828) 877-6527; www.dupontforest.com
Maps: DeLorme: North Carolina Atlas & Gazetteer: Page 53 D7

Finding the trailhead: From the junction of US 276 south and US 64 in Brevard, drive south on US 276 for 10.8 miles. Turn left onto Cascade Lake Road and travel for 2.4 miles to a right turn onto Staton Road. Continue on Staton Road for 4.6 miles before turning right onto Sky Valley Road (SR 1260). Travel for 1.5 miles to a large parking area on your right at the sign for Guion Farm Access Area.

From the junction of US 64 and US 276 north in Brevard, drive east on US 64 for 3.6 miles. Turn right onto Crab Creek Road (SR 1127) at the sign for DuPont State Forest and travel for 4.2 miles to a right turn onto DuPont Road. Continue on DuPont Road for 0.7 mile before turning left onto Sky Valley Road. Travel for 1.5 miles to a large parking area on your right at the sign for Guion Farm Access Area.

The trailhead is located at the southwest corner of the parking area. GPS: N35 12.679/W82 35.295

The Hike

While you may end up sharing this trail with some horseback riders or mountain bikers, it is unlikely that you'll see much, if any, foot traffic on your way to Wintergreen Falls. The trail begins by crossing the grassy field before leading back into the forest, where you stay for the remainder of the hike.

The trail is well marked as you navigate past three forks. The final leg leads past some horse hitching posts before reaching the creek.

Wintergreen Falls is one of six waterfalls located within DuPont State Forest. I highly recommend that you visit every one of them. Although Wintergreen is smaller than the others, it easily rivals them in beauty.

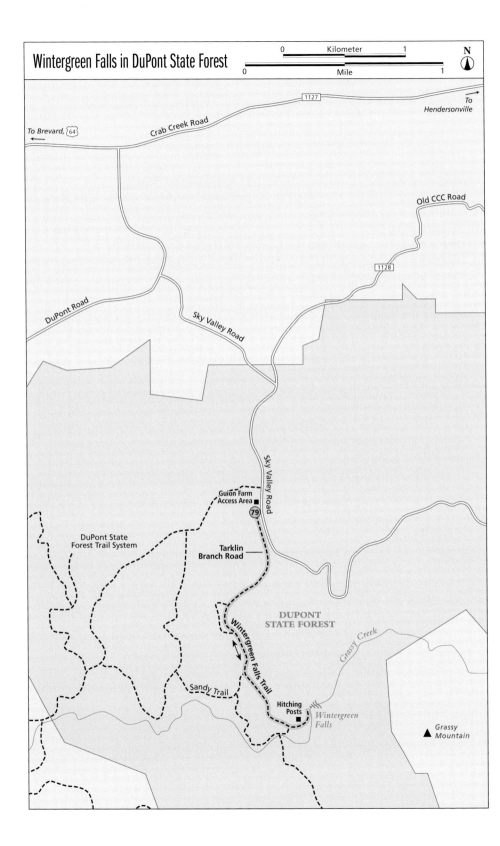

Wintergreen Falls in DuPont State Forest

0   Kilometer   1

0   Mile   1

N

To Hendersonville

1127

Crab Creek Road

To Brevard, 64

Old CCC Road

1128

DuPont Road

Sky Valley Road

Sky Valley Road

Guion Farm Access Area

79

DuPont State Forest Trail System

Tarklin Branch Road

DUPONT STATE FOREST

Grassy Creek

Wintergreen Falls Trail

Sandy Trail

Hitching Posts

Wintergreen Falls

Grassy Mountain

The author enjoys the peaceful setting of Wintergreen Falls.

Miles and Directions

0.0 From the trailhead, follow the narrow dirt trail southeast across a grassy field, keeping the tree line to your right (west). After crossing the field, you soon enter into the forest.

0.5 Come to a fork with a wide, clear path on your left (southwest) blocked by two boulders. Go left here, following this trail downhill.

0.7 The trail unites with the Tarklin Branch Road. Go left (southeast) and continue downhill.

0.9 Arrive at another fork. Go left (southeast) here onto the Wintergreen Falls Trail.

1.2 Come to a third fork, with the Sandy Trail heading right (south) and down. Bear left (east), still following the Wintergreen Falls Trail.

1.3 Pass the hitching posts on your left; continue straight ahead (northeast) to the creek's edge. Go left (north) and follow the creek upstream.

1.4 Arrive at the base of Wintergreen Falls (N35 1.862 / W82 35.021). Return the way you came.

2.8 Arrive back at the trailhead.

80 Falls on Long Branch, Hendersonville Reservoir Dam, and Falls on Fletcher Creek

Peaceful! Whether hiking or biking, these beauties offer a wonderful place to sit and bask in the splendor of the forest all around you. I personally prefer the latter two waterfalls, but even the Falls on Long Branch offer a nice reprieve as you make the steady climb back to the trailhead.

Height: Falls on Long Branch, 25 feet; Hendersonville Reservoir Dam, 25 feet; Falls on Fletcher Creek, 4 feet
Beauty rating: Good for all
Distance: 3.2 miles out and back (Falls on Long Branch, 2.0 miles; Hendersonville Reservoir Dam, 3.0 miles)
Difficulty: Easy to moderate
Trail surface: Wide gravel forest road

Approximate hiking time: 1 hour, 30 minutes
Other trail users: Mountain bikers, equestrians
Blaze color: No blazes
County: Henderson
Land status: National forest
Trail contact: Pisgah National Forest, Pisgah Ranger District; (828) 877-3265; www.fs.fed.us
Maps: *DeLorme: North Carolina Atlas & Gazetteer:* Page 53 A6

Finding the trailhead: From the southern junction of NC 191 and NC 280 in Mills River, drive north on SR 191/280 for 0.8 mile. Turn left onto North Mills River Road at the sign for NORTH MILLS RIVER RECREATION AREA and travel for 4.9 miles to Wash Creek Road (FR 5000). Turn right onto Wash Creek Road and travel for 2.0 miles to a left turn onto Hendersonville Reservoir Road (FR 142), which crosses a small cement bridge. Continue on Hendersonville Reservoir Road for 0.5 mile to where it ends.

From the northern junction of NC 191 and NC 280 in Mills River, drive south on SR 191/280 for 0.2 mile. Turn right onto North Mills River Road at the sign for NORTH MILLS RIVER RECREATION AREA and follow the directions above.

GPS: N35 25.217 / W82 39.413

The Hike

From the parking area you will see a trail information signpost and two gated forest roads to the right of it. The road on the right, Fletcher Creek Road (FR 5097), goes uphill. The one on the left, Hendersonville Reservoir Road (FR 142), goes downhill. Hike west down FR 142—the gated road on the left, which you will follow the entire way. At the 1.0-mile mark, you will pass the Falls on Long Branch. After a short visit here, continue hiking for another 0.5 mile to where the trail dead-ends at the Hendersonville Reservoir Dam. A short jaunt from here takes you to Falls on Fletcher Creek. If water levels are low, you will be treated with a lovely sandy beach

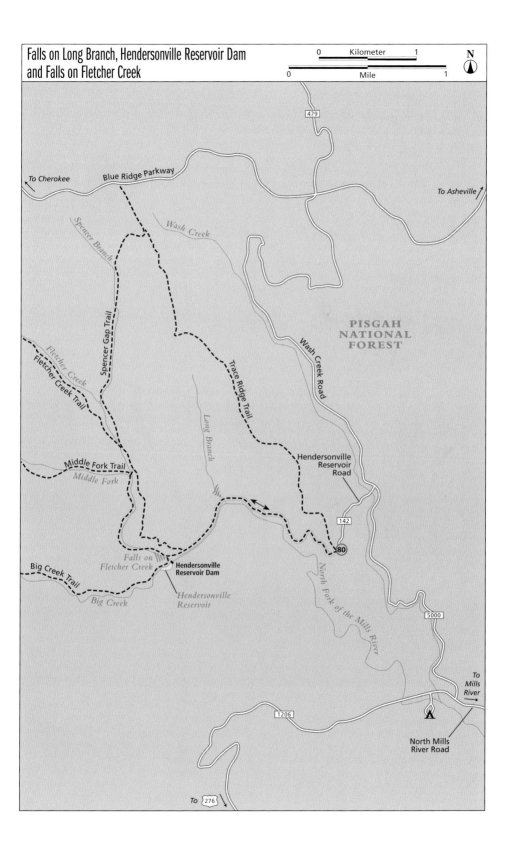

Falls on Long Branch, Hendersonville Reservoir Dam and Falls on Fletcher Creek

0 — Kilometer — 1
0 — Mile — 1

N

479

To Cherokee

Blue Ridge Parkway

To Asheville

Spencer Branch

Wash Creek

Spencer Gap Trail

Trace Ridge Trail

Wash Creek Road

PISGAH
NATIONAL
FOREST

Fletcher Creek

Fletcher Creek Trail

Long Branch

Middle Fork Trail

Middle Fork

Hendersonville
Reservoir
Road

142

Big Creek Trail

Falls on
Fletcher Creek

Hendersonville
Reservoir Dam

80

Big Creek

Hendersonville
Reservoir

North Fork of the Mills River

5000

1206

To
Mills
River

North Mills
River Road

To 276

at the base of the falls. The last 0.5 mile of this hike is far more enjoyable than the rest. It has an abundance of wildflowers, and you get to hike right alongside the river for most of the way.

More popular for mountain biking, Trace Ridge, Spencer Branch, Fletcher Creek, and Middle Fork Trails are all accessible from this trailhead. I found these three beauties while taking a day off from hiking to play on my mountain bike.

The reservoir is at the headwaters of the North Fork of the Mills River and provides drinking water for thousands of residents in Buncombe and Henderson Counties. The Big Creek Trail can also be accessed near the dam and is well worth exploring on foot, as it follows Big Creek for miles.

Hendersonville Reservoir Dam can be reached on foot, horseback, or mountain bike.

A log footbridge crosses over the top of Falls on Fletcher Creek.

Miles and Directions

0.0 From the information signpost, hike west down the gated forest road on the left (FR 142).

1.0 Arrive at Falls on Long Branch (N35 25.502 / W82 40.186). Continue hiking south-southwest and downhill. (*Option:* Return to the trailhead for a 2.0-mile hike of about an hour.)

1.5 Arrive at the Hendersonville Reservoir Dam (N35 25.183 / W82 40.528). Turn right (north-northwest) and follow the water's edge.

1.6 Arrive at Falls on Fletcher Creek (N35 25.188 / W82 40.540). Return the way you came.

3.2 Arrive back at the trailhead.

81 Lake Powhatan Dam

Timid! Hidden behind the lake and amid miles of mountain bike trails, Lake Powhatan Dam quietly flows in its own space and time, awaiting the occasional passerby to give a nod in its direction.

Height: 20 feet
Beauty rating: Good
Distance: 0.6 mile out and back
Difficulty: Easy
Trail surface: Wide gravel road; narrow dirt path
Approximate hiking time: 20 minutes
Other trail users: Mountain bikers
Blaze color: No blazes
County: Buncombe

Land status: National forest
Trail contact: Pisgah National Forest, Pisgah Ranger District; (828) 877-3265; www.fs.fed.us Lake Powhatan Campground; (828) 670-5627; www.cradleofforestry.org
FYI: A fee is charged to park inside the Lake Powhatan Recreation Area
Maps: *DeLorme: North Carolina Atlas & Gazetteer:* Page 53 A6

Finding the trailhead: From the junction of NC 191 and NC 112 in Asheville, drive south on NC 191 for 1.4 miles. Turn right onto Bent Creek Ranch Road (SR 3480) at the sign for LAKE POWHATAN RECREATIONAL AREA and travel for 0.2 mile to where the road bends left onto Wesley Branch Road (SR 3484). Follow Wesley Branch Road for 2.3 miles to a fork. Go left at the fork and travel another 0.2 mile to the gatehouse at the entrance to Lake Powhatan Campground. Pay the parking fee, and then drive straight ahead and down the hill for 0.2 mile before turning left onto the gravel FR 481F at the sign pointing to the fishing area. Continue for 0.1 mile to a small parking area on the right.

From the junction of SR 191 and the Blue Ridge Parkway in Asheville, drive north on SR 191 for 0.6 mile. Turn left onto Bent Creek Ranch Road (SR 3480) at the sign for LAKE POWHATAN RECREATIONAL AREA and follow the directions above.

GPS: N35 29.055 / W82 37.620

The Hike

This short but enjoyable hike takes you alongside the serene setting of Lake Powhatan. The falls are located just downstream of the fishing pier. If you enjoy fishing, bring a pole—but make sure you have a state fishing license before casting your line.

The Powhatan flourished in the late sixteenth century and were also known as the Virginia Algonquians. They were led by Chief Powhatan and controlled most of what is now eastern Virginia. It is said that the chief's hometown was near a waterfall, and so in the Algonquin language, *powhatan* came to mean "waterfall." Chief Powhatan is probably best known, however, for his daughter Pocahontas.

If you enjoy mountain biking, the Bent Creek Trail system can be accessed from the Lake Powhatan Campground and offers some of the best mountain biking in the area.

Lake Powhatan Dam

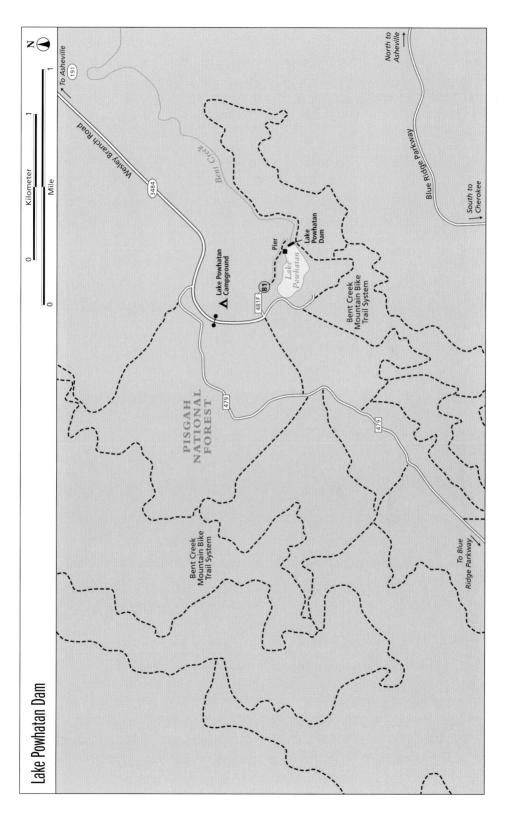

Lake Powhatan Dam is surrounded by the Bent Creek Experimental Forest—a mountain biker's mecca.

Miles and Directions

0.0 From the parking area, hike southeast on the gravel road toward the fishing pier.

0.2 From the fishing pier, go left (east) and you will see a few side trails on your right (south) that lead to the creek. Take any of them to reach the creek just downstream from the dam.

0.3 Arrive at Lake Powhatan Dam (N35 28.975 / W82 37.409). Return the way you came.

0.6 Arrive back at the trailhead.

82 Turley Falls

Primitive! Turley Falls waits in the distance, seeming to stand still in time. Peacefully flowing within the rugged wilderness, the waterfall seems untouched by the busy streets surrounding it.

See overview map on page iv.
Height: 100+ feet
Beauty rating: Good
Distance: Roadside
Difficulty: Easy
Blaze color: No blazes

County: Henderson
Land status: Private property
Trail contact: None
Maps: *DeLorme: North Carolina Atlas & Gazetteer:* Page 53 B7–C7

Finding the trailhead: From the junction of US 64 and US 25 (Main Street) in downtown Hendersonville, drive west on US 64 through town, staying on US 64 for a total of 3.6 miles. Turn left onto Turley Falls Road (SR 1215) and travel for 0.2 mile to a right turn onto Brightwater Drive. Continue on Brightwater Drive for 0.4 mile to where you can see Turley Falls in the distance on your left.

From the junction of US 64 and US 276 north in Brevard, drive east on US 64 for 13.5 miles. Turn right onto Turley Falls Road (SR 1215) and follow the directions above.

Be sure to stay on the road, or you'll be trespassing on private property. GPS: N35 19.563/W82 31.569

The Hike

Turley Falls is viewed from the roadside. The falls sit far off in the distance, so be sure to bring binoculars or a good zoom lens to appreciate its beauty.

Brightwater Branch flows down the north face of Jump Off Mountain to form Turley Falls, once known as Brightwater Falls. According to legend, more than 300 years ago an Indian maiden received word that her young chief had been killed in battle. She was so heartbroken by the news that she climbed onto a ledge at the summit of the mountain and jumped off. Some say that on moonlit nights, her ghost can still be seen atop the mountain.

It's worth waking up early to see these mountain views at sunrise.

83 Pearson's Falls

Charming! Pearson's Falls calms like the soothing sound of rain on the roof.

Height: 50 feet
Beauty rating: Very good
Distance: 0.5 mile out and back
Difficulty: Easy
Trail surface: Mulch path
Approximate hiking time: 20 minutes
Blaze color: No blazes
County: Polk

Land status: Private property, managed by Tryon Garden Club
Trail contact: Tryon Garden Club; (828) 749-3031; www.pearsonsfalls.com
FYI: A nominal fee is charged per person to visit the falls.
Maps: *DeLorme: North Carolina Atlas & Gazetteer:* Page 54 E1

Finding the trailhead: From I-26 take exit 59 (Saluda) onto SR 1142 (Ozone Drive). Drive south on SR 1142 for 1.2 miles to where it dead-ends at US 176. Turn left onto US 176 and travel for 2.5 miles to a right turn onto Pearson Falls Road. Continue for 0.8 mile and turn left into the driveway at the sign for PEARSON'S FALLS. After paying the fee, follow the signs to the parking area.

From the junction of US 176 and SR 1121 (Harmon Field Road) in Tryon, drive west on US 176 for 3.8 miles. Turn left onto Pearson Falls Road and follow the directions above.

GPS: N35 13.054 / W82 19.964

The Hike

This short, easily followed trail passes through a picnic area before heading uphill and upstream to the base of Pearson's Falls. The area is open year-round with varying hours of operation and is closed on Mondays except for holidays.

Pearson's Falls was named for Captain Charles William Pearson, an engineer who discovered the falls and surrounding glen while scouting passage for the Southern Railroad. Captain Pearson purchased the land for his family after the Civil War. In 1931 his son proposed to sell it to a lumber company, but thankfully the Tryon Garden Club stepped in and purchased the land. They have been nurturing it ever since.

With great plant diversity, including more than 200 types of ferns, Pearson's Falls glen is a botanist's dream.

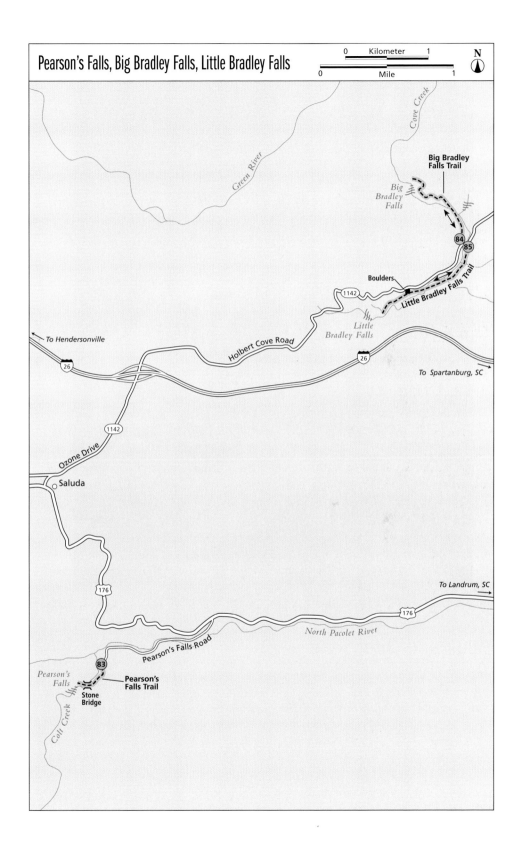

Pearson's Falls, Big Bradley Falls, Little Bradley Falls

Kilometer 0 — 1
Mile 0 — 1

N

Cove Creek

Big Bradley Falls Trail

Big Bradley Falls

84
85

Green River

Boulders

1142

Little Bradley Falls Trail

Little Bradley Falls

To Hendersonville

Holbert Cove Road

26

26

To Spartanburg, SC

1142

Ozone Drive

Saluda

176

To Landrum, SC

176

North Pacolet River

Pearson's Falls Road

83

Pearson's Falls

Pearson's Falls Trail

Stone Bridge

Colt Creek

The glen at Pearson's Falls is straight out of a fairy tale—picture perfect.

Miles and Directions

0.0 From the parking area, follow the sign pointing to the trailhead. Hike through the picnic area and upstream.

0.2 Cross the stone bridge and continue hiking upstream (west).

0.25 Arrive at the base of Pearson's Falls (N35 12.926 / W82 20.145). Return the way you came.

0.5 Arrive back at the trailhead.

84 Big Bradley Falls

Full-bodied! The cliffside overlook gives you a perfect vantage point to view each pool and dip that this full-bodied fall passes on its plunge to the base.

See map on page 221.
Height: 65 feet
Beauty rating: Good
Distance: 1.8 miles out and back
Difficulty: Easy to moderate
Trail surface: Wide, rooty, dirt path
Approximate hiking time: 45 minutes

Blaze color: Blue
County: Polk
Land status: National forest
Trail contact: Pisgah National Forest, Pisgah Ranger District; (828) 877-3265; www.fs.fed.us
Maps: *DeLorme: North Carolina Atlas & Gazetteer:* Page 54 D1

Finding the trailhead: From I-26 take exit 59 (Saluda) onto SR 1142 (Holbert Cove Road). Drive north on SR 1142 for 3.1 miles to a large pull-off on the left in front of an old gated road. The trailhead is located in the middle of the pull-off. GPS: N35 15.728 / W82 17.095

The Hike

The trail heads north from the trailhead and around the gate. Soon cross a large open field that was once an orchard owned by the Bradley family. After crossing the field, the trail heads into the cover of the forest, where it stays for the remainder of the hike.

As you make your way toward the falls, you will come to a creek crossing. Before crossing the creek, take a peek across to be gifted with a wonderful small waterfall on the other side. As you continue the hike, you will come across several small side trails, one of which leads to the base of the falls. Bypass these, and continue to the cliff-side overlook, which affords good views of not only the falls but also the surrounding mountains. Be sure to use extreme caution while enjoying the view. A fall from here could prove to be deadly.

In 2008 a forestry worker fell to his death while fighting a brush fire near the brink of Big Bradley Falls. Sadly enough, this was not the first life to be lost in the Cove Creek area. Prudence pays.

Miles and Directions

0.0 From the trailhead, hike straight across the open field (north-northeast). Bypass the trail shooting off to the left about halfway across the field, and continue straight ahead (north-northeast) back into the woods.

0.2 Come to a T junction. Go right (north) and follow the wide, blue-blazed path down to the creek.

0.25 Just before reaching the creek, look across it to view a lovely small waterfall on the opposite (east) side (N35 15.936/W82 17.130).

0.3 Cross the creek and head left (north-northwest).

0.6 Bypass the obvious side trail that heads off to the left (southwest) where the main trail makes a hard bend to the right (northeast); continue hiking northeast. Bypass the next two side trails as well. The main trail bends left (north) and takes you around a gap.

0.8 After hiking around the gap, take the second wide and obvious side trail shooting down to the left (south-southwest). Follow this trail steeply down to the overlook.

0.9 Arrive at the overlook for Big Bradley Falls (N35 16.151/W82 17.491). Return the way you came.

1.8 Arrive back at the trailhead.

85 Little Bradley Falls

Rebirth! With its perfect, clean-cut ledges to sit upon and a magnificently tiered flow, Little Bradley Falls brings rebirth to the creative soul. Something about the serenity of its catch pool or the strength of its sound draws you to sit and stay awhile.

See map on page 221.
Height: 35 feet
Beauty rating: Excellent
Distance: 1.8 miles out and back
Difficulty: Easy to moderate
Trail surface: Hard-packed dirt
Approximate hiking time: 1 hour, 45 minutes

Blaze color: Red
County: Polk
Land status: National forest
Trail contact: Pisgah National Forest, Pisgah Ranger District; (828) 877-3265; www.fs.fed.us
Maps: *DeLorme: North Carolina Atlas & Gazetteer:* Page 54 D1

Finding the trailhead: From I-26 take exit 59 (Saluda) onto SR 1142 (Holbert Cove Road). Drive north on SR 1142 for 3.6 miles to a small pull-off on your right. GPS: N35 15.722 / W82 17.052

The Hike

From the parking area, an obvious trail heads southwest into the woods and follows the creek upstream. Do not take this trail. Instead look to your left for a narrow, red-blazed trail that heads up and southeast. This is your trail. Climb up the hill; the trail immediately bends right (south) as it continues to rise and takes you high above the creek.

This enjoyable hike keeps you alongside the creek for most of the way. You also get to pass an old homestead site along the way. These factors, combined with the amazing beauty of Little Bradley Falls, add to its allure. I recommend making a quick visit to Big Bradley Falls and then coming to Little Bradley to spend the rest of the day picnicking or even taking a quick dip in the warmer months.

Aside from locals, this waterfall doesn't see much traffic, so you may have this serene yet mighty waterfall to yourself.

Both Little and Big Bradley Falls were named for an early settler who had a home and orchard in the area. As you make the hike to Big Bradley, you pass right through the remains of the old orchard.

Miles and Directions

0.0 From the trailhead, the trail heads south and continues to rise high above the creek.
0.1 Cross a small tributary and head right (west).
0.3 Come to a fork. Go right (west) as the trail leads you down to the creek. Cross the creek and again head right (west), following it downstream.

Little Bradley Falls has it all. Pack a lunch and spend the day basking at this beauty.

0.5 Cross the creek again and go left (southwest); the trail soon rises.

0.6 Cross the small boulder field. The path narrows as it continues to follow the creek west and upstream from high above.

0.7 Come to a fork with an old homestead in between the two legs of the fork. Go right at the fork and continue hiking west-southwest past the homestead.

0.9 Cross a small tributary and continue hiking west to the base of Little Bradley Falls (N35 15.283 / W82 17.717). Return the way you came.

1.8 Arrive back at the trailhead.

86 Shunkawauken Falls

Impressive! Flowing from the summit to the foot of White Oak Mountain, the massive height of Shunkawauken Falls is truly impressive, especially for a roadside waterfall.

See overview map on page iv.
Height: 150 feet
Beauty rating: Very good
Distance: Roadside
Difficulty: Easy
Blaze color: No blazes

County: Polk
Land status: National forest
Trail contact: Pisgah National Forest, Pisgah Ranger District; (828) 877-3265; www.fs.fed.us
Maps: DeLorme: North Carolina Atlas & Gazetteer: Page 54 D2

Finding the trailhead: From the junction of NC 108 and NC 9 in Mill Spring, drive west on NC 108 for 1.3 miles. Turn right onto Houston Road (SR 1137) and travel for 2.2 miles to a right turn onto White Oak Mountain Road (SR 1136). Continue for 2.0 miles to view the falls on your right. There is a pull-off a short distance before the falls on your left. I suggest driving past the falls and turning around prior to parking.

From the junction of NC 108 and I-26 near Tryon, drive east on NC 108 for 0.4 mile. Turn left onto Houston Road (SR 1137) and follow the directions above.

GPS: N35 16.325 / W82 12.884

The Hike

Shunkawauken Falls is viewed from the roadside, so you won't want to linger here.

The falls were known as Horse Creek Falls until 1891, when they were renamed by Frank Stearns in honor of the Native American Chief Shunkawauken. Stearns was a rich quarryman who saw great potential for commercial development in this area. He immediately purchased 3,000 acres, including all of White Oak Mountain, and is responsible for building the very road that you drove in on.

You don't even have to get out of the car to view Shunkawauken Falls.

87 Hickory Nut Falls

Empowering! Located inside Chimney Rock State Park, this beauty is well worth the visit, even if you have to go out of your way to get here. Chimney Rock Park is loaded with so many amazing natural features that I recommend spending an entire day here. Two different trails give you the best views of the falls.

Height: 404 feet
Beauty rating: Excellent
Distance: 2.2 miles
Difficulty: Moderate for Hickory Nut Falls Trail; moderate to strenuous for Skyline Trail
Trail surface: Wide dirt and gravel trail; many stair steps
Approximate hiking time: 2 hours
Blaze color: No blazes
County: Rutherford
Land status: State park

Trail contact: Chimney Rock State Park; (828) 625-9611 or (800) 277-9611; www.chimney rockpark.com
FYI: Entrance fee is charged per person; detailed trail maps available at the gatehouse; hours of operation vary through the year—call the park for info; trails are subject to closure during winter weather.
Maps: *DeLorme: North Carolina Atlas & Gazetteer:* Page 54 B2

Finding the trailhead: From the junction of US 74A and the easternmost NC 9 in Lake Lure, drive west on US 74A for 4.6 miles. Turn left into the entrance of Chimney Rock Park and follow the park road uphill. Pay the fee and continue to the parking area.

From the merger of US 74A and US 64 in Bat Cave, drive east on US 74A/64 for 2.4 miles. Turn right into the entrance of Chimney Rock Park and follow directions above.

GPS: N35 25.980 / W82 14.983

The Hikes

The story of Chimney Rock Park dates back to the late 1800s, when a young physician named Lucius B. Morse was diagnosed with tuberculosis. He was living in St. Louis at the time, and doctors there advised him to seek out a "healthier" climate. Heeding their advice, Morse made his way east, where he happened upon the monolith of Chimney Rock and was instantly entranced. In 1902, with the help of his brothers, Lucius purchased the first parcel of sixty-four acres for $5,000. Over time, piece by piece, the sixty-four acres grew to a thousand, as did the vision that came to be Chimney Rock Park. The park was owned and operated by the Morse family until 2007, when the State of North Carolina purchased it for $24 million.

Hike one trail, the other, or both. You'll get different views of the falls from each; Skyline Trail provides more scenery on the way up, but it's a bit more strenuous.

At 404 feet, the mammoth Hickory Nut Falls is quite a sight.

Hickory Nut Falls Trail

The Hickory Nut Falls Trail takes you to the base of the falls. From the lower parking area, a wooden boardwalk follows the road a short distance to the trailhead. From the upper parking area, a steep set of stairs leads down to a T junction less than 0.1 mile from the lower trailhead. Head left at the T junction to get to the base of the falls. Along the way, bypass the 4 Seasons Trail on the right and continue straight ahead as you make a slow and steady ascent to the base of Hickory Nut Falls.

Hickory Nut Falls

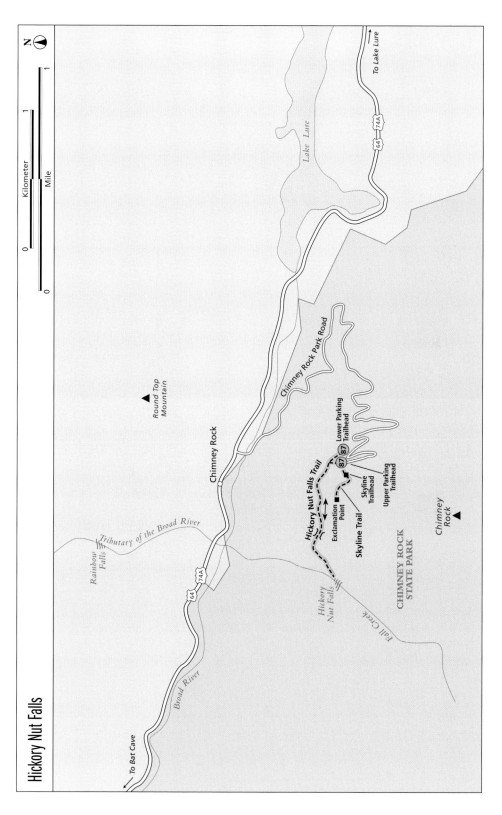

"Devil's Head" watches over the valley.

Miles and Directions

0.0 From the upper parking area, head northeast down the many steps that lead to a T junction at the Hickory Nut Falls Trail. (**Option:** Park in the Lower Parking Area and hike north-northwest toward the falls from the Lower trailhead.)

0.1 Arrive at the T junction. Go left here and hike northwest on the wide dirt trail. (If hiking from the Lower trailhead, bypass the steps to the left and continue hiking northwest on the wide dirt trail.)

0.2 Bypass the 4 Seasons Trail on your right (northwest) and continue to follow the wide, road-like trail as it slowly makes its way uphill.

0.4 Cross a wooden footbridge; continue hiking southwest.

0.75 Arrive at the base of Hickory Nut Falls (N35 25.999 / W82 15.535). Return the way you came.

1.5 Arrive back at the trailhead.

Skyline Trail

The Skyline Trail leads from the base of the Chimney Rock, up many stone steps, around some switchbacks, and then up to Exclamation Point. This trail offers splendid

TB FACTS

Tuberculosis (TB) is an infectious disease caused by bacteria that primarily affects the lungs. It was first discovered in 1882 by a German doctor named Robert Koch, who won a Nobel Prize for his discovery. TB can be spread from one person to the next via airborne transmission, meaning it is carried through the air in small droplets when an infected person coughs, spits, or sneezes.

Anyone can get TB, but some people, such as health-care workers, are more likely to be exposed to the infection. The symptoms can range from general weakness to shortness of breath. While TB is commonly treated with antibiotics, other treatments may also be needed. If left untreated, TB can be deadly.

views of Hickory Nut Falls and Lake Lure from high above. When water levels are low, however, the falls themselves are best viewed from the base.

Enjoy the sights along the way as the trail leads you past the Opera Box and Devil's Head—two natural features also worth seeing.

Miles and Directions

0.0 From the steps near the base of the "Chimney Rock" (near the "Sky Lounge") hike northeast up the stone steps.

0.1 Arrive at a T junction. Go left (south) as you continue to follow the switchbacks and steps.

0.35 Arrive at Exclamation Point to view Hickory Nut Falls from high above. Return the way you came.

0.7 Arrive back at the Skyline Trail trailhead.

88 Walker Falls

Quenching! As you travel the dry, bumpy forest road, you are greeted by this wonderful mass of water known as Walker Falls. While Walker is beautiful, it's still a roadside waterfall that's well off the beaten path.

Height: 70 feet	**Land status:** National forest
Beauty rating: Very good	**Trail contact:** Pisgah National Forest, Appalachian Ranger District; (828) 682-6146;
Distance: Roadside	www.fs.fed.us
Difficulty: Easy	**Maps:** *DeLorme: North Carolina Atlas & Gazetteer:* Page 32 D1-E1
Blaze color: No blazes	
County: Buncombe	

Finding the trailhead: From the junction of the Blue Ridge Parkway (BRP) and NC 128 (NC 128 is unmarked and leads to Mount Mitchell State Park), drive south on the BRP for 12.0 miles. Turn right into the Craggy Gardens Picnic Ground and go up the hill. After approximately 0.35 mile, make a sharp turn to the left and head downhill on the unmarked gravel road, which is FR 63. Follow FR 63, ignoring the road off to the left, which crosses the creek at 3.8 miles, and continue straight ahead. After 4.9 miles, FR 63 becomes paved. Continue on the paved road for another 1.5 miles until you come to a stop sign at Dillingham Road. (For the return trip, note that the paved part of FR 63 is named Stoney Fork Road.) Turn right onto Dillingham Road and travel for approximately 1.3 miles. At this point, Dillingham Road crosses a bridge and becomes dirt FR 74. Continue on FR 74 for 4.1 miles to view Walker Falls on your left, just after you pass the stone-faced cliffs on your left.

From the junction of the BRP and US 70 in Asheville, drive north on the BRP for 14.9 miles. Turn left into the Craggy Gardens Picnic Ground and follow the directions above.

Craggy Gardens is located between Mileposts 367 and 368 on the Blue Ridge Parkway. GPS: N35 45.338/W82 21.246

The Hike

Located well off the beaten path, Walker Falls is viewed from the roadside. While you're out here, I recommend taking the time to visit Douglas Falls as well.

On your way to Walker Falls, be sure to take note of the Great Craggy Mountains that surround you. The high slopes of the "Craggies" are known for their heath balds, which are visible from the valley floor as you head down Dillingham Road.

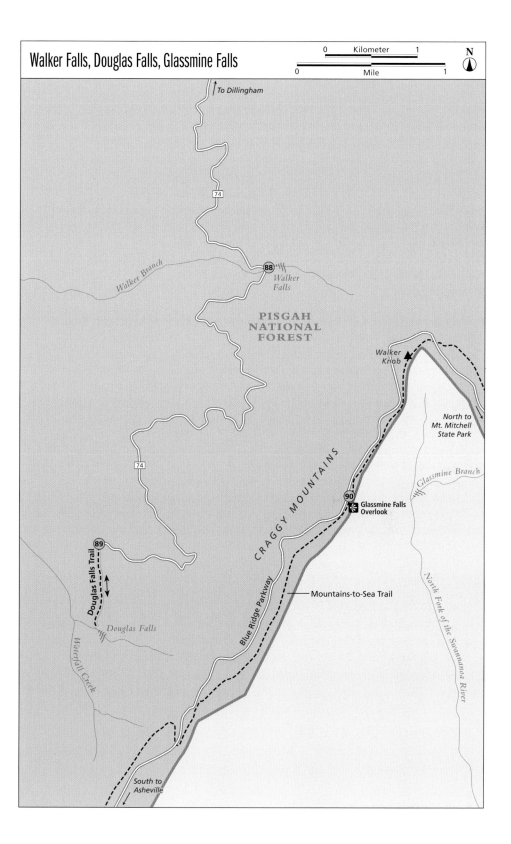

Walker Falls, Douglas Falls, Glassmine Falls

0 Kilometer 1
0 Mile 1

N

To Dillingham

74

Walker Branch

88 Walker Falls

PISGAH NATIONAL FOREST

Walker Knob

North to Mt. Mitchell State Park

Glassmine Branch

74

CRAGGY MOUNTAINS

90 Glassmine Falls Overlook

89 Douglas Falls Trail

Douglas Falls

Waterfall Creek

Blue Ridge Parkway

Mountains-to-Sea Trail

North Fork of the Swannanoa River

South to Asheville

89 Douglas Falls

Treasure in the mist! Tall and powerful, this beauty is unique as well. It's another of the few waterfalls that you can venture behind. As you stand beneath the mammoth rock overhang, the cool mist of the falls refreshes your body and spirit.

See map on page 235.
Height: 70 feet
Beauty rating: Very good
Distance: 1.0 mile out and back
Difficulty: Easy
Trail surface: Rocky dirt path
Approximate hiking time: 25 minutes
Blaze color: Yellow

County: Buncombe
Land status: National forest
Trail contact: Pisgah National Forest, Appalachian Ranger District; (828) 682-6146; www .fs.fed.us
Maps: *DeLorme: North Carolina Atlas & Gazetteer:* Page 32 E1

Finding the trailhead: From the junction of the Blue Ridge Parkway (BRP) and NC 128 (NC 128 is unmarked and leads to Mount Mitchell State Park), drive south on the BRP for 12.0 miles. Turn right into the Craggy Gardens Picnic Ground and go up the hill. After approximately 0.35 mile, make a sharp turn to the left and head downhill on the unmarked gravel road, which is FR 63. Follow FR 63, ignoring the road off to the left, which crosses the creek at 3.8 miles; instead continue straight ahead. After 4.9 miles, FR 63 becomes paved. Continue on the paved road for another 1.5 miles until you come to a stop sign at Dillingham Road. (For your return trip, note that the paved part of FR 63 is named Stoney Fork Road.) Turn right onto Dillingham Road and travel for approximately 1.3 miles. At this point, Dillingham Road crosses a bridge and becomes dirt FR 74. Continue on FR 74 for 8.7 miles to where it dead-ends.

From the junction of the BRP and US 70 in Asheville, drive north on the BRP for 14.9 miles. Turn left into the Craggy Gardens Picnic Ground and follow the directions above.

Craggy Gardens is located between Mileposts 367 and 368 on the Blue Ridge Parkway. The trailhead is at the far southwest corner of the parking area. GPS: N35 43.718 / W82 22.460

The Hike

Follow the Douglas Falls Trail (#162) on a slow and steady descent. While you can't hear any water flowing until you are almost at the falls, you're in for a real treat when you arrive at the base of Douglas Falls.

The falls were named for a true preservation pioneer. William O. Douglas was a Supreme Court justice for thirty-six years and a staunch advocate for wilderness protection. The longest-serving judge in the history of the courts, Douglas is credited with preserving many of our natural resources during his tenure.

The sheer size of Douglas Falls is made more noticeable by the family enjoying a picnic at the base.

Miles and Directions

0.0   From the trailhead, hike south on the dirt path as it slowly descends.

0.5   Arrive at the base of Douglas Falls (N35 43.262 / W82 22.467). Return the way you came.

1.0   Arrive back at the trailhead.

90 Glassmine Falls

On a clear day! And only on a clear day, will you get a good view of Glassmine Falls. If the Blue Ridge Parkway's fogged in, you won't even catch a glimpse, so pick the time you visit wisely.

See map on page 235.
Height: Over 100 feet
Beauty rating: Good
Distance: Roadside
Difficulty: Easy
Blaze color: No blazes
County: Buncombe

Land status: National forest
Trail contact: Pisgah National Forest, Grandfather Ranger District; (828) 652-2144; www .fs.fed.us
Maps: DeLorme: North Carolina Atlas & Gazetteer: Page 32 E1

Finding the trailhead: From the junction of the Blue Ridge Parkway (BRP) and SR 128 (SR 128 is unmarked and leads to Mount Mitchell State Park), drive south on the BRP for 5.7 miles to the overlook on your left signed for GLASSMINE FALLS.

From the junction of the BRP and US 70 in Asheville, drive north on the BRP for 20.0 miles to the overlook on your right signed for GLASSMINE FALLS.

The overlook is just south of Milepost 361 on the Blue Ridge Parkway, Glassmine Falls Overlook. GPS: N35 44.061 / W82 20.646

The Hike

If you do have the opportunity to spy Glassmine Falls, it is a beauty—just not a close-up beauty. Well out of reach across the valley, you don't get the personal experience with this waterfall that most others offer. But if you are in the area when the sky is clear, it's worth stopping at the overlook and enjoying from afar.

In the early 1900s mica was mined near the base of the falls. The mineral mica was also known as isinglass, or glass for short, hence the name "Glass-mine" Falls. Forms of the mineral are still being used in the production of insulation and some electrical components.

91 Setrock Creek Falls

Superb! Drop after drop, the many levels of this deep and gracious fall do impress. This makes for a great picnic spot as well.

Height: 100 feet
Beauty rating: Very good
Distance: 0.8 mile out and back
Difficulty: Easy
Trail surface: Gravel and hard-packed dirt
Approximate hiking time: 40 minutes
Blaze color: Yellow

County: Yancey
Land status: National forest
Trail contact: Pisgah National Forest, Appalachian Ranger District; (828) 682-6146; www .fs.fed.us
Maps: *DeLorme: North Carolina Atlas & Gazetteer:* Page 32 E2

Finding the trailhead: From the junction of the Blue Ridge Parkway (BRP) and SR 128 (SR 128 is unmarked and leads to Mount Mitchell State Park), drive north on the BRP for 3.3 miles. Turn left onto FR 472 and follow the gravel road for 4.7 miles until you come to a large Pisgah National Forest sign for BLACK MOUNTAIN CAMPGROUND. Just beyond the sign is a large parking area on the right.

From the junction of the BRP and NC 80 in Busick, drive south on NC 80 for 2.2 miles. Turn left onto South Toe River Road and drive across the bridge. After crossing the bridge, follow Neil's Creek Road (FR 472) for 2.1 miles to a fork (along the way, FR 472 becomes gravel). Go right at the fork, and continue on FR 472 for another 0.6 mile to a large parking area on the left, across from the Black Mountain Campground.

FR 472 is located between Mileposts 351 and 352 on the Blue Ridge Parkway. The trailhead is found within the Black Mountain Campground. GPS: N35 45.081 / W82 13.335

The Hike

From the parking area, cross the bridge and enter the campground. Once inside the campground, follow Briar Bottom Road toward the group camping area. You'll soon see where the gated road continues uphill and to the right. Don't go that way. Instead look left and you will see an obvious trailhead with a stone marker and white, yellow, and blue blazes on a tree. Follow this trail through the forest and then across the paved campground road. After crossing the road, follow the dirt path until you arrive at the base of Setrock Creek Falls.

There are several trails located within the Black Mountain Recreational Area. The most notable is the Mount Mitchell Trail, which leads from the campground all the way to the summit of Mount Mitchell. At 6,684 feet, Mount Mitchell is the tallest peak in North Carolina and the tallest east of the Mississippi River as well. If you have fresh legs and are up for the challenge, it's a worthy one. You can see five states from the summit.

Setrock Creek Falls, Roaring Fork Falls

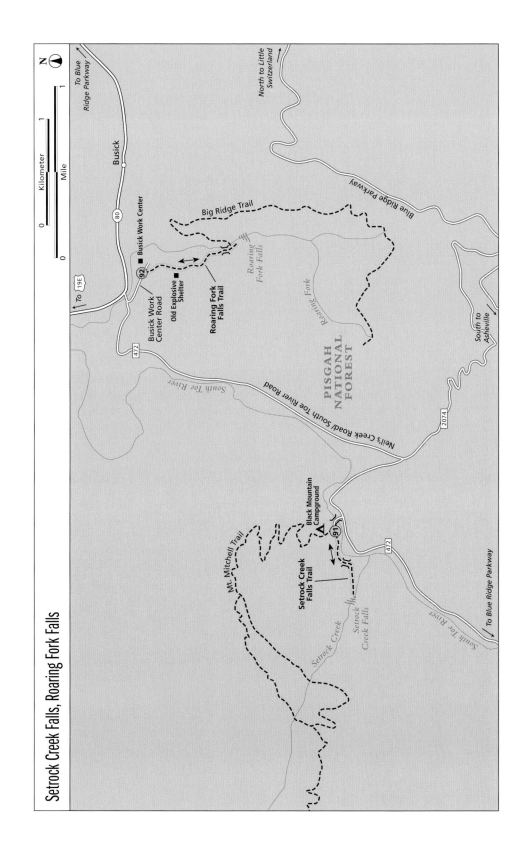

Miles and Directions

0.0 From the trailhead, follow the yellow blazes on the heavily used trail.

0.1 Bypass the Mount Mitchell Trail on your right, and continue straight ahead (west-southwest).

0.2 Cross the wooden footbridge and continue hiking south. Immediately after crossing the footbridge, you will see a blue-blazed trail that juts off to the right (west). Bypass this and continue for about another 50 feet to where the yellow-blazed Setrock Creek Falls Trail heads right (northwest) as well. Follow this trail across the road to a sign for SETROCK FALLS. Climb the few stone steps, and follow the dirt footpath west-southwest.

0.4 Arrive at the base of Setrock Creek Falls (N35 44.992 / W82 13.669). Return the way you came.

0.8 Arrive back at the trailhead.

92 Roaring Fork Falls

Outstanding! Brilliant with color, the mossy sides of the falls stand out brightly from their surroundings. Character oozes from this one.

See map on page 240.
Height: 100 feet
Beauty rating: Excellent
Distance: 1.0 mile out and back
Difficulty: Easy
Trail surface: Grassy and gravel roadbed
Approximate hiking time: 50 minutes
Blaze color: No blazes

County: Yancey
Land status: National forest
Trail contact: Pisgah National Forest, Appalachian Ranger District; (828) 682-6146; www .fs.fed.us
Maps: *DeLorme: North Carolina Atlas & Gazetteer:* Page 32 D2

Finding the trailhead: From the junction of the BRP and NC 80 in Busick, drive south on NC 80 for 2.2 miles. Turn left onto S. Toe River Road and drive across the bridge. Immediately after crossing the bridge, turn left onto Busick Work Center Road and travel for 0.2 mile to the gate in front of the work center. Park here, but don't block the gate. NC 80 is located between Mileposts 344 and 345 on the Blue Ridge Parkway. The trailhead is to the south, at the gated grassy road, with the sign reading Roaring Creek Falls—0.5 mile. GPS: N35 46.101 / W82 11.713

The Hike

Hike around the gate and head up the grassy road. The trail remains on this road for most of the way until you reach the creek. Once at the creek, a narrow path leads upstream to the base of Roaring Fork Falls.

The Busick Work Center is a USDA Forest Service hub that houses tools and equipment. Take note of the old bunkers along the trail. It is said that these once held explosives used for development of the area. Fear not; explosives haven't been stored here for years.

Miles and Directions

0.0 From the trailhead, hike up the grassy roadbed.

0.1 Bypass the grassy road that shoots off to the right (west), and continue hiking south.

0.2 Pass the old explosives bunkers.

0.5 Cross the small footbridge off to the right (south-southeast) and follow the rooty dirt path upstream.

0.5 Arrive at the base of Roaring Fork Falls (N35 45.609 / W82 11.512). Return the way you came.

1.0 Arrive back at the trailhead.

93 Crabtree Falls

Exceptional! Crabtree Falls creates a picturesque setting for all who visit. A single tree sits in the middle of the creek as the bold and powerful water passes it by.

Height: 70 feet
Beauty rating: Excellent
Distance: 1.8 miles out and back
Difficulty: Moderate to strenuous
Trail surface: Hard-packed dirt with rocky sections
Approximate hiking time: 1 hour, 30 minutes
Blaze color: No blazes

County: Yancey
Land status: National park
Trail contact: Blue Ridge Parkway; (828) 298-0398; www.nps.gov/blri
FYI: Campground open Apr 30 through Oct 30
Maps: *DeLorme: North Carolina Atlas & Gazetteer:* Page 32 D3

Finding the trailhead: From the junction of the Blue Ridge Parkway (BRP) and NC 80 in Busick, drive north on the BRP for 4.5 miles. Turn left into Crabtree Meadows at the sign for Crabtree Meadows Gift Shop; continue straight ahead for 0.2 mile toward the campground. At the campground entrance, turn right into the parking area at the sign for Crabtree Falls. If the campground is closed, park outside the gate and walk to the trailhead.

From the junction of the BRP and NC 226 near Spruce Pine, drive south on the BRP for 8.5 miles. Turn right into Crabtree Meadows at the sign for Crabtree Meadows Gift Shop and follow the directions above.

Crabtree Meadows is located between Mileposts 339 and 340 on the Blue Ridge Parkway. The trailhead is at the north end of the parking lot. GPS: N35 48.931 / W82 08.727

The Hike

Follow the trail as it rapidly descends through a rhododendron thicket and then leads you down to a T junction with a bench to rest upon. Head right, and continue your descent down three sets of stone steps as the sound of the falls beckons. After descending the steps, the rocky path takes you around a switchback before leading to the base of Crabtree Falls.

The crab apple tree (Malus sylvestris), or "wild crab tree," once flourished here. Orchards sat just above the falls with their showy pink blooms and tart crab apples. Very few crab trees can be found here today. Don't be discouraged: What the trail lacks in the tree's pink blossoms, it more than makes up for in wildflowers. This trail is home to more than forty species, making it an ideal place to hike during springtime.

Along with Crabtree Falls, this loop trail offers a wide variety of wildflowers in the springtime.

Miles and Directions

0.0 From the trailhead, hike north as you make your way downhill.

0.2 Come to a T junction with a sign for CRABTREE FALLS directing you to the right for another 0.7 mile. Go right (north) and continue hiking downhill.

0.4 Head down the stone steps and to the left (west) and soon hear the sound of the falls beckoning you.

0.5 Cross the footbridge and head down a second and then third set of stone steps.

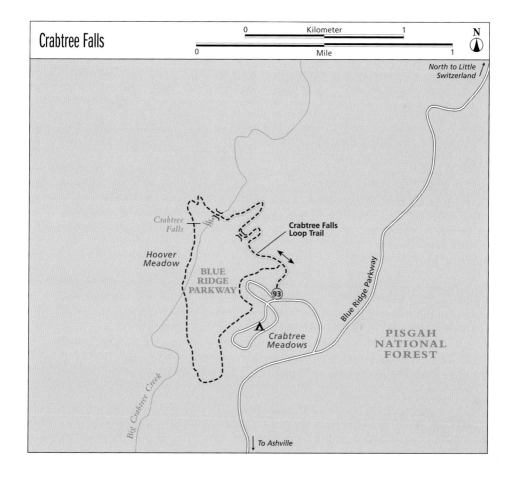

Crabtree Falls

North to Little Switzerland

Crabtree Falls

Crabtree Falls Loop Trail

Hoover Meadow

BLUE RIDGE PARKWAY

Blue Ridge Parkway

93

Crabtree Meadows

Big Crabtree Creek

PISGAH NATIONAL FOREST

To Ashville

0.9 Arrive at a footbridge at the base of Crabtree Falls (N35 49.183 / W82 08.954). Return the way you came. (***Option:*** Continue across the footbridge and up the switchbacks on the other side to make this a 2.5-mile loop hike. See below.)

1.8 Arrive back at the trailhead.

Option: Although I recommend you return the way you came, you can continue on the trail past the falls and up several steep switchbacks. If you do so, the trail makes a loop and brings you back to the T junction at the bench for a moderate to strenuous hike of 2.5 miles. A detailed trail map is posted at the trailhead.

94 Elk River Falls

Spectacular! Elk River Falls represents both beauty and grace as it flows into the plunge pool. Some say that the mysterious waters below the falls run so deep that they have yet to find the bottom.

Height: 65 feet
Beauty rating: Excellent
Distance: 0.4 mile out and back
Difficulty: Easy to moderate
Trail surface: Wide, hard-packed dirt
Approximate hiking time: 30 minutes
Blaze color: Yellow
County: Avery

Land status: National forest
Trail contact: Pisgah National Forest, Appalachian Ranger District; (828) 682-6146; www.fs.fed.us
FYI: Area open from 6 a.m. to 10 p.m.
Maps: *DeLorme: North Carolina Atlas & Gazetteer:* Page 12 E4

Finding the trailhead: From the junction of US 19 east and NC 194 in Elk Park, drive north on US 19 for 1.6 miles. Turn right onto Old Mill Road and travel for 0.25 mile to a left turn onto Elk River Road (SR 1305). Continue for 4.0 miles to where the road dead-ends.

From the junction of US 19 east and the North Carolina–Tennessee state line, drive south on US 19 for 2.5 miles. Turn left onto Old Mill Road and follow the directions above.

The trailhead is at the northeast end of the parking area. GPS: N36 11.845 / W81 58.203

The Hike

The wide dirt path follows the Elk River downstream the entire time. It leads first to the brink and then to the base of Elk River Falls. This is a popular spot for sunning and swimming, so you probably won't find seclusion here. However, the peacefulness of the waterfall itself is well worth a visit, even if you have to share.

Located in the town of Elk Park, the river, town, and falls are all named for the great eastern elk (Cervus canadensis). Known as wapiti to the Native Americans, this great beast could weigh up to 1,000 pounds and once lived here in abundance. Although they have not inhabited the area since the early 1800s, their name lives on. An experimental program is in progress within Great Smoky Mountain National Park to reintroduce the elk. Perhaps one day they'll be seen again in Elk Park.

Elk River Falls

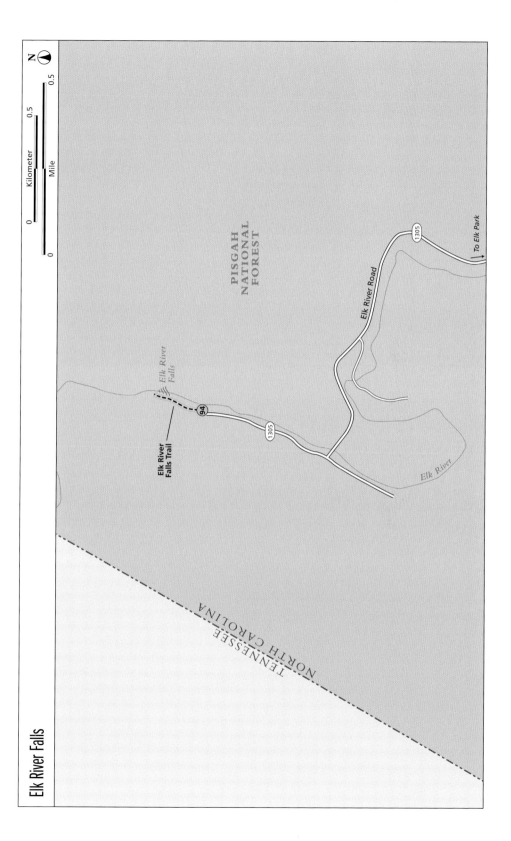

Kilometer
0   0.5

Mile
0   0.5

N

PISGAH
NATIONAL
FOREST

Elk River
Falls

Elk River
Falls Trail

94

1305

Elk River Road

1305

Elk River

To Elk Park

TENNESSEE
NORTH CAROLINA

Elk River Falls is a very popular swimming hole, so don't expect to have this beauty to yourself.

Miles and Directions

0.0 From the trailhead, climb the stairs and follow the wide, dirt trail north along the river's edge.

0.1 Arrive at the brink of the falls.

0.2 Arrive at the base of Elk River Falls (N36 11.952 / W81 58.145). Return the way you came.

0.4 Arrive back at the trailhead.

95 Lower and Upper Linville Falls

Extravagant! Each view is better than the last and each experience more powerful than the one before. Linville Falls and the gorge they're named for make for a must-do hike if you're anywhere in the area. Although the falls tend to be crowded, the experience will still put you in awe of the beauty this natural wonder has to offer.

Height: Upper Falls, 12 feet; Lower Falls, 60 feet
Beauty rating: Excellent
Distance: 1.6 miles out and back
Difficulty: Easy to moderate
Trail surface: Wide dirt path with short rocky sections
Approximate hiking time: 1 hour

Blaze color: No blazes
County: Burke
Land status: National park
Trail contact: Blue Ridge Parkway; (828) 298-0398; www.nps.gov/blri
Maps: DeLorme: North Carolina Atlas & Gazetteer: Page 33 B5

Finding the trailhead: From the junction of the Blue Ridge Parkway (BRP) and US 221 in the town of Linville Falls, drive north on the BRP for 1.0 mile. Turn right at the sign for Linville Falls Visitor Center and drive straight ahead for approximately 1.4 miles to where the road ends at the visitor center.

From the junction of the Blue Ridge Parkway (BRP) and NC 181 near Linville, drive south on the BRP for 4.2 miles. Turn left at the sign for Linville Falls Visitor Center and follow the directions above.

The turnoff for Linville Falls Visitor Center is located between Mileposts 316 and 317 on the Blue Ridge Parkway. The trailhead is located at the visitor center. GPS: N35 57.273 / W81 55.669

The Hike

The trail begins at the visitor center for Linville Falls Recreation Area. A trail map of the area is posted here as well. This trail affords you two very different and distinct viewing points of Linville Falls. I highly recommend seeing the falls from both points of view. The Chimney View lets you see the falls from high above, while the Upper Linville Falls Overlook gives you an up-close and personal experience of the water as it rushes by. Here you feel the power and might of Lower Linville Falls from the brink while simultaneously sensing the calming effects of Upper Linville Falls.

This trail is just a small taste of what Linville Gorge has to offer. The rugged and scenic gorge covers 12,000 acres and contains 39 miles of trail. The gorge was named for the explorer William Linville, who was attacked and killed in the gorge by Native Americans in 1766. At nearly 2,000 feet deep, Linville Gorge is one of the deepest natural gorges in the eastern United States.

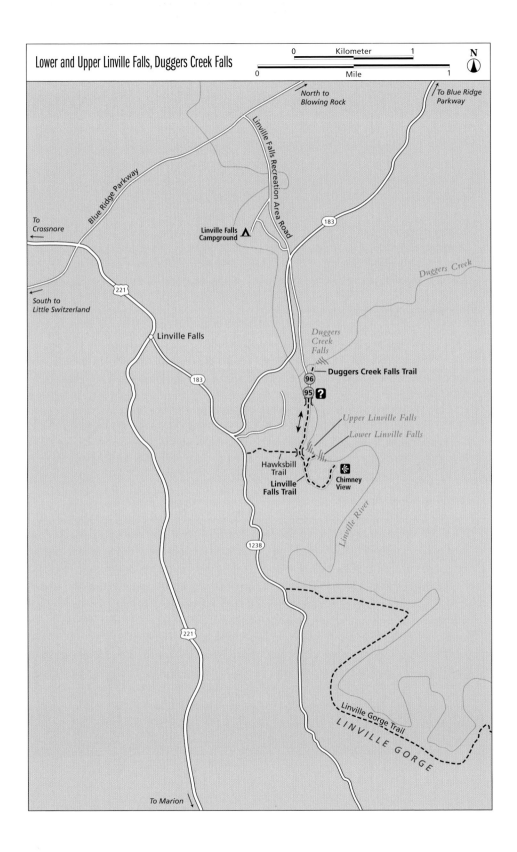

Lower and Upper Linville Falls, Duggers Creek Falls

0 Kilometer 1

0 Mile 1

N

North to
Blowing Rock

To Blue Ridge
Parkway

Linville Falls Recreation Area Road

Blue Ridge Parkway

183

To
Crossnore

South to
Little Switzerland

221

Linville Falls
Campground

Duggers Creek

Linville Falls

183

Duggers
Creek
Falls

96

95

Duggers Creek Falls Trail

Upper Linville Falls

Lower Linville Falls

Hawksbill
Trail

Linville
Falls Trail

Chimney
View

1238

Linville River

221

Linville Gorge Trail

LINVILLE GORGE

To Marion

Lower Linville Falls pours down into the gorge.

Miles and Directions

0.0   Start behind the visitor center and hike southwest; cross the bridge and head left (south).

0.3   Cross a second bridge and continue hiking east.

0.4   Come to a fork with a sign directing you to the left (north-northeast) to UPPER FALLS OVERLOOK—500 FEET and to the right (south) to the CHIMNEY VIEW OVERLOOK—0.3 MILES. Go right (south) toward the Chimney View and make your way uphill.

The peaceful waters of Upper Linville Falls soothe the senses.

0.6 A second fork awaits, with the right leading east-southeast to Erwin's View and the left leading north to Chimney View. Go left toward Chimney View.

0.7 Arrive at the Chimney View of Linville Falls (N35 56.950 / W81 55.522). (*Option:* Return to the trailhead for a 1.4-mile hike.)

1.0 Arrive back at the first fork, and now head north-northeast toward the Upper Falls Overlook.

1.1 Arrive at the Upper Falls Overlook (N35 56.999 / W81 55.628). Return to the trailhead.

1.6 Arrive back at the trailhead.

96 Duggers Creek Falls

A real gem! With a mossy gorge of its own, what Duggers Creek lacks in size it makes up for with lush greens and plant diversity.

See map on page 250.
Height: 18 feet
Beauty rating: Excellent
Distance: 0.2 mile out and back
Difficulty: Easy
Trail surface: Narrow, hard-packed dirt
Approximate hiking time: 15 minutes

Blaze color: No blazes
County: Burke
Land status: National park
Trail contact: Blue Ridge Parkway; (828) 298-0398; www.nps.gov/blri
Maps: *DeLorme: North Carolina Atlas & Gazetteer:* Page 33 B5

Finding the trailhead: From the junction of the Blue Ridge Parkway (BRP) and US 221 in the town of Linville Falls, drive north on the BRP for 1.0 mile. Turn right at the sign for Linville Falls Visitor Center and drive straight ahead for approximately 1.4 miles to where the road ends at the visitor center.

From the junction of the Blue Ridge Parkway (BRP) and NC 181 near Linville, drive south on the BRP for 4.2 miles. Turn left at the sign for Linville Falls Visitor Center and follow the directions above.

The turnoff for Linville Falls Visitor Center is located between Mileposts 316 and 317 on the Blue Ridge Parkway. The trailhead is located at the northeast corner of the parking area (opposite end from the visitor center). GPS: N35 57.273 / W81 55.669

The Hike

From the trailhead, follow the sidewalk to where it dead-ends. Take the small path that heads back into the woods toward the creek. Rock-hop the creek and follow the

LINVILLE CAVERNS

Not far from Linville Gorge lie the Linville Caverns. This giant recess gives you a peek into the heart of Humpback Mountain, just 4 miles south of the Blue Ridge Parkway.

A visit to the mammoth cave is like stepping back in time. Stalagmites and stalactites protrude from the stone, and occasionally bats can be seen hanging from the caverns' damp ceiling. The temperature stays at 52°F year-round, and dripping water seeps from the walls. If you visit, dress accordingly. For more information visit their website at www.linvillecaverns.com or call (800) 419-0540.

narrow path upstream. The trail soon takes you away from and then back to the creek before leading you to some stone steps and onto the base of Duggers Creek Falls.

You can cross over the footbridge at the base of the falls and continue hiking less than 0.1 mile. This route will bring you out into the parking lot just a little bit south of the trailhead.

While you're in the area, consider a trip to the nearby Linville Caverns. The caverns were discovered in 1822 by an angler who noticed a stream that flowed right out of the heart of Humpback Mountain, but it wasn't until 1937 that the caverns were opened to the public. Guided tours are given daily.

Miles and Directions

0.0 From the trailhead, follow the sidewalk north to where it dead-ends just before you reach the stop sign. Take the small path that heads back into the woods toward the creek. Rock-hop the creek and then go right (east), following the creek upstream.

0.1 Climb the stone steps and soon reach the base of Duggers Creek Falls (N35 57.400 / W81 55.648). Return the way you came. (*Option:* Continue past the falls less than 0.1 mile to where the trail ends at the parking lot just south of the trailhead.)

0.2 Arrive back at the trailhead.

97 Lower Falls of Upper Creek

Mother Nature's playground! Stones rise from the midst of the creek like islands in the sky as the water swiftly flows on either side.

Height: 15 feet	**County:** Burke
Beauty rating: Excellent	**Land status:** National forest
Distance: 1.8 miles out and back	**Trail contact:** Pisgah National Forest, Grandfa-
Difficulty: Moderate to strenuous	ther Ranger District; (828) 652-2144;
Trail surface: Rooty, rocky path	www.fs.fed.us
Approximate hiking time: 1 hour, 30 minutes	**Maps:** DeLorme: North Carolina Atlas & Gazet-
Blaze color: Yellow	teer: Page 33 B5

Finding the trailhead: From the junction of NC 181 and the Blue Ridge Parkway near Linville, drive south on NC 181 for 5.6 miles. Turn left at the sign for UPPER CREEK FALLS, and follow the road until it dead-ends at the parking area.

From the junction of NC 181 and US 64 in Morganton, drive north on NC 181 for 20.9 miles. Turn right at the sign for UPPER CREEK FALLS and follow the directions above.

The trailhead is located at the northeast corner of the parking area. GPS: N35 57.611 / W81 51.652

The Hike

The trail to Lower Falls takes you around many switchbacks as you descend to the falls. Please resist the temptation to shortcut. It destroys the vegetation, causes erosion, and makes the trail harder to follow.

If you happen to be visiting Upper Creek later in the day, after you enjoy the falls (both Upper and Lower), I recommend heading 2.0 miles south on NC 181 to the Brown Mountain Overlook. On a clear night, the mysterious "Brown Mountain Lights" can be seen wavering in the distance atop Brown Mountain. This strange phenomenon has mystified people for hundreds of years. Cherokee legend says the lights are the spirits of Indian maidens searching for their loved ones lost in battle. Others say that the ghosts of Civil War veterans are doomed to carry candles across the mountain forever.

Whether it's ghosts, spirits, foxfire, or a mirage, the lights do exist and have yet to be scientifically explained. You, too, can be spellbound by the mystery.

Lower Falls of Upper Creek, Upper Falls of Upper Creek

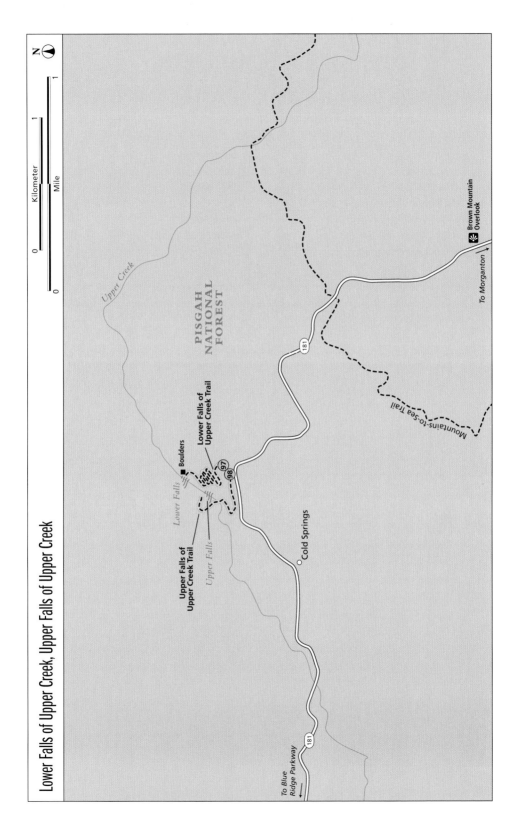

Lower Falls of Upper Creek are well worth the effort.

Miles and Directions

0.0 From the trailhead, hike across the grassy field, into the woods, and down some steps.

0.1 Come to a fork; go left (west) and continue following the yellow blazes.

0.6 Arrive at a second fork. Go right here and follow the rooty, rocky path northeast.

0.8 Mammoth boulders await. Head left (northwest) at the boulders and continue your steep descent.

0.9 Arrive at the base of Lower Falls of Upper Creek (N35 57.746 / W81 51.709). Return the way you came.

1.8 Arrive back at the trailhead.

98 Upper Falls of Upper Creek

Remarkable! The gifts given here are hard earned but most enjoyable upon receipt.

See map on page 256.
Height: 100 feet
Beauty rating: Excellent
Distance: 1.4 miles out and back
Difficulty: Strenuous
Trail surface: Rooty dirt path
Approximate hiking time: 1 hour
Blaze color: Yellow

County: Burke
Land status: National forest
Trail contact: Pisgah National Forest, Grandfather Ranger District; (828) 652-2144; www.fs.fed.us
Maps: *DeLorme: North Carolina Atlas & Gazetteer:* Page 33 B5

Finding the trailhead: From the junction of NC 181 and the Blue Ridge Parkway near Linville, drive south on NC 181 for 5.6 miles. Turn left at the sign for Upper Creek Falls and follow the road until it dead-ends at the parking area.

From the junction of NC 181 and US 64 in Morganton, drive north on NC 181 for 20.9 miles. Turn right at the sign for Upper Creek Falls and follow the directions above.

The trailhead is located on the west side of the parking area. GPS: N35 57.596 / W81 51.664

The Hike

Unlike its little sister, Lower Falls, this trail is easier to follow but makes a much steeper descent. The trail leads you around some switchbacks before reaching the creek at the brink of Upper Falls. The area above the falls is a wonderful playground, but be careful! This is the brink of a waterfall.

From the brink the path continues on a steeper downhill trek to the base of Upper Falls of Upper Creek.

I recommend hiking to both the Upper and Lower Falls of Upper Creek.

For those of you interested in road bicycling, the Piedmont Spur bicycle route begins less than 10.0 miles south of the parking area, where NC 181 meets Brown Mountain Beach Road. This 200-mile bike route offers astounding views and crosses creek after creek as it leads you through the countryside.

Miles and Directions

0.0 From the trailhead, hike southwest into the woods and follow the trail around a few switchbacks.

0.4 Arrive at the brink of the falls. Carefully cross the creek; head right (north) and follow the trail steeply downhill.

0.7 Arrive at the base of Upper Falls of Upper Creek (N35 57.696 / W81 51.763). Return the way you came.

1.4 Arrive back at the trailhead.

99 North Harper Creek Falls

Elegant! The free-flowing water of North Harper Creek seems to wrap its arms around the stone face of the falls.

Height: 40 feet

Beauty rating: Brink, Very good; base, good

Distance: 2.4 miles out and back

Difficulty: Very strenuous

Trail surface: Hard-packed dirt; short sections over stone

Approximate hiking time: 2 hours

Blaze color: Red and blue

County: Avery

Land status: National forest

Trail contact: Pisgah National Forest, Grandfather Ranger District; (828) 652-2144; www.fs.fed.us

FYI: The bushwhack portion of this hike should be attempted by experienced hikers only—no children.

Maps: DeLorme: North Carolina Atlas & Gazetteer: Page 33 B5

Finding the trailhead: From the junction of the Blue Ridge Parkway (BRP) and the northern-most intersection with US 221 (to Linville), drive south on the BRP for 6.0 miles. Turn left onto SR 1518 (Old Jonas Ridge Road) and travel for 1.7 miles until you arrive at a semi-fork at Mortimer Road (with the Long Ridge Baptist Church on your left). Go straight ahead onto FR 464 (Edgemont Road) and travel for 2.5 miles to a right turn onto FR 58. Follow FR 58 for approximately 0.25 mile to a small pull-off on the left at the sign for North Harper Creek Trail—#266.

From the junction of the BRP and NC 181 near Linville, drive north on the BRP for 0.8 mile. Turn right onto SR 1518 (Old Jonas Ridge Road) and follow the directions above.

SR 1518 is located between Mileposts 311 and 312 on the Blue Ridge Parkway. The trailhead is located at the far right end of the parking area. GPS: N36 00.419 / W81 51.062

The Hike

This can be a very difficult trail to follow, but I've done my best to give as clear and concise directions as possible. The trail leads from the far right (southeast) end of the parking area and heads down the wooden steps and into the forest. Follow the blazes as the trail leads to Harper Creek, which you'll cross three times.

As you follow the creek downstream, you find yourself hiking over the stony slopes beside it. The trail leads to the brink of the falls and then continues on a very steep and strenuous bushwhack down to the middle of the falls. This bushwhack should only be attempted by experienced hikers—no children.

Like its neighbor the "Lost Cove," the Harper Creek Wilderness Study Area is just that—a study area. It is managed and protected as a wilderness area by the USDA Forest Service, but its status is temporary while awaiting official approval from Congress. We can only hope that these areas remain under the wing of the Forest Service for years to come.

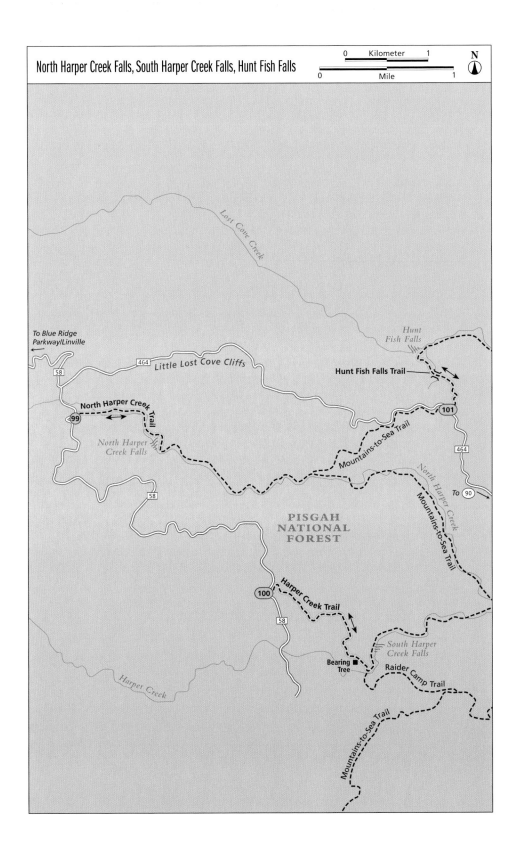

North Harper Creek Falls, South Harper Creek Falls, Hunt Fish Falls

0   Kilometer   1

0   Mile   1

N

To Blue Ridge
Parkway/Linville

Lost Cove Creek

Hunt
Fish Falls

464   Little Lost Cove Cliffs

Hunt Fish Falls Trail

58

North Harper Creek Trail

99

101

North Harper
Creek Falls

464

Mountains-to-Sea Trail

To 90

58

North Harper Creek

PISGAH
NATIONAL
FOREST

Mountains-to-Sea Trail

Harper Creek Trail

100

58

South Harper
Creek Falls

Bearing
Tree

Raider Camp Trail

Harper Creek

Mountains-to-Sea Trail

Hiking through a rhododendron tunnel is something a little different.

Miles and Directions

0.0   From the trailhead, hike southwest down the wooden steps, following the red-and-blue-blazed trail on its steep descent.

0.3   Cross Harper Creek and go right (southwest), losing the red blazes. Follow the creek downstream, crossing the stony slope until you pick up the red-and-blue-blazed trail again.

0.7   Cross the creek a second time and head left (south), continuing to hike downstream.

0.8   Just before reaching a primitive camping area with a large fire ring in the middle, go left (southeast) and cross the creek again. Once on the other side, head straight back (south) into the woods.

0.9   Arrive at the brink of the falls. To get to the base, head left (east) and make your way downstream. Follow the blue-and-orange surveyor's tape up and away from the creek.

1.0   The narrow path rejoins the blue-blazed North Harper Creek Trail. Head right (south-southeast) and continue downstream and steeply downhill.

1.2   The trail leads back alongside the creek. The blue-blazed North Harper Creek Trail continues left (east), but you want to go right (west) to reach North Harper Creek Falls (N36 00.179 / W81 50.341). Return the way you came.

2.4   Arrive back at the trailhead.

100 South Harper Creek Falls

Mythical! The cradle formed around the falls by the stony-faced walls creates a unique setting. You might expect an echo from the rush of water as it slides down the rock.

See map on page 260.
Height: 200 feet
Beauty rating: Brink, very good; base, excellent
Distance: 3.2 miles out and back
Difficulty: Moderate to strenuous
Trail surface: Narrow, overgrown, hard-packed dirt
Approximate hiking time: 2 hours
Blaze color: Orange

County: Avery
Land status: National forest
Trail contact: Pisgah National Forest, Grandfather Ranger District; (828) 652-2144; www.fs.fed.us
FYI: The hike to the base of the falls is recommended for experienced hikers only.
Maps: DeLorme: North Carolina Atlas & Gazetteer: Page 33 B6

Finding the trailhead: From the junction of the Blue Ridge Parkway (BRP) and the northernmost intersection with US 221 (to Linville), drive south on the BRP for 6.0 miles. Turn left onto SR 1518 (Old Jonas Ridge Road) and travel for 1.7 miles until you arrive at a semi-fork at Mortimer Road (with the Long Ridge Baptist Church on your left). Go straight ahead onto FR 464 (Edgemont Road) and travel for 2.5 miles to a right turn onto FR 58. Follow FR 58 for 4.1 miles to a large pull-off on the right marked by a sign for North Harper Creek Trail—#260.

From the junction of the BRP and NC 181 near Linville, drive north on the BRP for 0.8 mile. Turn right onto SR 1518 (Old Jonas Ridge Road) and follow the directions above.

SR 1518 is located between Mileposts 311 and 312 on the Blue Ridge Parkway. The trailhead is located on the south side of the road, just west of the parking area. GPS: N35 59.301 / W81 49.489

The Hike

Follow the trail as it heads into the woods and meanders through the forest. For now, the sound of solitude is all you hear.

As you follow the North Harper Creek Trail generally south, you will pass an open field and a bearing tree before making a steep descent to the creek. You soon arrive at the brink of the falls, where huge cliffs tower over the falls. From the brink, a small side trail leads downhill and around several switchbacks before reaching the creek again. Once at the creek, head upstream to the base of South Harper Creek Falls.

The trail to the base is very steep and dangerous. It is therefore recommended for experienced hikers only.

South Harper Creek Falls is actually located on Harper Creek. As a matter of fact, there is no South Harper Creek, only North Harper and Harper Creeks. The Wilderness Study Area that surrounds the creek is a protected black bear sanctuary, and the waters that flow here are excellent for trout fishing.

Miles and Directions

0.0 From the trailhead, follow the trail as it winds through the forest.

0.5 Come to a fork; go left (east) and continue following the sparsely placed orange blazes.

1.0 Reach an intersection with an obscure trail shooting off to the right between two trees marked with orange blazes. Bypass this trail, which leads down to private property. Instead continue hiking straight ahead (south) and pass an open field on the right (west).

1.2 Pass a bearing tree and the trail makes its final steep descent south-southeast.

1.3 Come to a T junction at the creek. Go left and continue hiking northeast.

1.4 Arrive at the brink of the falls. Go left (northeast) on the side trail and follow the steep switchbacks downhill.

1.5 Come to the creek. Continue hiking upstream (southeast).

1.6 Arrive at the base of South Harper Creek Falls (N35 58.867 / W81 48.655). Return the way you came.

3.2 Arrive back at the trailhead.

101 Hunt Fish Falls

Flawless! Two distinct and absolutely perfect drops create Hunt Fish Falls. With wrap-around stone surroundings and an incredible swimming hole at the base, this is a great place to spend a day.

See map on page 260.
Height: 30 feet
Beauty rating: Excellent
Distance: 1.8 miles out and back
Difficulty: Strenuous
Trail surface: Hard-packed dirt
Approximate hiking time: 1 hour, 10 minutes
Blaze color: White

County: Avery
Land status: National forest
Trail contact: Pisgah National Forest, Grandfather Ranger District; (828) 652-2144; www.fs.fed.us
Maps: *DeLorme: North Carolina Atlas & Gazetteer:* Page 33 B6

Finding the trailhead: From the junction of the Blue Ridge Parkway (BRP) and the northern-most intersection with US 221 (to Linville), drive south on the BRP for 6.0 miles. Turn left onto SR 1518 (Old Jonas Ridge Road), and travel for 1.7 miles until you arrive at a semi-fork at Mortimer Road (with the Long Ridge Baptist Church on your left). Go straight ahead onto FR 464 (Edgemont Road) and travel for 6.2 miles to an obvious parking area on the left.

From the junction of the BRP and NC 181 near Linville, drive north on the BRP for 0.8 mile. Turn right onto SR 1518 (Old Jonas Ridge Road) and follow the directions above.

SR 1518 is located between Mileposts 311 and 312 on the Blue Ridge Parkway. The trailhead is located at the southeast end of the parking area. GPS: N36 00.449 / W81 48.057

The Hike

Follow the white-blazed trail as it makes a steep descent and brings you across two rocky footbridges before reaching the creek just upstream from Hunt Fish Falls.

This waterfall is overcrowded on the weekends, but you may be lucky and have it to yourself on a weekday. Hunt Fish Falls is perfect for swimming or sunning and is ideal for a picnic.

This little beauty is located within the Lost Cove Wilderness Study Area. Along with neighboring Harper Creek, the wilderness area is awaiting congressional protection. Lost Cove itself is a black bear sanctuary and famous for the Lost Cove Cliffs. Home to roosting peregrine falcons, rare mosses, and stunted pitch pine trees, the cliffs can be best viewed from the Blue Ridge Parkway overlook at Milepost 310.

Found within the Lost Cove Wilderness Area, Hunt Fish Falls is incomparable.

Miles and Directions

0.0   From the trailhead, follow the white blazes east as you make a steep descent into the forest.

0.3   Come to a fork in the trail. Go left (north) and continue your descent.

0.5   Reach a small stream. Head downstream, cross it on the rocky bridge, and head right (north).

0.6   Cross a second small stream on a rocky footbridge and continue north. The trail heads away from the stream and continues downhill.

0.8   Reach the creek just upstream from the falls. Do not cross; instead go right (east) and hike downstream.

0.9   Arrive alongside Hunt Fish Falls (N36 00.844 / W81 48.235). Return the way you came.

1.8   Arrive back at the trailhead.

102 Harper Creek Falls

Stunning! Your imagination could not create the picturesque setting that is Harper Creek Falls. Its two-tiered nature adds the perfect touch to this amazing vision.

Height: 60 feet
Beauty rating: Excellent
Distance: 3.0 miles out and back
Difficulty: Easy to moderate
Trail surface: Hard-packed dirt
Approximate hiking time: 1 hour, 30 minutes
Blaze color: Orange

County: Caldwell
Land status: National forest
Trail contact: Pisgah National Forest, Grandfather Ranger District; (828) 652-2144; www .fs.fed.us
Maps: *DeLorme: North Carolina Atlas & Gazetteer:* Page 33 B6

Finding the trailhead: From the junction of the Blue Ridge Parkway (BRP) and NC 181 near Linville, drive north on the BRP for 4.0 miles. Turn right onto SR 1511 and travel for 4.3 miles to where SR 1511 becomes FR 981. Continue straight ahead onto FR 981 and travel for 4.5 miles until you come to a stop sign with the Edgemont Baptist Church straight ahead of you. This road is SR 90. Turn right onto SR 90 and travel for 2.0 miles. Turn right onto SR 1328 (Brown Mountain Beach Road) just past the Mortimer Recreation Area and travel for 1.4 miles to a large pull-off on the right at the sign for HARPER CREEK TRAIL #260.

From the junction of the Blue Ridge Parkway (BRP) and the northernmost intersection with US 221 (to Linville), drive south on the BRP for 2.8 miles. Turn left onto SR 1511 and follow the directions above.

SR 1511 is located between Mileposts 307 and 308 on the Blue Ridge Parkway. The trailhead is located at the north end of the parking area. GPS: N35 58.656 / W81 45.993

The Hike

Follow the dirt path steeply uphill and into the woods. The orange blazes take you around a switchback and up to the first fork. Head left, and the wide, sandy path flattens out before you come to a second fork.

Bear right at the fork and pass through a wonderful patch of holly and hemlock before arriving at a third fork. Again bear right, being sure to follow the orange blazes as you head uphill and come out alongside the creek from high above.

At the fourth and final fork, you stray from the Harper Creek Trail and soon see the rocky cliffs that loom above the falls. A steep, muddy path leads down to the creek at the base of Harper Creek Falls.

The Harper Creek Wilderness Study Area sits just south of the famed Grandfather Mountain. At 5,964 feet, Grandfather is one of the tallest peaks in the North Carolina Blue Ridge Range. The profile of the northern face resembles that of an old man.

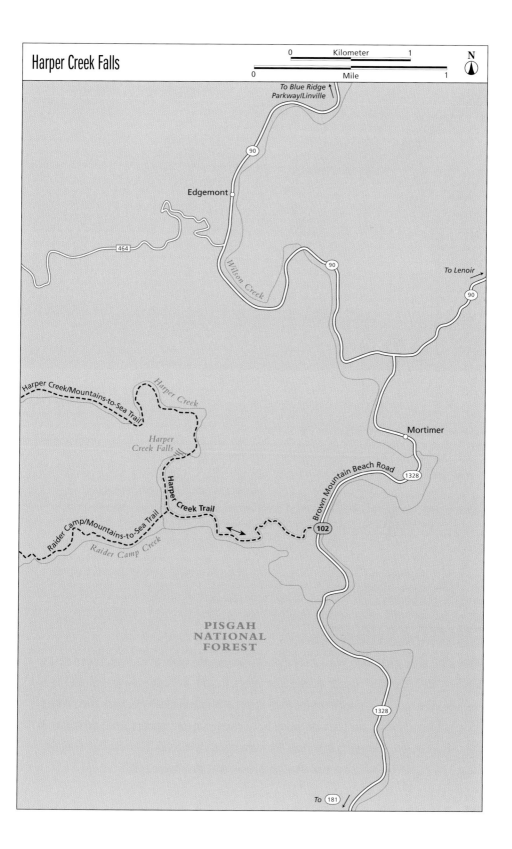

Harper Creek Falls

0 — Kilometer — 1

0 — Mile — 1

N

To Blue Ridge Parkway/Linville

90

Edgemont

464

Wilson Creek

90

To Lenoir

90

Harper Creek

Harper Creek/Mountains-to-Sea Trail

Mortimer

Harper Creek Falls

Harper Creek Trail

Brown Mountain Beach Road

1328

Raider Camp/Mountains-to-Sea Trail

102

Raider Camp Creek

PISGAH NATIONAL FOREST

1328

To 181

The colors of autumn begin to show at Harper Creek Falls.

Miles and Directions

0.0 From the trailhead, the trail leads steeply uphill and around a switchback.

0.25 Come to a fork with a red-blazed trail to your right (north) and the orange-blazed Harper Creek Trail to your left (northwest). Go left here as the wide, sandy path flattens out.

0.8 Come to a second fork. The left leads southwest down to a camping area. Take the right fork, which leads straight ahead (west) and continues to follow the orange blazes.

1.1 A third fork awaits. The left leg of the fork leads west to the Raider Camp / Mountains-to-Sea Trail (#440) and past a sign reading NC 181—8.3 MILES. The right is the continuation of the orange-blazed Harper Creek Trail. Go right here, hiking uphill (northwest) and alongside the creek from high above.

GRANDFATHER MOUNTAIN

If you have some extra time, you should visit Grandfather Mountain State Park, known for its 228-foot-long "mile high" swinging suspension bridge. It spans a chasm more than 80 feet deep at a mile above sea level. Acquired by the State of North Carolina in 2008, the park offers hiking trails and has a wildlife sanctuary harboring black bears, cougars, beavers, and bald eagles. A daily admission fee is charged per person. For more information contact Grandfather Mountain State Park at (800) 468-7325 or visit their website at www.grandfather.com.

1.3 Come to the final fork, with the orange-and-white-blazed Harper Creek Trail shooting up to the right (northwest). Stay left here, following the unblazed trail upstream (north).

1.4 As the trail bends to the right (east), you will see the rocky cliffs that perch above the falls. Take the steep, muddy path on your left (north) to the creek.

1.5 Arrive at the base of Harper Creek Falls (N35 58.976 / W81 46.795). Return the way you came.

3.0 Arrive back at the trailhead.

103 Silvervale Falls

Sad! Not the waterfall, but the individuals who have no respect for nature and have chosen to deface it. Sadly, those of us who do care must suffer the consequences.

See overview map on page iv.
Height: 80 feet
Beauty rating: Fair
Distance: Roadside
Difficulty: Easy
Blaze color: No blazes
County: Caldwell

Land status: National forest
Trail contact: Pisgah National Forest, Grandfather Ranger District; (828) 652-2144; www.fs.fed.us
Maps: *DeLorme: North Carolina Atlas & Gazetteer:* Page 33 A8

Finding the trailhead: From the junction of US 321 and US 64 in Lenoir, drive north on US 321 for 12.7 miles. Turn left onto Waterfalls Road (SR 1371) and travel for 1.8 miles to view the falls on your left.

From the junction of US 321 and the Blue Ridge Parkway in Blowing Rock, drive south on US 321 for 8.6 miles. Turn right onto Waterfalls Road (SR 1371) and follow the directions above.

GPS: N36 02.895 / W81 35.681

The Hike

Silvervale Falls can be viewed from the roadside, but the stone face of the falls has been littered with graffiti. Between the graffiti and the small flow of water, I would only suggest a visit if you're already in the area. Don't make any special trips here.

I do recommend a visit to nearby Blowing Rock, an unusual rock formation that juts out over the John's River Gorge from 1,500 feet above. The town of Blowing Rock was once inhabited by the Cherokee and Catawba, bitter enemy tribes.

According to legend, a pair of lovers, one from each tribe, were walking near the Blowing Rock. As the sun began to set, the sky beckoned the brave back to his tribe, but his maiden begged him to stay. So deep was his internal struggle that he threw himself into the gorge from atop the rock. As the maiden prayed to the Great Spirit to save her lover, the winds of the gorge blew so fiercely that they swept the brave up and into the arms of his fair maiden, where he stayed forever.

104 McGalliard Falls

Fabulous! Like a feather blowing in the wind, the flowing water of McGalliard Falls caresses the rock face as it flows into the fabulous plunge pool.

Height: 40 feet
Beauty rating: Very good
Distance: 0.4 mile out and back
Difficulty: Easy
Trail surface: Paved and dirt path
Approximate hiking time: 10 minutes
Blaze color: No blazes
County: Burke

Land status: Town park
Trail contact: Valdese Parks and Recreation; (828) 879-2132; www.ci.valdese.nc.us/ parks.htm
FYI: The park is open from 8 a.m. to dark; restrooms are open Apr to Nov
Maps: *DeLorme: North Carolina Atlas & Gazetteer:* Page 33 D8

Finding the trailhead: From the junction of US 70 and NC 18 in Morganton, drive east on US 70 for 6.9 miles. Turn left onto Church Street and travel for 1.35 miles to the neighborhood park on your right.

Take exit 111 off I-40 (Valdese exit) and turn right. Immediately turn right again, crossing the bridge and heading toward Valdese on Carolina Street. Follow Carolina Street for 1.2 miles to where it ends at a stoplight on Main Street (US 70). Go left onto Main Street and travel for 0.5 mile. Turn right onto Church Street and follow the directions above.

The trailhead is the gated, paved road at the southeast end of the parking lot. GPS: N35 45.849 / W81 34.185

The Hike

The paved road quickly leads you from the gate down to the brink of the falls. From the brink, a narrow dirt path leads to the base of McGalliard Falls. As you hike to the falls, a waterwheel comes into view alongside the creek, enhancing the picturesque setting. Although the park tends to be crowded, the beauty of the falls makes it well worth a visit.

Along with the waterfall, McGalliard Falls Park contains a playground, softball fields, picnic shelters, and volleyball nets. The original mill that sat beside the falls was the Meytre Gristmill. Built by Fred Meytre, it operated from 1906 to 1941. The mill you see today is a replica of the original and was built in 1982 when the park was created.

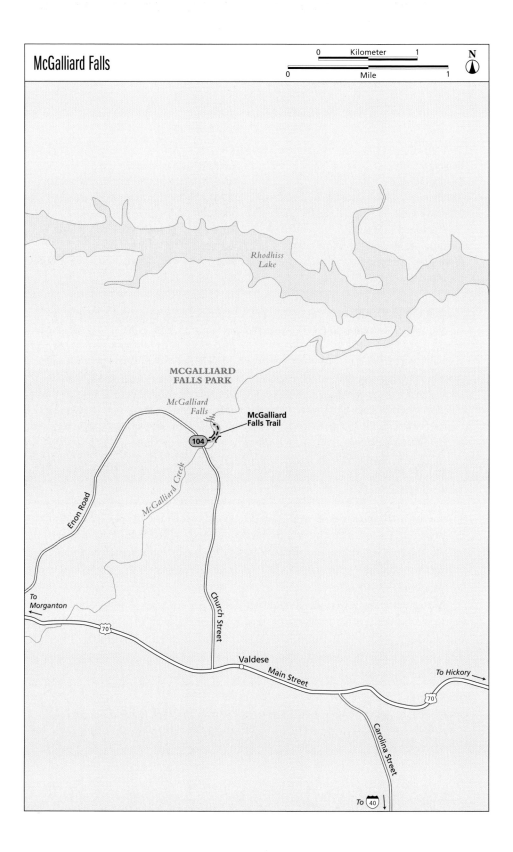

McGalliard Falls

A replica of the Meytre Mill sits beside McGalliard Falls.

Miles and Directions

0.0 From the trailhead, hike east on the paved path.

0.1 Cross the creek at the brink of the falls, and go left (north) on the narrow dirt path.

0.2 Arrive at the base of McGalliard Falls (N35 45.923 / W81 34.126). Return the way you came.

0.4 Arrive back at the trailhead.

105 High Shoals Falls in South Mountains State Park

Seductive! The sights and sounds of High Shoals draw you nearer and nearer. As each drop of water falls, it lures you like a first love, ensnaring your heart and causing you to catch your breath at the beauty before you.

Height: 80 feet
Beauty rating: Very good
Distance: 1.8 miles out and back
Difficulty: Moderate
Trail surface: Hard-packed dirt, gravel road, man-made steps
Approximate hiking time: 1 hour
Other trail users: Mountain bikers, equestrians
Blaze color: White triangles and blue circles
County: Burke

Land status: State park
Trail contact: South Mountains State Park; (828) 433-4772; www.ncparks.gov
FYI: Park hours vary through the year; closed on Christmas Day; contact South Mountains State Park for current info
Maps: *DeLorme: North Carolina Atlas & Gazetteer:* Page 33 F7. Detailed trail maps are available in the box at the west end of the parking area.

Finding the trailhead: From I-40, take exit #105 onto NC 18 in Morganton. Drive south on NC 18 for 11.0 miles to a right turn onto Sugar Loaf Road (SR 1913) at the sign for SOUTH MOUNTAINS STATE PARK. Continue for 4.2 miles to where Sugar Loaf Road ends at Old NC 18 (SR 1924). Turn left onto Old NC 18 and travel for 2.6 miles to a right turn onto Wards Gap Road (SR 1901). Continue for 1.3 miles to a fork and bear right onto South Mountains Park Avenue. Travel for 3.4 miles to where the road ends at a large parking area.

From the junction of NC 18 and NC 10 in Laurel Hill, drive north on NC 18 for 0.6 mile. Turn left onto Old NC 18 (SR 1924) and travel for 6.0 miles. Turn left onto Wards Gap Road (SR 1901) and follow the directions above.

The trailhead is located at the far left (southwest) end of the parking lot. GPS: N35 36.117 / W81 37.766

The Hike

This interpretive trail offers a wealth of information as you stroll along the river's edge.

Begin by hiking on the Hemlock Nature Trail as it follows the Jacob Fork River upstream. The trail soon becomes a gravel road and leads you into the Shinny Creek Picnic Area.

After passing through the picnic area, head up some steps and begin hiking on the High Shoals Falls Loop Trail as you return to the enjoyment of the forest. Along the way you will cross three footbridges before making your final ascent up the many stairs that lead to High Shoals Falls.

The 100,000-acre South Mountain Range encompasses three counties and once served as a buffer between the Cherokee and Catawba and the early white settlers.

High Shoals Falls in South Mountains State Park

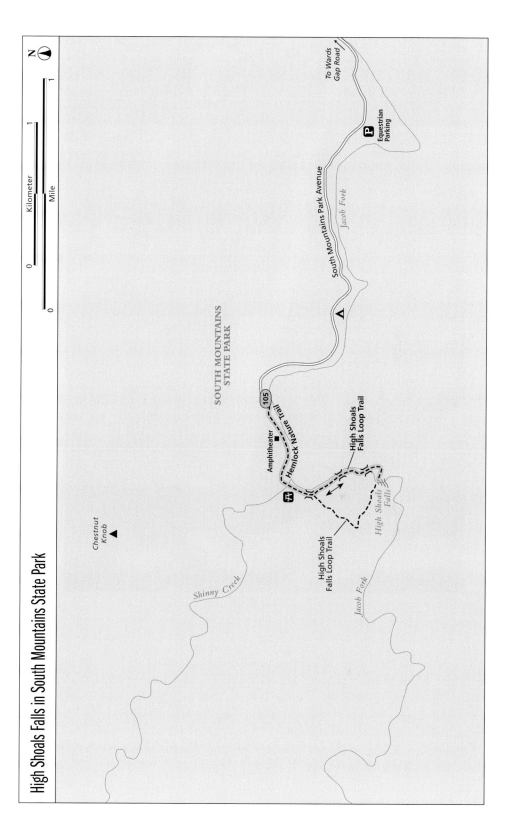

The view from the observation deck at High Shoals Falls is awesome.

In the 1930s the Civilian Conservation Corps began developing the land, and in the 1940s South Mountains State Park was proposed. It wasn't until 1974, however, that the funds became available and the first parcel of land was acquired. Today the park comprises more than 18,000 acres and contains a campground as well as hiking, mountain biking, and equestrian trails.

Shinny Creek supposedly got its name from the abundance of moonshine stills that once stood near its banks.

Miles and Directions

0.0 From the trailhead, hike west on the Hemlock Nature Trail and follow the river upstream.

0.3 Come to a T junction at a gravel service road; turn left (west) onto the service road.

0.4 Cross the bridge and hike through the Shinny Creek Picnic Area. When you enter the picnic area, you will come to a three-way fork with a gravel road heading straight (southwest), one going right (west), and a trail shooting off to the left (south) toward the creek. Go straight (southwest) on the gravel road.

0.5 Come to another fork, with a set of steps to the right (west) and a set of steps to the left (south-southwest). Go up the steps on the left. You are now on the High Shoals Falls Loop Trail. Continue hiking and cross the wooden footbridge. The trail soon leads you to the creek. Follow the creek upstream (south).

0.6 Cross another footbridge and then a boulder field.

0.7 Cross a final footbridge and then continue southwest up the many steep steps.

0.9 Arrive at an observation deck alongside High Shoals Falls (N35 35.693 / W81 38.131). Return the way you came. (**Option:** Continue past the falls for less than 1.0 mile to complete the High Shoals Falls Loop Trail.)

1.8 Arrive back at the trailhead.

106 Moravian Falls

Exquisite! Beautiful and pristine Moravian Falls is graced with a waterwheel to the left and perfect grassy flats at its sides. I advise visiting this one on a weekday; weekends tend to crowd the falls with tents and campers, tainting the natural beauty of the area.

See overview map on page iv.
Height: 50 feet
Beauty rating: Excellent
Distance: Roadside
Difficulty: Easy
Blaze color: No blazes

County: Wilkes
Land status: Private property
Trail contact: Moravian Falls Family Campground and Cabin Rentals; (336) 667-6150
Maps: *DeLorme: North Carolina Atlas & Gazetteer:* Page 34 A3-A4

Finding the trailhead: From the junction of NC 18 and NC 16 in the town of Moravian Falls, drive west on NC 18 for 0.4 mile. Turn left onto Falls Road and travel for 0.5 mile to a parking area on the right at Moravian Falls Campground. GPS: N3605.190 / W8111.417

The Hike

Moravian Falls is visible from the roadside. However, if you check in at the Moravian Falls Campground office, you can spend some quality time on the grassy banks of the creek. The falls are located on private property, so please check in at the campground office prior to visiting or you will be trespassing.

If you want this waterfall to yourself, you can rent the cabin that sits beside the falls and have it as your own backyard. If you prefer a more rustic setting, stay at the campground, which offers primitive camping, full hookups, and hot showers. Dogs are allowed.

Brothers of the Moravian faith first settled the area surrounding the falls in the mid 1700s. The brothers were originally from the province of Moravia, which is part of the present-day Czech Republic. As a Protestant denomination, the Moravians were branded as heretics, persecuted, and forced from their homeland. Upon coming to America they purchased a tract of nearly 100,000 acres, including the falls and the town that now holds their name.

107 Stone Mountain, Middle, and Lower Falls in Stone Mountain State Park

Glitter and gold! These three waterfalls are all located along the Stone Mountain Loop Trail. As they slide down the mountainside, each shimmers with its own beauty, like a shooting star in the sky.

Height: Stone Mountain Falls, 200 feet; Middle Falls, 40 feet; Lower Falls, 40 feet
Beauty rating: Very good for Stone Mountain and Middle Falls; excellent for Lower Falls
Distance: 4.8 miles out and back (Stone Mountain only, 3.2 miles; Middle Falls only, 3.0 miles; Lower Falls only, 3.8 miles)
Difficulty: Moderate
Trail surface: Wide, dirt and gravel
Approximate hiking time: 2 hours, 45 minutes

Blaze color: Orange for Stone Mountain Falls; blue for Lower and Middle Falls
County: Wilkes
Land status: State park
Trail contact: Stone Mountain State Park; (336) 957-8185; www.ncparks.gov
FYI: Park hours vary through the year; contact Stone Mountain State Park for current info.
Maps: *DeLorme: North Carolina Atlas & Gazetteer:* Page 15 C5

Finding the trailhead: Take exit 83 off I-77 onto US 21 in Elkin and follow US 21 north for approximately 10.7 miles. Turn left onto Traphill Road at the sign for Stone Mountain State Park and travel for 4.3 miles to a right turn onto John P. Frank Parkway. Continue for 2.3 miles to the gated entrance to Stone Mountains State Park. From the gate, travel for 2.9 miles to a parking area on the left.

From the junction of US 21 and the Blue Ridge Parkway near Sparta, travel south on US 21 for 4.4 miles. Turn right onto Oklahoma Road (SR 1100) and travel for 3.0 miles to where it ends at John P. Frank Parkway. Turn right onto John P. Frank Parkway and the gated entrance to Stone Mountain State Park is directly in front of you. From the gate, follow the directions above.

The trailhead is located at the southwest end of the parking lot, next to the restrooms and trail information sign. GPS: N36 23.858 / W81 03.098

The Hike

Begin by hiking on the Stone Mountain Loop Trail, which immediately takes you alongside a lovely trickling stream. The trail takes you past the Wolf Rock Trail and then past the old Hutchinson Homestead. After a quick visit here, you reach an open meadow with Stone Mountain standing gallantly before you.

Continue past the meadow, in awe of the nature before you, and soon you reenter the forest. Come to second fork at the trail for Wolf Rock and Cedar Rock. Continue hiking on the main trail over four footbridges before coming to another fork. Although I have you going left first, pick whichever route you choose. The left follows orange blazes and leads to Stone Mountain Falls. The right follows blue blazes and leads to another fork on the way to Middle and Lower Falls. Here, the right fork leads to Middle Falls and the left fork to Lower Falls. Again, choose whichever path you wish. If you head right, it takes you down a narrower footpath to the brink, affording fantastic views of Middle Falls. The left takes you across the creek and then leads uphill through the poplars and pines before descending again. You will cross the creek once more before finally arriving at the brink of Lower Falls. From here, continue for less than 0.1 mile to a sign reading FALLS TRAIL ENDS. Follow the narrow side trail toward the creek and soon arrive at the base of Lower Falls.

Established in 1969, Stone Mountain State Park is best known for the 600-foot-tall granite dome known as Stone Mountain. With a 4-mile circumference, the rock is said to be 360 million years old and is the largest plutonic monadnock in the state of North Carolina. Abruptly rising from the earth, Stone Mountain earned its designation as a National Natural Landmark in 1974. The park has a campground, and activities such as hiking, fishing, and rock climbing are all enjoyed here.

Miles and Directions

0.0 From the trailhead, follow the trickling stream, which leads to some steps.

0.1 Come to a fork. Go right and continue hiking southwest. Cross the footbridge and continue hiking north.

0.2 Come to a second fork. The right leads southwest to Wolf Rock. Go left here (southeast) and soon come to a footbridge. Cross the bridge and continue south.

0.3 Cross a third and fourth footbridge; continue to follow the creek upstream in a generally south to southeast direction.

0.4 Cross another footbridge; continue hiking south-southeast.

0.6 Pass the old Hutchinson Homestead and continue south-southeast toward the open meadow. Stay on the main trail and soon reenter the forest.

0.7 Come to another fork, with a sign for WOLF ROCK and CEDAR ROCK to your right (south). Go left here and hike southeast on the wide dirt and gravel trail.

0.8 Cross another footbridge; follow the trail south alongside the stream.

1.0 Cross another footbridge; continue south.

1.1 Cross another footbridge; continue southeast.

1.2 Cross another footbridge; continue south and come to a fork. The left leads southeast toward Stone Mountain Falls; and the right heads south toward Middle and Lower Falls. Go left for now, following the orange blazes. (*Option:* Hike south toward Middle and Lower Falls.)

1.5 Take the steps southeast.

1.6 Arrive at the base of Stone Mountain Falls (N36 22.864 / W81 02.141). Return to the last fork. (*Option:* Return to the trailhead for a 3.2-mile hike.)

2.0 Arrive back at the last fork and turn left (south) toward Middle and Lower Falls. The blue-blazed trail immediately leads you across the creek.

2.2 Come to a final fork. The right leads west-northwest to Middle Falls; the left heads south toward Lower Falls. Go right, down the narrower blue-blazed footpath. (*Option:* Hike south toward Lower Falls.)

2.3 Arrive at Middle Falls (N36 22.839 / W81 02.435). Return to the last fork. (*Option:* Return to the trailhead for a 3.8-mile out and back.)

Stone Mountain, Middle, and Lower Falls; Widow's Creek Falls

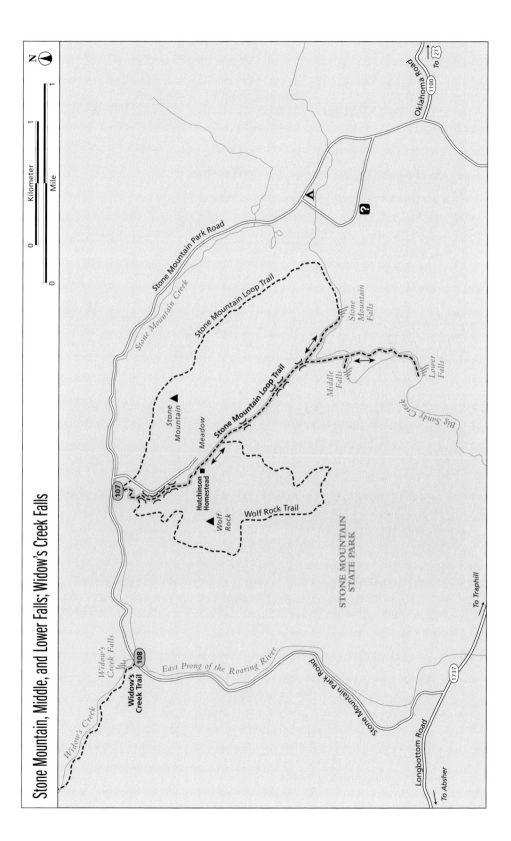

Stone Mountain Falls is one of many splendid sights within Stone Mountain State Park.

2.4 Arrive back at the last fork, turn right (south) and immediately cross the creek on your way toward Lower Falls.

2.7 Cross the creek again and continue hiking southwest.

2.8 Arrive at the brink of Lower Falls; continue a short distance farther.

2.9 Arrive at a sign reading FALLS TRAIL ENDS. A side trail on the left leads southwest toward the creek. Go left here and soon arrive at the base of Lower Falls (N36 22.491 / W81 02.481). Return to the trailhead.

4.8 Arrive back at the trailhead.

108 Widow's Creek Falls in Stone Mountain State Park

Marvelous! Located within Stone Mountain State Park, this waterfall outshines them all. Of the four waterfalls located within the park, Widow's Creek has the most character by far.

See map on page 281.
Height: 40 feet
Beauty rating: Excellent
Distance: 0.2 mile out and back
Difficulty: Easy
Trail surface: Gravel
Approximate hiking time: 15 minutes

Blaze color: No blazes
County: Wilkes
Land status: State park
Trail contact: Stone Mountain State Park; (336) 957-8185; www.ncparks.gov
Maps: DeLorme: North Carolina Atlas & Gazetteer: Page 15 C5

Finding the trailhead: Take exit 83 off I-77 onto US 21 in Elkin, and follow US 21 north for approximately 10.7 miles. Turn left onto Traphill Road at the sign for STONE MOUNTAIN STATE PARK and travel for 4.3 miles to a right turn onto John P. Frank Parkway. Continue for 2.3 miles to the gated entrance to Stone Mountain State Park. From the gate, travel for 3.9 miles to a pull-off on the right at the sign for WIDOW'S CREEK FALLS.

From the junction of US 21 and the Blue Ridge Parkway near Sparta, travel south on US 21 for 4.4 miles. Turn right onto Oklahoma Road (SR 1100) and travel for 3.0 miles to where it ends at John P. Frank Parkway. Turn right onto John P. Frank Parkway and the gated entrance to Stone Mountain State Park is directly in front of you. From the gate, follow the directions above.

GPS: N36 23.787/W81 04.019

The Hike

From the parking area, the gravel trail leads directly to the base of Widow's Creek Falls. A short trail then continues up the left side of the waterfall to a picture-perfect swimming hole and picnic site amidst the falls. Widow's Creek Falls earns two thumbs up from me.

Miles and Directions

0.0 From the trailhead, hike northwest up the gravel path.
0.1 Arrive at the base of Widow's Creek Falls (N36 23.829/W81 04.062). Return the way you came.
0.2 Arrive back at the trailhead.

109 Hidden and Window Falls in Hanging Rock State Park

Celestial! This trail graces you with two small yet refreshing waterfalls. The first to greet you is Hidden Falls, although I'd call it "Not So Hidden Falls." Nestled away in the woods, this small but lively waterfall makes a great place to picnic.

Height: Hidden Falls, 15 feet; Window Falls, 30 feet
Beauty rating: Good for Hidden Falls; very good for Window Falls
Distance: 1.4 miles out and back (Hidden Falls, 0.8 mile)
Difficulty: Moderate
Trail surface: Wide gravel path

Approximate hiking time: 45 minutes
Blaze color: Orange and white
County: Stokes
Land status: State park
Trail contact: Hanging Rock State Park; (336) 593-8480; www.ncparks.gov
Maps: *DeLorme: North Carolina Atlas & Gazetteer:* Page 16 C4

Finding the trailhead: From the junction of NC 8 and NC 89 north of Danbury, drive south on NC 8/NC 89 for 1.4 miles. Turn right onto Hanging Rock Park Road and travel for 3.2 miles to a left turn leading toward the visitor center. Follow this road to the far end of the parking lot, and park before the road makes a loop back down to the visitor center.

From the junction of NC 8 and NC 89 south of Danbury, drive north on NC 8/NC 89 for 5.1 miles. Turn left onto Hanging Rock Park Road and follow the directions above.

The trailhead is by the picnic area, at the east end of the parking lot. GPS: N36 23.733/W80 15.895

The Hike

Follow the wide gravel road downhill through the picnic area to a signpost for INDIAN CREEK TRAIL, WINDOW FALLS AND HIDDEN FALLS. Continue to follow the white-and-orange-blazed trail as it descends the entire way before reaching a T junction with a sign for HIDDEN FALLS to the right and WINDOW FALLS to the left. Head right here; the path quickly leads to the base of Hidden Falls.

To get to Window Falls, backtrack to the T junction at the sign and head the other way toward Window Falls. The trail continues its downhill trek before reaching an observation deck overlooking the "window." Continue a bit farther to a second set of steps, which lead down to the base of Window Falls. Window Falls makes a freefall in front of a small cave, with giant cliffs looming above. Mother Nature carved a hole out of the rocky bluff, creating the "window" at Window Falls.

If you're in the mood to keep hiking, the white-blazed Indian Creek Trail continues to follow Indian Creek downstream for another 3.9 miles to where it ends near the Dan River.

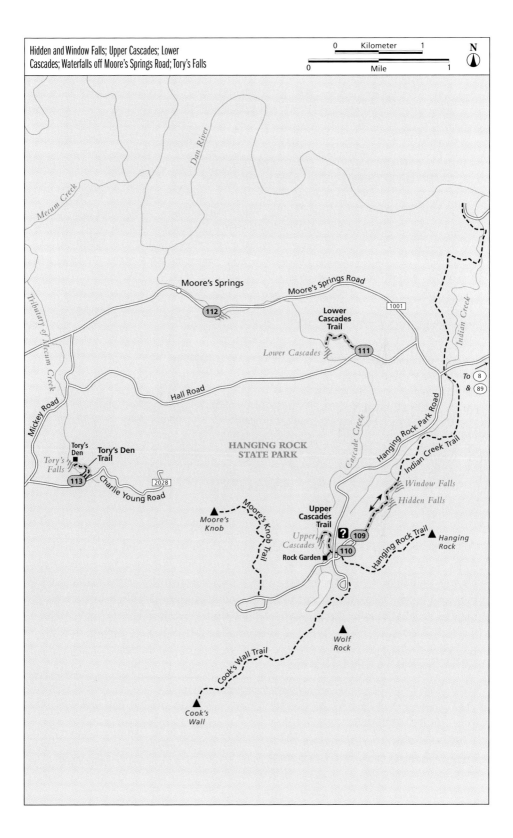

0   Kilometer   1

0   Mile   1

N

Dan River

Mecum Creek

Tributary of Mecum Creek

Moore's Springs

Moore's Springs Road

112

1001

Indian Creek

**Lower
Cascades
Trail**

Lower Cascades

111

To 8
& 89

Hall Road

Mickey Road

Hanging Rock Park Road

Cascade Creek

**HANGING ROCK
STATE PARK**

Indian Creek Trail

Tory's
Den

**Tory's Den
Trail**

*Tory's
Falls*

113

Charlie Young Road

2028

Window Falls

Hidden Falls

Moore's Knob Trail

**Upper
Cascades
Trail**

?

109

Hanging Rock Trail

▲
Moore's
Knob

*Upper
Cascades*

110

▲ Hanging
Rock

Rock Garden ■

▲
Wolf
Rock

Cook's Wall Trail

▲
Cook's
Wall

A tail feather lies upon the path.

Hanging Rock State Park is located within the Sauratown Mountains and contains six fabulous waterfalls to visit. The park is known for its unique geological features, including the "Hanging Rock" for which it is named. Cook's Rock, House Rock, and Wolf Rock are among other outstanding geological features worth seeing.

The park has a visitor center, picnic areas, and offers cabin and boat rentals. Activities such as camping, hiking, fishing, and swimming can all be enjoyed here.

Miles and Directions

0.0 From the trailhead, hike east-northeast through the picnic area.

0.4 Arrive at a T junction. Go right and hike southeast to the base of Hidden Falls (N36 23.957 / W80 15.628). Return to the T junction. (**Option:** Hike to Window Falls first.)

0.5 Arrive back at the T junction and hike north toward Window Falls.

0.7 Arrive at the base of Window Falls (N36 24.076 / W80 15.574). Return to the trailhead.

1.4 Arrive back at the trailhead.

110 Upper Cascades in Hanging Rock State Park

Flamboyant! Located within Hanging Rock State Park, Upper Cascades, with its two distinct sections, is a great spot for a picnic in the sun along the creek's edge.

See map on page 285.
Height: 35 feet
Beauty rating: Very good
Distance: 0.6 mile out and back
Difficulty: Easy to moderate
Trail surface: Wide gravel path
Approximate hiking time: 30 minutes

Blaze color: No blazes
County: Stokes
Land status: State park
Trail contact: Hanging Rock State Park; (336) 593-8480; www.ncparks.gov
Maps: *DeLorme: North Carolina Atlas & Gazetteer:* Page 16 C4

Finding the trailhead: From the northernmost junction of NC 8 and NC 89 north of Danbury, drive south on NC 8 / NC 89 for 1.4 miles. Turn right onto Hanging Rock Park Road and travel for 3.2 miles to a left turn leading toward the visitor center.

From the southernmost junction of NC 8 and NC 89 south of Danbury, drive north on NC 8 / NC 89 for 5.1 miles. Turn left onto Hanging Rock Park Road and follow the directions above.

The trailhead is located at the far west end of the parking area (opposite end of the picnic area). GPS: N36 23.650 / W80 16.027

The Hike

Take the steps down from the trailhead and cross the main park road. The paved path then leads to a fork. The left is a wheelchair accessible paved path that heads southwest less than 0.1 mile to a rock garden. The right fork heads northwest toward the waterfall. Go right and follow the wide gravel path through the forest and then downhill to an observation deck at the upper section of the falls. From here, a set of steps takes you steeply down to the base of Upper Cascades.

Miles and Directions

0.0 From the trailhead, hike down the steps. Cross the park road and soon come to a fork. Go right (northwest) at the fork.

0.3 Come to an observation deck. Continue south, down the steps, and arrive at the base of Upper Cascades (N36 23.730 / W80 16.147). Return the way you came.

0.6 Arrive back at the trailhead.

111 Lower Cascades in Hanging Rock State Park

Pleasant! The view from the overlook is just that. However, if you hike to the base, pleasant is a huge understatement. With massive cliffs dwarfing the falls from above, a pristine and private swimming hole awaits at the base of Lower Cascades.

See map on page 285.
Height: 25 feet
Beauty rating: Excellent
Distance: 0.8 mile out and back
Difficulty: Easy to moderate
Trail surface: Wide sandy path
Approximate hiking time: 45 minutes
Blaze color: No blazes

County: Stokes
Land status: State park
Trail contact: Hanging Rock State Park; (336) 593-8480; www.ncparks.gov
FYI: The gate is open from 8:30 a.m. to 7:30 p.m.
Maps: *DeLorme: North Carolina Atlas & Gazetteer:* Page 16 C4

Finding the trailhead: From the northernmost junction of NC 8 and NC 89 north of Danbury, drive south on NC 8 / NC 89 for 1.4 miles. Turn right onto Hanging Rock Park Road and travel for 1.5 miles. Turn right onto Moore's Springs Road (SR 1001) and continue for 0.25 mile to a left turn onto Hall Road. Follow Hall Road for 0.4 mile to a parking area on the right at the sign for Lower Cascades.

From the southernmost junction of NC 8 and NC 89 south of Danbury, drive north on NC 8 / NC 89 for 5.1 miles. Turn left onto Hanging Rock Park Road and follow the directions above.

The trailhead is at the northwest end of the parking area. GPS: N36 24.887 / W80 15.896

The Hike

Follow the old roadbed as it meanders through the forest and soon leads to some steps that take you down to an overlook of the falls from above. From the overlook, follow the stony staircase steeply down to the base of the Lower Cascades.

Of the six waterfalls within Hanging Rock State Park, Lower Cascades seems to be preferred by the locals, so don't expect to have this one to yourself, especially on weekends.

Lower Cascades at Hanging Rock State Park is very popular with the locals.

Miles and Directions

0.0 From the trailhead, hike west on the old roadbed. Bypass the gate in front of you and continue hiking north-northwest as the wide sandy trail meanders through the forest.

0.3 Come to an overlook of the falls from above. Head south down the steps.

0.4 Arrive at the base of Lower Cascades (N36 24.908 / W80 16.115). Return the way you came.

0.8 Arrive back at the trailhead.

112 Waterfall off Moore's Springs Road in Hanging Rock State Park

Surprising! Located within Hanging Rock State Park, you pass this beauty on your way to Tory's Falls. Although it may go unnoticed by some, I thought this little gem deserved to be mentioned.

See map on page 285.
Height: 20 feet
Beauty rating: Good
Distance: Roadside
Difficulty: Easy
Blaze color: No blazes

County: Stokes
Land status: State park
Trail contact: Hanging Rock State Park; (336) 593-8480; www.ncparks.gov
Maps: DeLorme: North Carolina Atlas & Gazetteer: Page 16 C4

Finding the trailhead: From the northernmost junction of NC 8 and NC 89 north of Danbury, drive south on NC 8 / NC 89 for 1.4 miles. Turn right onto Hanging Rock Park Road and travel for 1.5 miles to a right turn onto Moore's Springs Road (SR 1001). Continue for 2.0 miles to a pull-off on the left just before the bridge.

From the southernmost junction of NC 8 and NC 89 south of Danbury, drive north on NC 8 / NC 89 for 5.1 miles. Turn left onto Hanging Rock Park Road and follow the directions above.

GPS: N36 25.105 / W80 16.978

The Hike

The falls are located west of the parking area, on the south side of the road, and can be viewed from the bridge. When water levels are high, this beauty really booms.

Enjoy this little extra bonus while visiting the other waterfalls of Hanging Rock State Park.

113 Tory's Falls in Hanging Rock State Park

Inquisitive! While the falls are not that impressive, the intrigue of Tory's Den—a 30-foot-deep cave carved out of the mountainside—is.

See map on page 285.

Height: 100 feet over several sections
Beauty rating: Fair
Distance: 0.6 mile out and back
Difficulty: Easy to moderate
Trail surface: Hard-packed dirt
Approximate hiking time: 30 minutes
Blaze color: Blue/Green

County: Stokes
Land status: State park
Trail contact: Hanging Rock State Park; (336) 593-8480; www.ncparks.gov
FYI: The parking area is open from 8:30 a.m. to sunset.
Maps: *DeLorme: North Carolina Atlas & Gazetteer:* Page 16 C4

Finding the trailhead: From the northernmost junction of NC 8 and NC 89 north of Danbury, drive south on NC 8 / NC 89 for 1.4 miles. Turn right onto Hanging Rock Park Road and travel for 1.5 miles to a right turn onto Moore's Springs Road (SR 1001). Continue for 3.1 miles and turn left onto Mickey Road. Travel for 1.1 miles to a left turn onto Charlie Young Road (SR 2028). Follow Charlie Young Road for 0.35 mile to a parking area on the left.

From the southernmost junction of NC 8 and NC 89 south of Danbury, drive north on NC 8 / NC 89 for 5.1 miles. Turn left onto Hanging Rock Park Road and follow the directions above.

The trailhead is located at the far northeast end of the parking area at a sign directing you to TORY'S DEN. GPS: N36 24.116 / W80 17.966

The Hike

A narrow, dirt footpath leads you downhill toward the faint sound of the falls. As you enjoy wonderful views of the valley below, the trail leads you to a T junction. The left heads south to Tory's Falls; the right heads north to Tory's Den. I recommend taking both routes, first heading to the cliffside overlook of Tory's Falls and then backtracking and taking the short jaunt to the unique cave known as Tory's Den.

Many questions arise when you first come upon this cave, some of which still lie unanswered. The most popular legend about Tory's Den is that it was a place of refuge for Loyalist soldiers during the Revolutionary War. Whatever tales the den might tell, it certainly is an intriguing place that lets your imagination run wild.

Tory's Den stirs the imagination.

Miles and Directions

0.0 From the trailhead, hike north-northeast down the narrow dirt path.

0.1 Cross a footbridge over the creek and continue northeast. Soon come to some man-made steps; head west down the steps.

0.2 Come to a T junction. The left leads south to Tory's Falls; the right heads north to Tory's Den. Go left for now and arrive at the cliffside overlook of Tory's Falls (N36 24.151 / W80 18.007). Backtrack to the T junction and hike north toward Tory's Den.

0.3 Arrive at Tory's Den (N36 24.185 / W80 18.023). Return to the trailhead.

0.6 Arrive back at the trailhead.

Falls Index

About the Author

Waterfall hunter, nature enthusiast, tree hugger, and avid hiker, Melissa Watson is truly at her best when she's in the forest. Her passion for waterfalls and nature in general stems back to childhood, and she continues to fulfill that passion to this day. For more than twenty years Melissa has been exploring the forests of North Carolina—hiking by day and camping by night as she continues her quest for new trails and new waterfalls. And whether searching out new waterfalls or revisiting old favorites, she has come to be known as a local expert in the field.

Melissa has been a career firefighter and paramedic since 1993. She started adventure racing in 2000 and continues to master her skills as a navigator and mountaineer. She is also the author of FalconGuides' *Hiking Waterfalls in Georgia and South Carolina*.

For more about Melissa, visit her website www.trailtimenow.com.

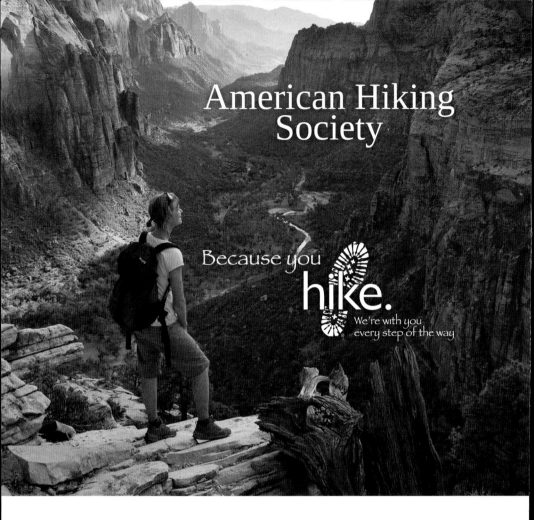

American Hiking Society

Because you hike.
We're with you every step of the way

As a national voice for hikers, **American Hiking Society** works every day:

- Building and maintaining hiking trails
- Educating and supporting hikers by providing information and resources
- Supporting hiking and trail organizations nationwide
- Speaking for hikers in the halls of Congress and with federal land managers

Whether you're a casual hiker or a seasoned backpacker, become a member of American Hiking Society and join the national hiking community! You'll enjoy great member benefits and help preserve the nation's hiking trails, so tomorrow's hike is even better than today's. We invite you to join us now!

American Hiking Society